To Roz
Merry Xmas '99
and a very Good New Year 2000
Much love
Karen xxxxx

Essex

NEW YORK

PENNSYLVANIA
DUTCH COUNTRY

Shartleville

Paradise

Shenandoah
National
Park

Skyline Drive

NASHVILLE   Asheville

Blue Ridge
Parkway

MEMPHIS   NORTH CAROLINA

TENNESSEE   Cherokee

OXFORD

MISSISSIPPI

DALLAS

LOUISIANA

AUSTIN   Breaux   July 4th
HOUSTON   Bridge
            NEW ORLEANS
    Galveston

Victoria

KFC

D1639587

I & CLAUDIUS

I & CLAUDIUS

travels with my cat

Clare de Vries

BLOOMSBURY

First published 1999

Copyright © 1999 by Clare de Vries

The moral right of the author has been asserted

Bloomsbury Publishing Plc,
38 Soho Square, London W1V 5DF

A CIP catalogue record for this book
is available from the British Library

ISBN 0-7475-4444-1

10 9 8 7 6 5 4 3 2 1

Typeset by Hewer Text Ltd, Edinburgh, Scotland.
Printed by St Edmundsbury Press, Suffolk
Endpaper illustration by Lucinda Rogers

to Sonya de Vries

Acknowledgements

The following people helped, supported and made Claude's and my trip fantastic and I would like to thank them:

Kate Alvarez, Clara Lee Arnold, Christian Bandler, Diane Bandler, Gail Barnes, Peggy and Richard Bright, Jane Rule Burdine, Keith Butt and Peter Arbeid – the best vets in London, Piki Chappell, Esther Cohn, Ken Decker, Dana Dickey, Jonny Dymond, Gary Fisketjon, Hoot Gibson, Jim Grace, Jenny Greenhalgh, Neil Hamilton, Kelly Hay, Philo Hayward, Eric Heinberg, Richard and Lisa Howorth, Charles Lambert, Angela and Paul Lehman, Heidi Levy, Wendy and Stanley Marsh, Barbara Murphy, Diana and Jeff Nayer, Walter Chappell and Linda Piedra, Tifany Richards, Howie Richey – the Texpert tour guide, Dale and Carolyn Smith, Saied and Solaimon, Grayson Splane, Hebe Splane, James Strait, Anne and Anne Dyer Stuart, Ed and Terry Sullivan, Kate Walker, Dan Wente, Brandt Wood. Mark Alward at Buick; Adolphus Hotel, Dallas; The Cat Practice, New Orleans; Skip and the Mansions Hotel, San Francisco; Neil Rosenbaum and the Las Palomas, Santa Fe, and the Hotel Santa Fe. But most especially thanks to: Dr Tony Shipp, LA's outstanding vet and Derek Cockle, who picked up the pieces.

Thank you so much to my editor Liz Calder and my agent Vivienne Schuster, who had faith and took a risk with me.

Chapter One

It Happened One Night

Lying in bed, ermintruminating over my life. Something's got to give. For too long now, I've been wasting my life in a numbingly dull job. I'm fed up of pouncing from my bed, my hair loobrushingly angry, having snored and snorted my way through a nightmare-ridden doze, to struggle to work, there to do battle with attitudes and personalities that would not be out of place in Papa Doc's regime. I feel as though I've given up before I've even begun. I need to feel alive, live the best life possible, fulfil a dream. Before I resort to kids. Tomorrow I'm going to work. On the dot of nine I'll throw up my arms, shout 'I'm outy!' run home and be back in bed by ten.

Then what? I can't decide what to do, because any 'normal' job might eliminate the possibility of adventure, excitement and lack of routine. But I'm twenty-eight now and have been flibbertigibbeting from job to job ever since university. Every time I move it seems to be either sideways or downwards. I have to stick at something longer than five minutes if I'm to be a focused expert (cf., Mozart, Michelangelo, Monty Roberts). What if at the age of forty I'm some wandering uncommitted hippie rather than the diversely experienced but successful boho I'm aiming for?

What shall I do? Aaaargh. Think, think, think. An astronaut once told me that

There are stars,
Realms that glow
Around the skies,
Velvet lights dim
Emanating from
Life as we know it, Jim

I never knew what he meant. But I'd love to see the skies I haven't seen. Get away from this orange star-free London night. Live life as a film. *Thelma and Louise* (no rape scene). A roadtrip around America has been playing on my mind for some time now. New York to San Francisco via the southern states.

So why not bugger off then? Because I'm in love. With my cat Claudius. He's a nineteen-year-old (133 in human years), chocolate-brown, green-eyed Burmese dreamboat who is curled snorily in my left arm right now, as he is every night. There is no way in the world I could ever leave him. He sits by my bath when I'm in it, follows me around everywhere, only drinks from a glass (I take two up to bed at night), eats chocolate, ice cream, crisps, cheese and chips. I leave videos on while I'm at work to keep him company. He's often quoting them at me. He's rather deaf, has no gnashers, but nevertheless is the world's most beautiful cat.

Why not wait until he dies? *Dies?* Did you say *dies?* You unthinking unfeeling monster. For a start he may be nineteen, but he looks and behaves like a ten-year-old. He could live for another five years and I can't put my life on hold for ever. My sister gave me Claudius when I was ten years old. I chose him when he was the length of my little finger – a blind brown mouse. We grew up together and when I was messing around London looking for jobs and places to live he stayed with my mother. They loved each other dearly, but she got pancreatic cancer, and even though he kept a careful vigil on her bed, she died two years ago. He came back to live with me. Now after years of breathing together in our sleep, we are too bonded to be separated.

Anyway, when we are apart, my heart starts to ache, not unlike a mother whose breast milks when she hears her baby cry. The last time I went travelling, Claude went down with kidney disease two days before I departed. I was terrified about leaving him but left it to Fate since I was on the verge of barking mad-dom. I spent two weeks in Egypt alternately being hassled by carpet sellers or in veils of tears thinking Claude was going to die. I came back to find him preparing cocktails with the entire veterinary staff, I mean everyone from the receptionist to the nurses to the vets themselves, at his beck and call, popping in to see how he was, wondering if there was anything they could get. 'Yes, do you have any of those maraschino cherry things?' replies Claude, the words dancing through his whiskers like notes on a musical stave. 'Oh never mind here she is,' as he hops down from his place by the window and saunters out to the Lancia where I am standing flabbergasted, holding the door open like his chauffeur, as he gently climbs in and plumps down on the front passenger seat.

'Yowser,' he purrs.

Mull, ponder, think, wonder, muse.

This is not the first time I have been cogging it over. Yet this is the night that the answer comes, crystal clear in its confidence.

I'll take him with me.

I do a little 'By Jove' right-arm punch across the midriff gesture just to punctuate the point, waking Claude up as I do so. So what if the received wisdom is such that cats don't travel? Pah! I say, and then pah! again say I to living life by the rules. Anyway Claudius is not a cat. Well he is, but he's a special cat. My instincts tell me that his spirit is that of a traveller. As long as we're together we'll both be fine.

He's awake now so I might as well broach the subject.

'Claude. I want to go travelling. But no "finding myself" mission. Good God, if I haven't found myself by now, then surely there is nothing to find.'

Dramatic paws.

'Will you come with me?'

He blinks greenly, sleepily at me.

' "The only excitement I've known is here with me now. So I'll go with you and I won't whine and I'll sew your socks and I'll stitch you when you're wounded and I'll do anything you ask of me. Except one thing. I won't watch you die. I'll miss that scene if you don't mind." ' He turns round and curls back down in my arm crook.

'Riiiiight,' I think frowningly.

'What about quarantine?'

'Forget it – you're nineteen, you haven't got for ever and I want us to be together. Six months is a long time at this stage.'

'I agree. So it's simple then. We just keep going.'

On to practicalities: what does a cat about town wear in New York? A dark brown wool suit? A fur coat – it's so cold in winter. Or just a very chic Donna Karan catsuit? I mentally tick off the most important things to pack.

For me:
Wind chime (to induce sense of calm when panicking).
Facial sunblock (to prevent wrinkles when indulging in guilty but inevitable sunbathing).
Gucci pencil-line skirt (no explanation needed).

For Claudius:
Litter tray.
Yellow water bowl.
Blue food bowl.
Green cardigan (to remind him of home).

I get out my savings and rent out my flat, to secure us a budget. I find an airline that allows Claude in the cabin with me: Air France, which means we go to New York via Paris. At the check-in desk, the stewardess starts with a 'No Animals on Board' approach until she reads the small print. I unzip Claude's travelling bag and he pops his head out with an 'I'm getting out' look on his face.

'Wow! What a face.'

'Thank you.'

'I mean your cat. What type is he?'

'Burmese.'

'And you can't be without him?'

'That's it.'

'Hmmm . . . I love my tabby too.' She sighs contentedly, tappety-tappeting.

'You know, I think this screen is showing a technical error. You just have to pay fifty pounds. He's excess baggage.'

'She's excess baggage.'

'Claude. Behave.'

'I'm sorry?'

'Nothing. Here you go.'

In the departure parlour, I let him out of his bag. He hates travelling cooped up like an animal. He wanders around Bally umming and ahhing over strappy ankle stilettos and passé platforms before spending an overly long time looking up wistfully at the Oyster Bar.

The plane speeds down the runway and I put a comforting hand on him, but he is remarkably sanguine about it all, more interested in finding the most comfortable position in his bag than in the roaring engines.

As we tilt backwards promisingly I think about the London I am leaving behind. A city whose corners are sprouting with Spy shops. A city whose Sainsburys have four choices of trolley in a faux-American attempt at efficiency. A city whose TV stations manage to show simultaneously the flick you've just chosen from your local video shop.

Once we're airborne, I take Claude out and he settles on my lap for a sleep. After a while, when a whimper of a snore is just getting ready to roll, a steward insists he go back in his bag, prefacing every sentence with the equivalent of 'I love cats, some of my best friends are cats, but . . .' I ask to see the head stewardess. A thin-lipped unsmiling-eyed Parisian Madame approaches. She is not tickled pink by the sight of the brown fur.

'Put him back in his bag.'

'Why?'

'He might jump out.'

'But the windows don't open – or do they? In which case why don't we all have nosebleeds?'

'Put him back NOW.'

'And if I don't?'

'I believe you're in transfer. I'll tell your next flight and he'll have to go in the hold.'

I narrow my eyes to a murderous slit. I put him in but leave the top undone so he can still see out.

'Shut the bag.'

'Bugger off.'

From Paris to New York everyone is much more relaxed. The plane isn't full so Claude has a seat to himself to curl up on. I pull out his personal television screen. The film is *Midnight in the Garden of Good and Evil*.

'Ask them to put on *Breakfast at Tiffany's*.'

'They don't have it.'

'Who says? Ask them.'

'There's no choice, Claudius. We all watch the same film.'

'I've seen this.'

'You've seen *Breakfast at Tiffany*'s.'

'But I . . . oh for God's sake.' He settles down.

He curls up and tries to sleep. The steward looks at him and his thoughts slide across his eyes like lasers on a visor. *That's a cat. I don't think he's meant to be a) in the cabin b) out of his bag. I think I'll just ignore the situation.*

'Would you like a drink, madam?'

I enjoy my Nicorettes, filling myself with nicotine the entire seven hours. How I love not smoking. After about four hours Claudius is bored: tired but can't sleep. He starts to wander the aisles, up and down, up and down. I follow behind to keep him out of the steward's wheels. People see him, look away and then double-take around the backs of their chairs. I try not to catch anyone's eye because I don't want to come over all 'proud mum'.

As we settle back in our seats I experience a startling moment of truth. We are running. We can't come back. We have to keep going. I am effectively taking your beloved granny out of her nursing home for one last whizz around the world in her wheelchair.

Eight hours later and we are stepping off the plane at JFK. It's damn exciting. Claudius is alive and there is no problem at immigration and no problem at customs. In fact I could have brought a horse in and they wouldn't have noticed. The airport staff are totally unimpressed by a cat setting off on his last journey. Then I remember. This is New York. This is the town where you take dance classes at 3am, visit your in-laws at 4am and grab some sushi at 5am. Nothing is weird. Nothing is out of place. Not even Claudius's swan song.

Chapter Two

Chitty Chitty Bang Bang

Connecticut

So Claude and I are over the pond and over the moon and we decide to start the trip with a little holiday: a few days' rest and calm at my godmother's house in Connecticut. My mother's best friend, Janie, is English and her husband, Mikey, is New York Jewish. The last time I was in this white wooden house was ten years ago, just after my A levels, when I spent most of my days lying face-down in their pool, playing dead, in a bid for attention while their son Mark Lee raced around on his bike screaming. Janie remembers this well – Mikey does too because at that time I had a penchant for swimming naked – and is a little wary of my coming to stay. So on our arrival, Claude walks her to the other side of the house.

'My dear I love this decoration . . .' I hear seep through his whiskers. She is enchanted by him, and immediately calls him the Chocolate Soldier.

'Such a brave boy undertaking such a trip at such a fine old age,' she coos. 'Cosmo, come and meet your Great-Uncle Claudius.'

Cosmo takes one look at Claude, sticks his haunches in the air, slaps his ears to the back of his head and hisses for the devil.

Claudius looks away. He is not impressed by the manners.

*　　　*　　　*

Mikey takes me by the arm and leads me to the pool.

'So, ya still look like a boy when you're naked?'

'Hmm, charming. Aren't you too old to get it up?'

'No, baby. Now, when are you leaving on this ridiculous trip of yours? You realise there are more psychotics down south than there are anywhere else in the world? You mustn't flash your bee stings down there. No nudie swimming. Cover up at all times. They're real prudes.'

'OK, Mikey. How's the Mafia?'

'I'm a Jew not a wop. So when ya goin'?'

'Well, it looks very, very comfortable here. I think a couple of months' rest and then Claude and I might saunter off.' I settle down into one of their long sofas.

'I'm givin' ya a week tops. Then ya gotta get out. Mark Lee is comin' home from school, and we don't want both you idiots around at the same time.'

'But Mikey we're both grown up now and anyway the car doesn't arrive until next week . . .'

'Shame. If ya don't get out I'll get my Connections to get ya out.'

'I thought you said you were . . .'

What is essential for a road trip? A cat. I have one. Some Gucci slingbacks. I have some. Am I forgetting something? How about a car? I have that too. It is being shipped over as we speak. My precious Lancia Fulvia Coupe 1.3S Rallye. Go on. Go and look it up in a car manual in your local book shop. It's a classic Italian sports car, ideally suited for rallies hence the Rallye (why do they spell it with an e?). And what is a road trip if not an extended rallye? This car is my dream car. I took years to save up for it, love it almost as much as Claude, and wasn't about to leave it behind. I spent a certain amount on tarting it up and shipping it over. When I mentioned this casually to my family at the Last Supper, a cacophony of sibling whinnies and yells filled the air.

'It's a death trap!' (Sister Mandy.)

'You're a fool!' (Brother Phil.)

'Be careful!' (Sister Antonia.)

'What's on TV tonight?' (Brother Alex.)

This all for a couple of reasons: driving back from Gloucestershire one Sunday evening with my friend Sophy (why does she spell her name with a y?), we heard a strange ticking noise. A garage was up ahead so we pulled in there. I phoned Classic Car Rescue Line. They came after an hour and took a brief look at the engine.

'Anything serious?' I ask.

'You forgot to put oil in the engine, madam,' he replies.

'Hmm, what would have happened if I hadn't stopped then?' carrying on as though nothing to be ashamed of at all.

'The engine would have seized up, the wheels would have stopped turning and you would have gone into a roll-over situation.' (This last with obvious relish at the thought of it all being on a motorway at 80mph.)

Another time I was having trouble starting the car, so I took it to the local garage.

'The drive shaft's loose – hanging on by the last thread of the last bolt,' they said.

'Ah I seeee,' I replied knowingly. 'Just remind me what that means?'

'That means that the next time you drove it, it would have worked loose, come up through the floor of the car and taken your legs off.'

'Indeed,' I said in one of those clever tones that could either mean 'Really?' or 'Of course I knew that.' In spite of such moments, I am still hoping/thinking/praying it will make it to California.

So as my baby sails the seas, I am already installed in Connecticut, having a nice suburban time of it. Claude and I spend our days by the pool, me sunbathing, him sniffing the roses. Cosmo is friendlier now, but prefers to keep out of our way as much as possible, which suits us fine.

This is not really the America I am yearning to see. The lone road into the distance, the run-down neon-lit motel and diner, the mountains-on-the-horizon America I have been dreaming of. In fact it looks just like England, which accounts for the name given to these parts – um, New England. The houses, on neatly manicured lawns, are made of white wooden slats with slanting grey roofs. The white lace-latticed window fronts surround coloured wooden frames. The roads are clean and pretty, usually grass-edged or tree-lined and everyone pootles along at 35mph. All is comfort and security. The only crime is when old ladies back their cars into shop windows by mistake.

As the days wear on Claude and I get more and more settled. In between the odd saunter out to the cinema and plunge into the pool, we watch telly. You don't have to wait until Fridays for 'Frasier' here, it's on every night and 'Seinfeld' is about to finish for ever. I've never watched it, but I get the impression that I've missed out on a great cultural event. The casts of other sitcoms have recorded messages for Seinfeld and sometimes they even interrupt the news to deliver them.

Tonight I take Janie and Mikey to see *The Horse Whisperer* so that they can get the gist of Monty Roberts. He has devoted his life to talking to animals and I have his address in California and plan on meeting him at the end of my trip. Talking of which, I think fear has me by the throat. I am in this great house, with Claudius well fed, happy and comfortable and all America is out there waiting to be discovered. Yet part of me doesn't want to go. Each night I won't know where I'll be staying. I'll be lugging bags from one place to another. Why didn't I think of this before? It's as though I fear the experiences I crave.

Mikey catches me mid-track as these thoughts cross my mind.

'Forget it, baby. You're still going.'

'But Mikey. I think all I needed was a change from London. Do I have to go? I can just send e-mails to my friends pretending I'm in Lackawanna, Dahlonega, Homosassa . . .'

'No, baby. I'm looking forward to fielding calls from sheriffs all over the south. You're going and you're going soon.'

So I prepare to leave, which is easy as I hadn't really unpacked in the first place. I call the shipping company to check up on the car. Any moment now. I bid farewell to the pool and feel vaguely guilty about dragging Claude away from all the comfort. The Day of Departure starts off in a shiny shoe, out of bed the right side sort of way. The angels – who resemble Donny and Marie's Ice Angels – are singing in high-pitched Hollywood timbres. I celebrate by dressing up for the occasion. Short pink Jean Muir shift dress, high-heeled black slingbacks, dark glasses. Janie and I have a vague tussle at the front door as she tries to stop me making a fool of myself.

'That's really not appropriate for the south.'

'Jane, I'm not arriving in the south for a good long while. And I'm pushing thirty. Please. Let me wear what I want.'

'Do you think that's comfortable for a long car drive?'

'Pain is beauty. Beauty is pain. Please, Jane, the door?'

Claude and I and the bags are dropped at the dock by Mikey – 'And don't come back,' he hollers cheerily, driving off. It will take the morning to organise the car and then we'll set off for the south, the west, America! in the afternoon. To cut a long bureaucratic/paperwork story short we see the boat dock, and we wait for hours, my pins aching tottering on those shoes, while it sorts itself out. Finally we are reunited with the darling Lancia, gleamingly white with its red leather interior. Claude and I settle in, he on my lap, his ears pricked up, watching the road through the steering wheel. We zoom off, in the direction of the interstate. We are ridiculously small compared to the other cars and lorries on the road beside us. We haven't been driving ten minutes when I start to have misgivings. Is there something strange in the air? Like seeing a Frenchman in a Barbour, I know there's something amiss but just can't pinpoint it. Maybe it's the fact that my foot is flat on the floor and we're pootling along at 40mph.

'35. 30. 25. 20.'

'All right, Claudius. I don't need a running commentary of the speedometer thank you.'

Just before we grind to a complete standstill I pull off to the emergency lane. My shoulders shoot up to my ears in hyper stress mode. This is when the angels, screeching laughter, turn to me and say:

'You thought it would all be fine! But today is one of the worst of your life! And we are no Ice Angels . . .'

'Oh my God,' first quietly and then a thunderous scream. 'Oh my GOD.' The world carries on around me in slow motion as I experience two silent moments of utter helplessness. I realise with a heavy heart that Claudius and I will not be making as much progress today as we were hoping. And that I look faintly ridiculous in my shift dress, slingbacks and sun specs pushing back hair. I totter for miles along to the roadside phone.

'Jon! Booty!' are the only two words the pick-up driver utters as he delivers Claude, the Lancia and me to the local garage several hours later.

Jon is his name, fuck-ups is his game, his badge and face simultaneously tell me. His manner is irritatingly slow and he's clearly unmoved by the serious state of my car. He seems to have read *Zen and the Art of Motorcycle Maintenance* because he insists that we look at the facts one at a time to work it all through, referring incessantly to *method*.

'The facts are very simple,' I toot. 'My car has broken down and needs fixing. Immediately.'

'Sweet little kitty. Here kitty kitty kitty.'

'For fuck's sake. Could we please concentrate on the matter in hand?'

'Now ma'am, if ya cain't keep this clean I cain't carry on the conversation. Cussin' jess takes mah mind off the work. Now there are two ways of looking at it. Either you accept the rule of the universe and work at it methodically which is what me an ma boyz are gonna do or you fight against it and get yourself nowheres.'

'Fine. When will my car be ready?'

'Couldn't rightly say. Ain't never seen one a these before.'

God knows where that accent's from – we're not even out of New York state yet.

Faced with such pub philosophy I invent specific methods not to punch him in the face. Either I bite a part of myself to release the sheer violence inside (ideally I'd hurl glasses at walls like Elizabeth Taylor in *Cat on a Hot Tin Roof*, but we're outside so it's not practical) or I blaspheme silently in an expletive-type way about Jesus because I am convinced, due to my Catholic upbringing, that if the devil thinks he has won your soul, he brings about your dearest wish, which in this case is that Jon, quite simply, explode. Of course I realise I am compromising my own soul and security in the next life with this, but still, it seems worth it. Anyway back to the biting . . .

'Mikey? Mikey? Is that you?'

'What do you want, baby?'

'Hi! Hi! How are you?'

'You know how I am. You saw me this morning. Where are you?'

'Oh, Mikey. Lovely talking to you. Actually I wondered if I mightn't ask a favour?'

'For cryin' out loud. If I haven't already driven four hours today for you.'

'Um, there's been a slight problem, and I was wondering if you mightn't come and pick us up?'

'Why? Why don't you drive yourself back here if you have to come home?'

'Well, the car is not what you'd call in working condition. It broke down ten minutes out of the docks.'

My dream of road-tripping around America seems temporarily stuffed. Luckily, Jon's partner is more useful. He puts me in touch with a local classic enthusiast, who offers to buy the Lancia. This is not my ideal scenario, but I realise that if we continue with the Babe-mobile, it might take some time to get to California. I can't face breaking down every ten minutes, which is what Claudius assures me will happen. He takes the money and runs. I totter after him in my blistered high trotters unable to believe that I don't have my little Lancia any more.

So today I go to buy a car. Negotiations with the local dealer are swift but firm and I think we both get our points across.

'What are you doing?'

'Crossing the States.'

'So you need a family car.'

'No, I want a convertible.'

'Or an SUV.'

'No, no jeeps, but something large, American . . .'

'But you need something which doesn't use too much gas. Like a Dodge Shadow.'

'No, God no. I think something from the Fifties. Classic. A Cadillac, pink if poss.'

'And you need something you can sleep in if lost.'

'No, I'll be bedding down in beds as I was designed to do, thanks. Basically something sporty and cool.'

'So you want Japanese.'

'Absolutely not, no.'

'. . .'

Eventually he sways me from the Classic Car scene, mainly because none of them has any air conditioning, and apparently it's hot down south. So in the end we shake hands on a Buick LeSabre. Classic American, if er, brand new. Not a 70s muscle car *à la Starsky and Hutch*, not a see-sawing huge convertible ship *à la Thelma and Louise*, but a comfortable family-sedan thing. Plenty of room to stretch the legs. It seems neither classic nor cool but I am open to suggestions. Anyway I have never driven a new car before. I get in and smell the smell of new and it smells good. It looks good too – shiny bottle-green. It has air con, a CD player, cruise control, the works, and all of these can be manned from buttons on the steering wheel.

So once again we set off, this time with Janie and Mikey waving from the steps of their home. Claude and I set off for Pennsylvania on the 184. But when we get to the Taconic Parkway and see signs to New York, I can't resist. I've been there before but Claudius hasn't. Ridiculous to come to America and not spend some time in the world's most exciting city. So we point the nose of the quietly humming Buick towards the skyscrapers . . .

Chapter Three

Breakfast at Tiffany's

New York

After a quick roadside phone call, we have a place to stay with a friend on the Upper East Side. Negotiating the traffic and getting lost about seventy-four times are highly stressful events. Buses stop suddenly in the inside lane and cabs play some advanced form of 'Death' with me. They pull out in front, they swerve behind, they do the hokey cokey and they blow my mind. Coming into the city without a map was a marvellous idea. It's all very hairy, and I drive slowly so as not to jerk Claudius from his seat, which simply *infuriates* everyone around us. He sits on the passenger side next to me, his litter tray on the floor in the back, his water cup in the holder next to my Coke, his food bowl on the floor-divider between us. We listen to Barry White, the one where he says, 'Take it off. Take it all off. I don't want to see no panties. And take off that brazeer, ma dear,' which in normal circs would keep us in playful mode but now? Oh no. It stands in stark contrast to the furore and mayhem around us.

I've never stayed in this swish part of town before and am excited about possible luxury. Yes there is a uniformed doorman who helps me with my bags. Yes there is a gold lobby and fast lifts. Yes the apartment is minute as only New York apartments can be. After settling Claude on the sofa bed (he's a tad tired after the journey and wants to catch up on his sleep), I meet an old school friend, Kate, for a cocktail at the Izzy Bar on First Ave. We down margaritas before going on for supper at Bistro Jules in St Mark's Place. The later it gets the more everyone comes alive. We watch the girls. They are unusual and beautiful – not just blonde and big-titted but interesting-looking, clear-skinned and *lovely*.

Kate and I gossip, and acknowledge each other's love-life/laughable careers/haircuts with clipped New Yorker 'Right's. Actually, asherlee, actuerlee, I'd been practising mine in England.

A few examples of the many situations we used it in:
   'I'm going to have the tuna frisé salad.'
   'Right.'
   'Bruno was an arsehole.'
   'Right.'
   'Do you only change your knicks when they smell of marmite?'
   'Right.'
   'I'm having a sex change.'
   'Right.'

On the subway home at about 12.30, a group of unscared German tourists yodel songs at the other end of the carriage while I fantasise about the damn glam week Claude and I are about to have: the parties, the shopping, the cocktails.

Then, the night from hell. It is boiling hot so I constantly turn the air conditioning on and off, on for the cool air, off because of the noise. Not that it makes much difference. Claude and I might as well kip down on Lexington Ave itself. Ambulances, police cars and lorries holler their way through the Manhattan night sounding horns fit for chemical carriers in the foggy Pacific. One siren plays a disco tune rather than the usual howl, the DJ driver scratching out blipped suppressed bubbles at full pelt. Anyone heading for the hospital in one of these will have to be treated for cardiac arrest or deafness on arrival.

Lunch with Dala, a special-projects editor on one of the Condé Nast magazines. She gives me the most valuable piece of advice I've heard since I thought up this trip. She walks me along Madison wearing brown suede trousers, white T-shirt and white cowboy hat. She is stopping traffic – quite irritating as I would rather do it myself. No one gives me a second look even though I have on a charming light blue mini skirt, matching T-shirt, very expensive deep-pink cardigan from Voyage, and matching pink suede mules that I bought in Clarks in London. (I was stopped by the fashion police on the way in but they were so impressed by the bargain price – £17 – they let me off.) She takes me out for lunch and I debate whether to get my hair cut in a salon chain store or go for the more expensive option. Dala is adamant. 'You can't mess this up. Remember, when you're down south, your haircut is all you'll have to fall back on.' So at Bumble and Bumble on the corner of 56th and Lexington, Shawn (a girl) cuts my hair with one of those tools my father used to cut my brothers' hair with back in the 70s.
'Was he a barber, your dad?'
'No, a barrister.'
'Oh, similar then.'
All hairdressers the world over have one characteristic in common: they have dreadful haircuts. Shawn's is sawn off in the most unlikely places and coloured red and orange in various patches. But she's a wizard with one of those thingummies. She cuts and shapes for hours as I feel more and more guilty about leaving Claudius alone. In the end she opts for the tousled look. Which means I walk out looking like a matted-carpet-tramp-creature from the bog. The whole experience is extortionate but very satis-

fying. I trip along Lexington feeling most Audrey afterwards.

Today we are surrounded by skyscrapers as we wander through the financial district, downtown. It's awesome, but Claude hasn't seen a tree in a while and he has decided that today's burning question is this: can trees commit suicide? Can they stop osmosis or whatever it is and just refuse to let the juice in? Take one, stuck by itself in the middle of Fifth Avenue surrounded by pollution through no fault of its own. Can it bail out? His clear green eyes ask me this question and then turn back to the people hurrying to and from Wall Street. They are in too much of a hurry to notice him and when they do they are already out of patting range, because they are moving so fast. A cat with questions, a human with no answers.

Lunch with Claude, Kate and her boss, Jaron (who invented Virtual Reality), in the Empire Diner on 10th Ave. A silver-chrome art-deco classic American diner – reputedly Bette Davis's favourite – with a fat old lady in a pink gingham waitress coat and pink lipstick above her lips playing Sinatra tunes on the piano in the corner. After ordering we sit outside so that Claudius can bask in the sun on the fourth chair. The place is great, just the sort of atmospheric diner I had fantasised about.

'I hope the rest of America is like this.'

'Don't be fooled by the nostalgia for the old days,' says Jaron. 'People want the homogenousness around them. They want the easy life it entails.' (From the man who invented the means to access the entire world from your living room.)

'Problem is, it's making everywhere like everywhere else. Seeing McDonald's and Burger King in any international city merely encourages people to be set in their ways rather than try something new, and people who are rigid tend to close down the world for people trying to push out less conventional ideas.'

'How original. I've not heard that one before.'

'Oh shut up, Claude.'

Just then the waitress storms up and tells me to get my 'mutt' outta here. Claudius cocks one ear to the back of his head and looks away.

'My what?'

'Your old mutt. He's unhygienic.'

'Not as dirty as you by the looks of things. And he's a cat, a cat, do you see? Anyway, we're outside.'

She raises her eyes to the sky and then slams our food down. She buggers off returning with the check which she almost throws at me.

'Can I have a pen, please?'

'No. I don't have an extra pen,' she spits, her nose up to mine. My blood's up.

I borrow one from the other (smiley) waitress and take it back.

'There, was that such a big deal?' I turn and walk to our table.

She storms up.

'Excuse me, why do you come up to me in such an aggressive manner?'

'Aggressive? Have you taken a look at yourself lately? You've been unbearably impolite.'

'Well, that's very interesting.' Huffs off. Pounces back.

'You know what? It takes one to know one.'

'Oh well, now you've said it. I'm crushed. I am tot-al-ly crushed.'

I'm on some weird adrenalin high, charged from having stuck up for us, but Claude seems slightly sheepish, if you can imagine, and Jaron is looking as though I've just admitted to having lesbian sex with my sister. Vaguely titillated but essentially horrified.

*   *   *

I'm still psyched so to cool off I decide to take Claude for a walk in Central Park. Appropriately, as we climb into the cab, the driver plays the Eartha Kitt seat-belt tape.

'Cats have nine lives – grooawrh – but unfortunately you have only one – so buckle up!'

At the entrance I put Claude down while I search my pockets for his purple halter.

'Don't even think about it,' he says as he stalks off in the direction of the Wollman Rink to watch the rollerbladers. Pottering after him I hear several people stage whisper, 'Only in New York,' as he passes. He elicits a lot of attention, mainly from under-five-year-olds, who crowd round him, over-pat him and murmur 'Kitty' to themselves. The place is full of nutters. One girl, who has rollerblades without the rollers, but with springy little bridges that lift her two feet off the ground, is explaining to the crowd around her that these are 'Kangaroo Jumps', before bouncing off.

Then a guy in T-shirt and sweat shorts gets off his bike to talk to Claudius. We strike up a conversation; he explains about his engineering/building job, I tell him about my trip. After a while he starts repeating himself, and I foresee that our acquaintanceship will not develop into a deep and lasting friendship.

And then it pops out. I look down and his wiener is looking at me blackly from the leg of his shorts. I wonder whether he realises. Then he says, 'There are so many beautiful sights in the Park.'

Juh right.

Claudius, meanwhile, is ruminating towards the tramps. Kale (Kale? Dala? Jaron? These people should be extras on *Star Trek*) wakes from her afternoon nap to find him staring into her face from a distance of 5 cm. After a brief 'argh!' she sits up and we chat. I mention thirst and she says she'll go get us a drink. I give her the rest of my money and then wonder guiltily if I'll ever see her again. I need the change to take a cab home, as the subway might scare Claude. After a while she returns and I feel worse for having doubted her.

'Haven't you any family you could stay with, Kale?'

'My husband he beat up on me. Thas why I leave.'

'How long have you been homeless?'

'A yea now. Comin on fo a yea. It ain't easy. Livin out. It ges cold in winner.'

'What about your family?'

'Ah don know whey they are.'

'Or your friends?'

'Nor them neither.'

'How will you get off the streets?'

'There you go gin axing another question I don know the answer to. Ah tried. Ah went to one of them half way houses, but I couldn stay. I had to go. I got into fights with the other girls. Cos they was tryin ta take mah stuff. And I don want nobody touching mah stuff. It's mine. Here kitty kitty kitty. Was her name?' She strokes Claudius who gives her his most chocolate whiskery face, half closing his eyes in warm pleasure, purring like a machine gun.

'His. He's a boy. Claudius.'

'Christmas?'

'Claudius.'

'Claws are us?'

'Claudius. Claw-di-us.'

'Clowdeearse. Hmm. Sounds classic to me.'

'Yes that's right. He's a classic.'

'Well he sho is perty.'

'Thank you.'

After a pause we talk about the warm summer and the cool drinks and the cool cat sitting on the grass watching the world go by, because it's easier than the real issues. I want to help, but in order to do that I would have to commit, I would have to stay with her and have her stay with me. My middle-class rationalisations kick in; I don't know her from Adam, she might steal everything, I don't know the truth of her situation. As if that matters. The bottom line is this: I'm homeless out of choice. I'm ashamed of my own thoughts and my inability to stay anywhere long enough to do anyone any good.

This morning Claude made a startling revelation.

'I don't like this part of town.'

'Why not, my kitkat? It's rather Audrey.'

'If that's what you call rich, old Jewish women having manicures and waiting for the winter so they can emigrate to Florida, then so be it. Personally I would prefer somewhere rather more hip.'

'Um, let me see what I can do.'

So, on to the task of finding the kitten somewhere more pleasing to stay. Luckily, my sister's best friend Derek lives in Chelsea. His apartment is immaculately designer with a terrace, a state-of-the-art music system, walls and walls of hardback books about the fashion and music industries and a silver Bengal cat named Pearl. I think Claudius will feel it a home from home so we're moving in today.

As we settle in, Pearl hisses angrily. For the first time ever I'm grateful that a cat has had its nails removed. Claude of course refuses to lower himself to a snarling situation – probably due to his lack of teeth. Instead he curls up on the sofa and catches up on some sleep. I case the joint and look at all the silver-framed photos on the walls. Derek has lived here since 1974 and has obviously made a lot of friends.

'They're all dead,' he says as he watches me scan them for pictures of my sister.

'It's the wall of fame. They all died of Aids. Of these,' he points to one picture of eight friends partying on Fire Island, 'I'm the only survivor.' With that, he stalks off to the bathroom to prepare us some coke.

Which seems to be addictive. Ten lines later (and a little pill to stop the jitters), we go to a diner. No hunger. Then we hit a gay bar – pow! right in the kisser. A bald type with a tiny cropped T-shirt, having his huge beer gut massaged by a stranger, asks a passing Derek, 'What are *you* into?'

'Forget it,' he replies.

I'm the only girl there, and receive no attention whatsoever, until a guy eventually comes up and asks, 'What are you *doing* here?' I pacify him by giving him change to play on the slot machine, where you pair up various male faces and bodies in a certain time, to be rewarded by a huge picture of a guy doing something *filthy*. I've always been rather good at Pelmanism. Eventually we get home and pop another pill to sleep. In the morning I feel a bit strange, so Derek gives me another pill to make me feel better. Claudius on the other hand is sitting at the other end of the bed ignoring me.

I feel instinctively that he didn't sleep in my arms last night. I move towards him but he plays hard to get. He's ignoring me. I burst into tears. Yes, my cat has the power to make me cry. I lie in my sofa bed gazing at the sun brushing the Manhattan roofs, in my favourite city in the world, and I cry solidly (keeping an eye on him to see whether he feels at all guilty). I can't remember a night in two years when he hasn't slept in my arms. After a while he shifts towards me looking concerned. But he says not a word.

I presume that travelling isn't always going to be easy. Regardless of serious problems like illness on either part, there is also the question of everyday moods. He's in a sulk, but he'll get over it. Having said that, I feel very panicky when all is not well with him. What if he hates it here so much that he starts to get ill and then dies? Even though he is at an advanced age and this event must take place sooner rather than later, I can't see through it, I can't see past it, I can't see it at all. Sometimes I almost wish that he would die just so that I can get it over with, because I know it has to happen. Then I fear the pain and I feel like a heroin addict. I'll do anything in my power to prevent it from happening. So rather than take the risk I have to find a way to make him sweet again. Oh for God's sake, I don't know. At least I've started smoking again. Thank God.

Today a call from Jaron with the number of a friend of his, a Famous New York Novelist who has done a similar trip and wants to meet me. I can't take Claudius because I now know what these restaurants are like about health regulations. I dress up in kitten heels, purple silk skirt, no knicks so as to avoid VPL, little DKNY cardi draped around shoulders. All the clocks in the apartment say different times, and I can't ask Claude which is the correct one because he's still sulking, so I choose the most likely and leave under the impression that I can saunter down Eighth Ave to West 4th in the Village. On the way out I hear the postman telling someone it's five minutes before our lunch date. I bomb it, but get pushed by a nutter on to the subway things Marilyn stood over to feel the cool air in *The Seven Year Itch*. I don't remember Marilyn's heels getting caught with her legs in a dreadful knock-kneed position. And of course she had pants on when the train came. Red-faced and sweating, I run into the restaurant. When we talked on the phone and I mentioned that I didn't know what he looked like, he suggested, after a disgusted pause, that I go to a bookstore and look up his face on the back of one of his many bestsellers. Juh right. I haven't done this but I wish I had because he's incredibly attractive.

'So what's your route?'

'Um. It's this way,' drawing a large smile across the bottom of an imaginary America.

'Yes, but the roads. And where you're stopping.'

'Well I'm not that organised. I'm more of a fly by the seat of my pants kinda gal' – this last in the sort of transatlantic twang I swore I'd never adopt.

He is not overly impressed.

Hungover, witless and spark-free, henceforth I bore him so rigid that he spends most of our lunch with his eyes glued to the door, his face at a 90° angle to mine, evidently searching for someone prettier/more interesting to walk in and amuse him.

Afterwards, to cheer myself up before facing the sulky kitkat, I have my first manicure. The girl speaks not a word of English, so when she asks whether I want them square or curved, and I reply curved, she instantly blocks my nails off so that I can do handstands on them.

I should have an early night, but am too depressed to have Claudius reject me again so I'm off to drink with a friend of Janie and Mikey's, whom I first met when I was seventeen. I was terrified of him then, thinking he was one of the Mafia, but now in my late twenties I think I might be able to handle him better. Also, he knows people all over the States and I'm hoping for the odd contact or two as well as a fat dinner somewhere fabulous. He is a lawyer, pushing seventy, short, fat and his crooked hook of a fat nose has two huge warts at the end. So no Prince Charming then. He decides that an English girl would feel at home in – an English pub, Churchill's on Third Ave. Great. Just what I came to New York for. There are three old winos propping up the bar. Good to know I'm at the hub of New York society. Don insists on kissing me on the mouth which leaves me vaguely queasy.

'What to drink, Young Lady?'

'I'll have a Scotch on the rocks, please.' I hoist myself up on to the bar stool, as his hand brushes my bum in a misplaced attempt to help me up.

'Sure you don't want a beer? They're very good here.'

'No, sure, I'll have a Scotch on the rocks, I love that.'

'And it's cold too. Fresh from the casket and cold. Jim, get the little lady a pint of your beer. She's English. She'll love it. What'll ya have to eat?'

I peruse the menu.

'A steak – rare please.'

'But you're in America! Cam ahn. Have a hamburger. Jim! Get her a Monster Burger. So, my dear, long time no see.'

'No, Don. How long has it been? Let me see . . .' I start mentally totting up but stop mid-sum as he slams his hand on to my forehead, almost causing a frontal lobotomy.

'Stop frowning! It'll give ya wrinkles!'

'Oh! Well I am almost thirty now, Don, so a few wrinkles would show a life well lived. No?'

'Are ya kidding? You'll never get a husband with that attitude. Don't drink that!' He whips away his Perrier which I'm about to swig. 'It'll give ya cellulite!'

'Nothing could make my cellulite worse. How come you're an expert on these matters?' And what about your paunch and balding head? What are we going to do about those? my mind yells out.

'Hey, now don't get shirty. I remember now. I remember that temper. Yeah. Yeah,' chuckling to himself. 'You need to be dominated.'

'And you're the guy to do it, *right*?'

'Now listen, if fifteen-year-olds can be satisfied, I don't think you should be quite so fussy.'

'What *are* you talking about?' and instantly regret asking.

'Let me tell ya a story.' (My burger arrives so I tuck into it while I listen to his shaggy-dog story. Simultaneously I become obsessed with finding his top teeth. As he talks and smiles I notice they never appear. I become convinced they don't exist and wonder how he pronounces his esses.)

'A few years back, a very good friend of mine asked me to look after her daughter one evening while she went out with her boyfriend. She was a very well-to-do New York society lady. So I say what's she like, yer daughter? And she says, fifteen. She's pretty. Don, I'll leave her in your capable hands.'

'OK. I don't believe this already. No mother that loved her daughter would leave the girl with you.'

'Shirty again, huh? Well, wait till I've finished. So this girl comes around. She's dressed head to toe in Chanel. I buy her dinner, we go back and watch TV. She swings her legs up on to my sofa and and falls asleep. I phone her mother. "What shall I do? She's asleep," I say. "Let her sleep," says her mother. "Just make sure she gets to her hairdressing appointment tomorrow at eleven." So, I move her to my spare room and tuck her up and go to bed. In the middle of the night, she comes into my room. I wake up to find her staring at me. "You didn't touch me did you?" she asks. "No, of course not," I reply. "I want you to make love to me," she says. "Are you kidding?" I say. "You're fifteen." "So?" she says. "You're not the first. You have to, please," she says. Well, anyway, I won't do it. Next night she comes over and the same thing. Then the third night . . .'

'Let me get this straight. You say you have a beautiful fifteen-year-old begging you to have sex with her.'

'That's right. On the third night I do, and afterwards she jumps up and down on the bed, naked, shouting, "I'll never do a preppy again! I'll never do a preppy again!" '

'Because your technique is so fantastic?'

'Well, I guess. Anyway she has her best friend whom she introduces me to. "I want you to make love to her," she said. "But you can't come inside her. You have to come inside me." '

'I think I'm going to be sick.'

'So this friend comes round. She too is from one of New

York's foremost society families and she too is dressed exclusively by Chanel. And so we go to bed. Then this one has a friend too.'

'How many more are there, Don?'

'That's it, three of them. So for a while all three of us slept in the same bed together. And I made them all read the newspapers and study hard. And if one of them didn't get good grades she would be excluded from group activities, like –'

'– don't tell me.'

'I was going to say like going out to dinner. Then one day the first girl's father comes on the phone.'

'Sticky.'

'Very tricky. But he says, "Don I don't wanna know how ya did it. But Kimberley's grades are fantastic. She's helpful and sweet at home. She's no longer the grouchy teenager she was. And I want to thank you. Let's go out to lunch." '

'So if I have understood correctly, Don, the moral of the story is that you are a healer of some sort.'

'Well I'm just saying –'

'– rather than a child molester?'

'Child molester? What are you talking about? These girls were begging me. And anyway they were hardly vestal virgins. They had done most of the football team between them.'

'Two wrongs don't make a right. Children who are grossly neglected by their parents, who fuck around for affection, and then you come along, someone who could make a difference and help them, and you *fuck them too?*'

'Their grades went up and their parents were happy.'

'Were they happy? But I want to know why you're telling me this?'

'I just think, Clare, you could do with a little help. You know this cat thing is a little weird . . .'

'Do you know what, Don? Strange as it may seem I'm

going to pass up on the fantastic opportunity to be touched by your healing spermatozoa this evening. Put it down to hereditary insanity, but I just don't think it's a good idea.'

'Well, have fun in the south. You realise of course that the cops down there have fake radar readers. When they see your out-of-town licence plates, they'll stop you, claim you're over the limit and slam you in jail for the night. But it'll do ya good. You're a piece of hoity-toity shit. You think your fancy education makes ya special and ya know everything. Well, it doesn't and ya don't. Those girls had better manners than you. And they were more reliable, too.'

Back home I relate the story to a pretending-not-to-be-interested Claudius (who has spent all evening watching documentaries on Studio 54 up in Derek's bed) and decline Derek's offer of the odd pill or sniff to cheer me up. I pull out the sofa bed and settle in. To my relief Claudius settles in my arms and motor-purrs us to sleep. In the night I can sense him taking a break and sitting up straight to watch me. I have often woken to find him like this, patiently waiting for me to forget my slumbers and give him breakfast. Sometimes he gets bored and bites me on the nose to hurry things up a bit. Which he does this morning at 6am.

Today I feel distinctly 'there's a great party going on and I haven't been invited'. It might be the coke, it might be New York, whatever, I'm not happy. I flick through the papers until I notice a small box advertising Lee Day, a pet celebrity hair stylist. What does this mean? Is she a celebrity, or does she just deal with celebrities' pets or pets that are celebrities? How many celebrity pets are there anyway? Isn't Lassie dead? Must be a lean living she's making. I phone and she invites us to her place in Bloomfield, New Jersey. Claude and I hop on a bus at Grand Central – I would take the car except I can't remember where I parked it. The journey is bumpy and uncomfortable through some ugly parts of town and Claude is slightly bad-tempered when we arrive.

'I just want to make people and animals happy,' Lee yodels as we step down off the bus. She's short, squat, and her Annie-orange curls surround a tiny yellow face in a large head. She leads us back to her flat, which features

1 Framed signed pictures of Joan Rivers, Liz Taylor and Doris Day;
2 a picture of Lee herself in classic showbiz garb, top hat and tails holding a pooch in her arms, and
3 stomach-churning doggie catty smells.

Her own cat, a ginger mog named Lucas Lorenzo Spencer, is the size of a small St Bernard. She cured him of diabetes. Probably by bursting into song, which she does every ten minutes. Her smooth-haired dachshund, Dr Doogie, sings along whenever she opens her mouth – a kind of howling prayer. He's the pooch in the picture. She sings loudly to Claudius who turns to me with a firm 'Get me out of here now' look on his face. I change the subject.

'Are you related to Doris Day?'

'I always loved her. So I took her name. And I have her voice' – brief excerpt of *Pillow Talk* in American Les Dawson/Marge Simpson tones – 'she was born eleven days before me. And my brother – he's a film editor – he was looking through all these old photos recently and he found one of her. It was taken 11 January 1961 at 11.15 in the morning – funny how I remember that?' She talks faster and faster, her face approaching mine with every word, the saliva forming strings and bubbles at the side of her mouth. 'Isn't it all a bit too close for comfort?'

'It certainly is. And have you ever spoken to your idol?'

'Yes, once, back in 1975. You know it's sad. One of my

clients' father was Doris's son's highschool headteacher.
So I got hold of his yearbook, and contacted him that very
day – that very day! Of course he was thrilled to be sent a
copy, but Doris never wrote to thank me. Did I have to do
any of that? No, it was because I love from the bottom of
my heart.'

'So why did you only speak once?'

'Because a lesbian friend of mine stole Doris's number
from my phone book, and kept calling her. She bothered
her repeatedly and Doris blamed me and never called me
again. Our friendship ruined just like that because of that
lesbian. And then Doris's photo – take this as an example. I
became friends with Liz Taylor and she sent me a photo.
Look at this: "With all my love always, Liz" – not Elizabeth
Taylor. But Doris just wrote "To Lee from Doris".'

'How did you become friends with Liz?'

'I wrote to her sending her some health suggestions for
her little dog.'

'Oh great. Did you then meet her?'

'No.'

'Did you ever talk on the phone?'

'No.' She sighs. 'Ya know? Doris didn't go to Frank
Sinatra's funeral. She's meant to love animals. But I don't
think she can love animals if she treats humans that way.
Clare, can you imagine how it feels to realise that your idol
is a piece of caca?'

'When are we going home?'

'Claude, shh, boy.'

'He is talkative, isn't he? So is Lucas. Lucas, talk to us
honey!'

'Meoow. Meow meow meow meow meoooooooooow.'

'There you go!'

Claude and I exchange looks.

'So where are you going on this trip?'

'We're heading for California across the southern
states.'

'Great! Here is Doris's number. Call her. You tell her. You say Lee is the most fascinating, wonderful person and all England thinks so, and she's keeping you alive, because everyone thinks you're dead.'

I ask her about her career and what exactly does she do? What's the celebrity part of all this? She turns on the video and plays us tapes of her

i   Performing a bark mitzvah for Joan Rivers's dog, Spike;

ii   marrying a West Highland terrier in miniature top and tails to some other tiny white ball of cutesy fluff dressed in a white veil – 'If anyone objects to this wedding let them bark, meow or grunt now', and

iii   presiding over some cattychisms.

No, really.

Turns out she has appeared on 'Wogan' and several other TV shows. Back in the 80s, as a result of 'Wogan', Princess Di (*Prinny Di!*) had invited her to sing to the boys' rabbits at Ken Pal.

'Wasn't it sad when she died? I felt awful,' I venture.

'You felt awful? Imagine how I felt knowing her. You know the night before she died I was feeling very low. I hadn't been acknowledged by Show Business, Doris had treated me badly, I was blue. I was falling asleep and suddenly there was a flash of light and an angel before me. Now, I had taken a pill but that wouldn't bring flashing lights into my room, now would it? The angel said, 'Lee. Your work with Dr Doogie is not yet finished.' And next day Princess Di died. Isn't that strange? I was told the news by my best friend who coincidentally used to be Doris's secretary. So I immediately sent angel keyrings to all Diana's relations. You know her boys sent me personal

Royal Letters.' She proudly shows me typed notes from their private secretaries. 'Now those boys wouldn't have written to me unless I had been a friend of their mother's – right?' She sighs. 'I hate sex. I think it's disgusting and nasty. I'd like to create a cute little Disney world. I dunno. Maybe I'm too deep for most people.'

'I'm *sorry?*'

'Claude, shh.'

I turn back to Lee who says, 'Now, do you want to see me blow Lucas out?'

'Oh! No thank you.' This very quickly.

'Come on you'll love it.'

She plumps her cat-dog in the kitchen sink, turns the hose on him and lathers up some baby shampoo. Then out with the hairdryer. All the time she sings lustily, 'A lick on the face may be nice, wet and sloppy, but pet treats are a pet's best friend . . .'

'OK. When's the next bus back to Planet Earth?'

'Claude – be patient, she's very sweet.'

The last few bars ring out from her lusty lungs, and she turns smiling towards us.

'Now then, would you like me to do Claudius?'

My brow frowns but a wicked glint of possible revenge for the recent sulks makes my mouth say:

'Yes. I think he'd love that.'

'*What?*' says a horrified Claude who then turns and races around the room with both me and Holly Golightly's nemesis after him. Up curtains across chairs a clear leap over the bed up on to the video all her tapes scattering to the ground through the draining crockery on the sink on the soggy tuna sandwiches waiting on the kitchen table over the fridge down the stairs and into the dark cellar.

'I don't think he's keen, Lee,' I heavy-breathe to her. She hasn't had such a good workout in years. 'We'd better go.'

'What a shame.'

It only takes me two hours to find Claude and give him

the all-clear. Weirdly, he is silent all the way back to the city.

To make up for yesterday's fiasco and my naughty behaviour, I take Claude to Tiffany's. Unfortunately I oversleep so by the time we get there the day has developed into a fully blown Saturday shopping day and the place is heaving with Japanese tourists. There is a slight kerfuffle at the door as the doorman refuses to allow Claudius in. Claude in his turn refuses to get in my rucksack and absolutely will not brook his purple silk harness. I am slightly peeved at the doorman as I am sure he allows New Yorkers' irritating little lap dogs in. Be that as it may, we are out on the street and can but admire the jewels from the windows.

'So what do you think Claude? Should one wear diamonds before the age of forty?'

'I thought you said we were having breakfast here. I'm hungry.'

I open a tin of sardines in tomato and we share it straight from the tin squatting on the pavement outside. Not the glamorous scene I had envisaged. Worse, people stop and stare.

'We're a couple of no-name slobs. We belong to nobody and nobody belongs to us. We don't even belong to each other.'

'Claude, don't say that. In fact, why don't we take this moment – please don't eat that, that's on my side – to discuss how you feel about New York. I've got the impression recently that you aren't totally keen.'

'I was hoping it would be like *Taxi** but it's much cleaner and richer. Of course that makes it less heady than the Studio 54 days.'

'Which you knew masses about, being a cat.'

* Claudius was around in the late 70s, albeit only just and in kitten form, but already an avid observer of all things cultural – telly.

He ignores this.

'New York has chewed us up and, by the looks of your baggy eyes and over-thin frame, is about to spit you out. I, luckily, am still sleek and brown. We should leave.'

'But there are plenty of other things to do here that we haven't done. I haven't told you about Wigstock, when all the drag queens parade through Central Park wearing two-foot platforms and silver-foil-covered-loo-roll-wigs, and we haven't yet watched a movie on the Hudson river from a boat like in *Cinema Paradiso* or posed for Spencer Tunick starkers on Brooklyn Bridge . . .'

'No matter. We should leave.'

'Right.'

After a protracted search for the car, we leave the city and hop on the I84 in the direction of Pennsylvania. Our time in NYC has been bitter-sweet. Bitter because I wanted a piece of the action – to do the supermodel thing and hang out at the best parties and the newest most infamous clubs, in spite of the fact that I am neither a supermodel nor famous – and failed miserably. Sweet because in New York, even when you end up in a tacky English pub on Third Ave with repulsive, frog-like Mafia-lawyers, sur-rounded by low-life over-drinking bar-proppers, you still feel like you're in a film. It may be a C going straight to the Korean video market, but at least it's celluloid.

Chapter Four

Witness

Pennsylvania Dutch Country

OK so here we are on the road driving towards Amish country, and what a lovely if very bland road it is too. We've crossed into Pennsylvania and the view isn't even slightly different from England or Connecticut, just greenery at the side of the road and nothing else to see. We've been going for ages now. I have no idea how close we are to our first stop, Shartlesville, but I think it's a while yet. Dum di dum. Here comes a sign. That's weird. It's indeed for the ville of Shartle, but on the road 61, whereas I was expecting Interstate 78. What shall I do? Maybe this is a short cut, except if it's a normal road it could take hours longer. What do I do? What if there isn't an interstate near Shartlesville as I thought? Aaargh, I can't decide nor can I slow down because I want us to get there before dark. Only problem is if I miss the turning it'll take us even longer to get there. We're at 70 in the outside lane and there's the turning up ahead. Shall I take it? Or? Oh God there's a lorry on my inside I can't get over. Oh fuck. Oh fuckit. Too late. Oh shit. I'm lost. Help. We're in the middle of America and I have absolutely no idea where I am or where I'm going and my map isn't detailed enough and I think I'm going to cry. I hate everything. Waaaah.

'Well you're a relaxing companion.' Claudius awakes and stretches.

'I've just missed our turning.'

'Were you asleep?'

'Sadly, not all of us can afford the luxury of catching up on our zeds while driving.'

'How long have we been in the car?'

'Seven hours.'

'Wasn't this leg meant to take us three?'

'Yes,' through gritted teeth.

'How much longer in the car?'

'Five months so shut it.'

'What's that up ahead?'

'A sign, to, I can't read it yet, um, Interstate 78! Fantastic! We're OK.'

We choose our first motel, the appropriately named Dutch Motel, and settle in. I don't tell them about Claude because it's just for one night. And because there's a huge sign saying 'No Pets'. I'm just too tired to look for anywhere else. Finally in the room. A small white asbestos-ceilinged box, thin brown curtains, plastic cups, thin worn coverlet on the bed, face-less. Claude sniffs around discontentedly and then sits on the bed looking grumpy.

Right, now what? No carousing in the nearby diner or going to a bar drinking beers for me. I'm (a) alone (b) feeling shy and (c) too tired. So I'll try to sleep. I can't. The motel is right on the highway and therefore incredibly noisy. It's also hot so there's a choice of air conditioning and deafening noise, or open windows and deafening noise. Toss turn toss turn. Claudius's tail gently twitches and tickles against the side of my body, letting me know that he didn't enjoy today. Guilt and overwhelming self-doubt prevent me from sleeping. I want to cry and after just one day of travel am wondering exactly why I wanted to drive around America with my cat so badly. Is this freedom? I don't think so.

*   *   *

A Gloria Vanderbilt biography on TV doesn't knock me
out, so I finally think 'shove it' and do just that: shove
down my throat one of Claudius's emergency tranquilli-
sers the vet had given me for the flight over, which he
hadn't needed. As I down another, I notice the red-lettered
'For animal use ONLY' on the package. I then refuse to
sleep in case I fall into a coma.

Today I'm groggy, but alive. And actually have no idea
what we're meant to do now. Maybe some sightseeing? So
we pack and up and set off to discover the Amish and all
things truly American. I'm not dressed too outlandishly
today. As a concession to the Amish, I have taken off my
red nail-varnish (on my fingers – takes so much concen-
tration to do the toes that I couldn't quite bear to remove
that). And I'm wearing a *long-sleeved* pink T-shirt which
a) is swelteringly hot and b) says 'Born Free Babes' on it. A
little feminist cajoling to the Amish girls can't go amiss.
   Our first stop is Roadside America, the world's largest
miniature village. The old ducks running it allow me to
carry Claude around in my arms, because the owner,
Alberta, whose grandfather built the entire village, loves
cats and has seven of her own. Her own whiskers are long
enough to tie into a bow. She is thrilled to see Claude, once
she's sure I'm not dumping him on her, which happens
regularly as she's the local cat-nut. Roadside America is
8,000 square feet. There's a canyon and lake with water-
falls, canals, highways, turnpikes and every other type of
scene or building you'd find in a 1941 rural town. There's
a cathedral with forty-four hand-painted windows which
took 400 hours to make, an airport, and several train
stations. There's even a butcher complete with dog begging for scraps. I press the various buttons designed for
audience participation, and Claudius's head shifts sharply
left to right as he watches the train run back and forth. The
village was built by two brothers at the turn of the century.

Back in those days before telly and joy-riding, youngsters enjoyed good clean fun like hiking. A ten-year-old named Laurence Gieringer and his brother Paul climbed nearby Mount Penn and looked down on the tiny village of Reading in the distance. Said Laurence: 'Say, Paul, wouldn't it be swell to make little houses the way they appear from here. Future generations could see how things are now.' To which Paul appropriately replied: 'Swell!'

'See, Claude, what you get when you devote yourself properly to something for yars and yars?'

'An overgrown toy?'

'Do you like it?'

'Swell!'

For smutty and childish reasons we drive off to look for a town called Intercourse. I'm happily following the long and correct road, when without warning it suddenly turns into a different and incorrect road.

Panic, turn around several times, get lost and promptly burst into tears. Then startle because Dodge pick-up truck has stopped and (good-looking) bald guy with Richard Gere eyes (all stitched in), scars on face and naked (brown) torso is standing at the window.

'Can I help you, ma'am?'

'I'm looking for Intercourse.' This last bit quietly.

'Uh huh.'

'I thought I was on the right road, but suddenly it changed and now I'm lost.'

'Just carry on the way you are, miss. That way you can't help but find what you're looking for.'

'Thank you.'

I follow his advice but the road still leads nowhere. Well, how unhelpful.

En route to another unlikely-named town, we notice a classic car rally. We stop for a breather and to admire the old Caddies and Chevvies and Fordies. The sun beats down, upping the temperature to 86°. Claude finds a Le Mans 326 and plumps himself down under the engine to escape the sun.

'Well jess look at that. Someone's left their kitty-kat to guard the car.'

In town I call Derek precisely so that in answer to his inevitable 'Where are you?' I can say:

'Paradise.' Pause. 'Pennsylvania.'

I've found us another motel, somewhere to stay for to-night, a nice clean place with beautiful large gardens which Claude wants to walk around in. Unfortunately they also have a 'No Pets' sign. I can see that travelling with him is going to be like harbouring an escaped convict. I'll have to keep schtum and pray that any other guests who notice him do the same.

As we are in the vicinity of the Amish, the very air seems pervaded with upright, honest molecules. Claude, in the room, is slightly peeved that he is not allowed to walk around outside. I leave guiltily to look for some lunch for us at the local shop. The motels are more expensive than I had bargained for and I predict a shortage of expensive dinners out in the future.

A couple of horse-drawn buggies are standing outside the shop. I go in excitedly. There are several women in there with baskets. They are all dressed identically, with plain nurse-like blue dresses and black aprons and white bonnets on their heads. They wear not a stitch of make-up between them and their long hair is tied back in a bun at the nape. The oldest has a parting so wide she looks bald, presumably from years of this austere coiffure. Presently they are joined by a couple of men who are dressed identically – to each other I mean, not that they're in blue dresses. They wear blue shirts with grey trousers held up by braces and straw boaters on their heads. Their long

pubey beards look strangely bare without a moustache –
in fact the circle of hair around their entire face makes
them look like the monkeys from *Planet of the Apes*. I try
not to stare but am fascinated by the rigidity of dress codes
and their conformity to one another.

Outside there are three tiny tots dressed in miniature
versions of their parents' clothes hanging out of the buggy.
I ask them whether they hire them out. They of course
have no idea what I'm talking about. Shy, I get back in the
car, but on the wrong side, forgetting that the driver's seat
is on the left here.

Back at the motel I tell Claude about them.

'How am I ever going to get near them? They're so
different.'

'Why don't you worry about when I'm next going to be
allowed outside?'

'What if they chuck us out?'

'Am I to be indoors for the next five months?'

So I go to the front desk ready to come clean about
Claudius. The old folks working the front desk aren't
there. Instead there's a girl about my age dressed very
neatly in Ann Taylor garb, with small gold earrings and
the slightest hint of make-up. She is clearly not Amish. She
tells me she is the daughter of the owners. Falteringly I tell
her why I'm here.

'I wondered if you would mind if he took a walk in these
lovely gardens of yours?'

A horrid pause.

'Of course.'

Relief. We chat and Grace tells me she is a Christian
Baptist missionary. 'My parents are Amish-Mennonites
but my grandmother was Amish. She died recently leaving
10 children, 65 grandchildren, 184 great-grandchildren
and 19 great-great-grandchildren – 278 descendants in
total.'

I start pummelling her with questions. I can understand the Amish life a hundred years ago, but what can it be like now, seeing these brand-new flash cars with people designered up inside them. Don't they wonder what our life is like? Don't they want Gucci stilettos? Don't their children all run away to the big city?

'Some do and some don't, like any group of people. Their numbers aren't depleting. They've been seeing big new cars all century. They're really not into material things. If you're interested you might want to come to my cousin's wedding, tomorrow. The reception will take place at the next farm down the road. You can bring your cat if you like.'

Buoyed up with excitement, I deliver the good news to Claude and take him for a walk. This evening we are living as the Amish do – no telly and no phone. We've been staring at the wall for hours.

I spruce up for the wedding. I've put on my rather nifty black Rifat Ozbek jacket with white bone-rib motif on the front. Claude raises his whiskers when he sees this but then just polishes them extra hard. Grace comes for me at nine – we have to start early because the service takes about four hours.

Claude sleeps at the motel during this bit and I come back for him at lunch time. He can join us for the reception in Grace's aunt's garden. While in the bathroom (I've been dying to go since 9.05), I shout through to his endless questions from the other room.

'I didn't understand a bloody word. The entire thing was in German.'

'Well, what did you expect? That's where they come from.'

'Yes, but three hundred years ago. You'd think they might have picked up the lingo since then.'

'They have, but considering they're a people who were

persecuted for their religious beliefs in Alsace, it's not surprising they hold on tightly to their culture.'

'All right, all right. Anyway, you'll be glad you weren't there. The entire service took place in a barn on hard *backless* benches. I wanted to die. And it wasn't really a service. It was one preacher sermoning the couple for *four hours*.'

'And the lovely couple?'

'I didn't know who they were at first. She wasn't in white. She was in the same as everyone else, and there wasn't a flower in sight.'

Grace comes along and I pick Claude up. At her aunt's house, I put him in the garden and immediately he acts as a magnet for all the children in a ten-mile radius. I offer to help in the kitchen but the women smile, shake their heads and look down silently. Plates and plates of bread and chicken and salads and celery and cookies and fairy cakes are being carted outside. The walls are a glossy brown, the hall is green and the sitting room is blue – the colours of nature. There are no photos of the family or portraits anywhere. Just rural scenes on the walls. Instead of curtains, green shades roll neatly at the top of each window frame. The décor is unbelievably simple and contrasts with the enormous amount of female bustle going down.

'Grace. How come there are some gadgets in the kitchen? I thought the Amish didn't use anything modern,' I whisper, staring at an electric egg whisk.

'They're not opposed to modern, just things that are attached to the physical world, like phone and electricity lines. The kitchen stuff is run by battery, as are all tape recorders and CD players.'

'CDs? They have CDs?'

'Yes, and the Internet. As long as the machine does not belong to them and isn't in the house.'

'You're kidding.'

'My uncle has a phone in a booth in the garden, it just can't be heard from the house. That's how he runs his business. People know when he'll be in the booth.'

I wander outside and watch the proceedings. Everyone is singing – it's the Waltons on a grand scale. Good clean earthy fun. I don't know the words so I can't join in. Some people smile at me but always look away, others don't smile. After the singing everyone eats at trestle tables covered in white cotton cloths. I go for a plate but soon realise this is not the wise thing to do. They eat in order: men first then boys then women then girls. Oh for God's sake. When it's my turn, I jump in with the women behind Grace, take a small plate and eat on the grass next to Claudius, quietly feeding him bits of chicken when no one's looking. In other words all the time. I would sit at a table but I just don't feel right about it. Later a group of teenage boys plays a ball game, watched by some girls who are helping clear up the trestle tables. The men are talking in groups – the women are working. The bride's girl-friends are crowded around her. It is fun, I suppose, but I feel strangely lonely. No one comes to talk to me, although they all seem to crowd around Claude. As the time to leave draws nigh, Grace comes up with one of her sisters.

'Would you like to come for the clean-up tomorrow?'

'The what?'

'The clean-up. It's such fun. The newly-weds do the laundry and us friends try to prevent them from finishing it – we cut down the clothes line and let the whole lot fall into the mud so that they have to start again!' The two girls giggle behind their hands demurely.

'Wild! You guys sure know how to have a good time. Thank you so much but I think we'll have to get going.'

Claude and I wander back to the motel, along the single-lane road that winds past fields of crops. The sun is setting in a large orange globe behind us. The sounds of singing (they're off again) recede behind us as we amble.

'I had a good time.'

'I'm not surprised. Everyone paid you so much attention.'

'Feeling a tad left out, are we?'

'Well, Claude, not a soul spoke to me. I've been lonely.'

'Have you considered it might be because of your jacket?'

'My what?'

'Your jacket looks like a military jacket. It's well known that the Amish are pacifists – they deplore all things warlike because of their own persecution by the military in the 1700s. They don't even have buttons on their clothes or lapels; and that's why none of the men wear moustaches.'

'Claudius. Thank you for the history lesson. But this is a Rifat Ozbek and it cost me a fortune. It is perfectly suitable for a wedding.'

'In London. But we're in Pennsylvania Dutch country. It's rather rude to wear something like that at a do like this, wouldn't you say? It's not surprising they shunned you.'

'I didn't mean to be rude. I didn't know.'

'Think, my dear. In Rome . . .'

'All right. All right. Come on.'

Sulks. On my part.

Today I apologise to Grace for my inappropriate garments and she is sweet about it. 'It wasn't the best idea, but don't worry. They're very strict and you are an outsider. We're family and even we still get slightly shunned because my parents are Amish-Mennonites and not pure Amish.'

I think. Therefore I'm mad. Move on. I have hunger in my soul which leaves little room for peace. We leave the Dutch country in search of the Skyline Drive and the Appalachian mountains.

Chapter Five

The Big Chill

Drive, drive, drive.

Let's just examine the facts.

Let's remember them one by one.

In October my aunt died from cancer. At the time Ma was planning to retire from her work – she was sixty-eight. Within a matter of weeks she had coughing and vomiting fits that seemed more than just routine. She went to the doctor and after a series of tests was diagnosed with cancer of the pancreas. She phoned me and I went straight home.

From the moment she phoned I knew she was going to die. We had jumped off the cliff. We just had to hit the bottom.

'It's palliative,' she said.

'What's that?'

'There's no cure.'

Claudius stayed on Ma's bed keeping vigil every day she was ill. He didn't leave her room except to pee and eat and never ventured out into the garden in case she might miss him.

That Christmas things were very different from the matriarchal shindig we had enjoyed in former years. Ma was not cooking an enormous lunch, ordering the boys to open champagne, or handing out present after present from under the tree. She was upstairs in bed, dying. The rest of us had a silent Christmas lunch, and my sister took up a tray fit for a doll, a little turkey on a saucer (Claudius thought it was for him), a spoonful of stuffing next to it, a couple of sprouts, a tiny glass bowl of Christmas pudding. An egg cup of champagne. A lone cracker on top with a sprig of holly sitting dolefully beside. It came down untouched.

In desperate need of escapism I drove to my best friend's house in the country for New Year's Eve, overpowering December sun shining in my eyes the entire drive down, as though trying to blind me from flight, a message I didn't want or was unable to grasp. Not much of a New Year considering what I had to look forward to. On New Year's Day I left Hampshire and couldn't stop crying. Once I knew Ma was dying I wanted to be strong for her, and so never cried in front of her, which only created a barrier between us. When I arrived at my sister's house, I found her walking Ma back to her bed from the bathroom. Ma's pain had bent her back over, gnarled her limbs into tight sinewy knots, and emitted from her mouth wailing, wounded, animal screams. Her pain cut into me so deeply it left nothing behind, just a very black mirage that occasionally changes location, but sometimes makes its empty presence felt. She had stopped talking and had trouble focusing. When I squeezed her hand she didn't know me.

From then on my sisters and I took turns nursing her through the night. We relieved her by means of a bed pan, removing marmitey-pungent thick black treacle, the fruits of a rotting body. So much for never being too thin. Her yellow paper skin was stretched in soft wrinkles over very old sinewy chicken-like bones that showed not a hint of fat or muscle. A most impressive impression of a Belsen victim. Night after night we sat through the dark watching Ma breathe, waiting for the change. One night was particularly bleak, the dead of it creeping into our blackness and nesting there coldly.

But at seven in the morning dawn broke and the sun came up and I went outside for a breath of fresh air and looked up. The night had been replaced by that strange crystal light which makes you think the world is as it should be. The street was silent except for a dog barking. My sisters and I reconvened around the bed discussing Ma's favourite topics – Venice; Placido Domingo, the thinking older woman's Tom Jones; books we had read at her instigation; her garden of wild flowers; opera; whisky; bridge – when she sat up and started smiling and laughing.

'I thought you said that dog was called Sonya!' the morphine in her system chortled in one of those extraordinary dream jokes that are hilarious in sleep and mean nothing by day. I looked at the new day and the sun and my sisters smiling at my darling mother and I thought everything would be fine, the world is so intangible, who knows what will happen? Why shouldn't there be some miracle cure? Why shouldn't it all have been a mistake?

At eight o'clock, her breathing started rasping through her body like a tornado. It came slower and slower until you couldn't believe there was any left but then just as you thought it was over, another whisper from the crypt blew up. We asked the nurses to give her more morphine, and then we waited around her bed, my sisters, my brothers and Claudius. At ten o'clock, her tongue protruded slightly in protest as though she were turning a grape seed out of her teeth. She was dead. Claudius climbed off the bed, padded downstairs, pushed open the catflap and flipped out into the backgarden. He stayed out all day.

I was blind awake from then on regardless of the lack of sleep but I couldn't stay in the room with my mother's corpse, I was scared. What of? That she might rear, mummy-like from her death bed? Wouldn't this be a dream come true rather than a scene from a horror film? I wanted to see it all, acknowledge this moment of being alive, take the raw memories with me to my own grave. I watch the undertakers whip back the sheets and lift up Ma's scrawny dead yellow body to place her in a zipper bag. Her white nightie starts to ride up, and just as we are about to see her, one of the men hastily pulls it down. But this is the last image I have of her and the inappropriateness of it has shut some valve in my heart that will take years to open up again. I will try to confront it later, but like a weight on a door, it pulls itself shut whenever I try to throw light on it.

That was it. Six weeks from retirement to zipper bag. Did she fight it at all? Or did this disease cut her a blow to the back of the legs so blinding that she could never really get up again, and then continue to beat her till she was just a pulpy bloody unrecognisable mess?

For days afterwards I can still hear that breathing. Then I obsess over when the grapefruit-sized tumour which slowly spewed its toxins through her body had developed. Had it accompanied us on our Saturday outings to the Royal Academy of Art or to the cinema? Had it participated in conversations discussing the merits of various unsuitable boyfriends? Had it been there, albeit in foetal stages, when I told her I had lost my virginity (surely not that far back!) and she replied, 'I thought you looked flushed. Go and have a bath and then we'll talk about it'? Had it been there hands on hips when she barged into the bathroom one day and said, 'Clare how many times have I told you not to wash your hair every day?' and then to my bewildered 'Why not?' in rabbit-in-headlight uncertainty, 'Because it overstimulates the fagglecytes.'

Then the perfunctory three months of kind friends, before the majority feel you should be better by now, not realising that a part of your soul has died, your arm has been ripped out of your socket and there is a gaping bloody hole left to deal with that they can't see. Then my other aunt died. The three sisters gone in six months in an unrealistic artistic symmetry. Laughable, really.

Chapter Six

Clueless

Virginia – North Carolina

Claude and I stop in Front Royal, Virginia, where we book into the Pioneer Motel, ready to set off on the Skyline Drive tomorrow. The room smells musty, the carpet is sticky, the loo seat is hairy and there's a lonely little poo in the bowl waiting to be flushed, the immediately surrounding water and porcelain stained browny-red from the long delay. I pull back the covers to find stains all over the sheets. I make a fuss but refuse to allow the owners in the room to clean up.

'No I'll do it,' I snap as I grab the sheets and shut the door lest they spy Claude curled up on the bed. He's resting with open eyes. His very sensitive nose likes neither the smell of the place nor the vibes.

Today we commence the Skyline Drive. This is one of America's classic drives, best done in the autumn when the leaves are turning, following the line of the beautiful Appalachian mountains. The curving road allows just 35mph, and there are many, many stop-out points with incredible views. I stop at the first, which happens to have a good-looking guy sitting on top of his red BMW smoking a huge cigar. At ten in the morning. 'Well *hello*,' my internal George Sanders voice chimes. Claude sniffs the grass and twigs and generally becomes one with nature.

The guy introduces himself to Claudius. His name is Dan, originally from Indiana, now living in Texas.

'Texas! I'm going there!' I say brightly, hoping for an invitation. From a complete stranger. Well you know how it is when you're travelling and fed up of motels (even though you've only been on the road a few days). Over eager. Over friendly. Desperate.

As we chat, getting on to heavy topics fairly quickly – his recent divorce, his son's near-death experience, our views on religion (he's an Episcopalian), my mother's death, my slightly obsessive love for Claudius – it becomes clear that we get on very well and so decide to travel together for a day or two. We drive in tandem, he quite speedily as he tests his new Beamer which he's driving home across country, me all over the road as I struggle to put Claude on my lap, change the CD and put on my make-up all in one go.

We stop at various look-out points to admire the trees and vegetation, which neither of us can identify to save our lives, until we stop at one of the inns for the night. These are quite comfortable affairs and so are peopled by retired couples driving brand-new Lincolns and Cadillacs. We discuss sharing a room, and even though I've only just met him I think I'll go for it. I've no intention of doing the dirty but I am aware that if he wants to a) steal my stuff or b) have his evil manly way with me against my will, I don't have a leg to stand on. Still, shove it. I like his company.

This evening I have someone to eat with rather than the junk-food-in-bedroom deal Claude and I have recently indulged in. The inn's restaurant has a great Skyline Drive rolling-trees-and-hills-type view. I drink as much as possible to make up for the lack of booze over the last couple of days, and am pretty squiffy but not yet ugly, if a little one eye here and the other eye there, before Dan even finishes his starter. If he's intending to do me down, I'm only making things easier for him, I realise through a haze of alcohol. We have an intelligent (one-sided) conversation which is interrupted every few minutes by an over-zealous waitress wanting to know if we're all right. She insists on wading in wondering whether we want the blackberry gat-*tow* or not.

'Do you know what you can do with your raspberry gat-tow?' I turn to her after her third attempt. Dan looks a little taken aback.

Back to the room. I am a little nervy about the fact that this guy might be the equivalent of Lester in *Clay Pigeons*, or the male version of Sharon Stone in *Basic Instinct*, you get my drift. No doubt Claude will protect me, I think as I walk in to find him curled up snoring in a tight furry ball in the middle of my bed, completely oblivious to the world. Maybe not. In the bathroom I wonder if Dan can hear me peeing like a horse. Then when he goes in and does the same, I realise yes, definitely. I must be giving off scared vibes because finally he says.

'Now, listen. Relax. I won't make a pass at you, so long as you promise not to be insulted in the morning.'

'Scuse me?

Today we drive more and admire the scenery more and ah-at-Claude-smelling-the-flowers more. He slinks around looking chocolate with his green flinty eyes. He seems quite happy. He likes it when I'm happy and I relax when I'm with other people. SO. Good to know that I've under-taken a six-month road trip *solo* then. In the afternoon we visit the Luray caverns to look at the stalactites and mites and cave formations. The extremely fat girl guiding us asks us not to touch anything in the cave as the rocks die at the touch of nasty oily human skin. She points out the dream lakes, pools of water that reflect the ceiling so perfectly you are unable to tell where the ceiling starts and the water begins.

Water dripping down from the stalactites is meant to be lucky if it drips on you, so I hold Claudius under a likely one.

'Could you move on please, miss?'

'Yes just a sec, I want Claude to have good luck drip on him.'

'But miss we've been waiting here for some time and we're losing the group.'

'Won't be long now.'

'Just another thousand years or so.'

Some of the cave formations are dripped on so often they've developed a sort of primaeval goo on the surface.

I turn to Dan.

'The locations manager from Paramount has an option on this cave. He comes here and scrapes off that gunk by the bucketful whenever there's a new *Star Trek* film.'

'Please be quiet.'

'OK.'

Claudius is being an angel. He's actually quite interested in it all, looking this way and that. Draped across my arms I carry him for a good forty-five minutes until my arms give out. Then I let him walk like the rest of us. After a while I hear the sound of rain pattering. Strange as we're underground.

'Miss, is your cat drinking the dream water?'

'Er . . .'

'Miss, these rocks are protected by the law. Please come with me.'

'Oh God no, I'll pick him up. Look, I've picked him up.'

'Follow me please.'

'Oh for FUCK's sake.'

Several points to note here. First, I'm losing my temper. Nothing new there. Second, I'm swearing loudly, not the best way to win support from the cuss-hating, law-abiding folks in these parts. And yet I find that letting out a good long 'FU-U-UCK' is the only way of dealing.

She frog-marches me upstairs, Claudius perched on my arms trying to get down. After a drawn-out debate, which could have been much curtailed had I been polite, not used bad language and apologised, none of which I did, I'm fined for defacing public property or something and finally released back to Dan.

'That's quite a temper you have on you,' he says. 'I heard you all the way back there.'

'Shut it,' I smile back.

'Not until I've introduced you to these lovely people I've just been talking with. Their children were admiring Claudius.' A good-looking family is standing behind him, two parents, five children and four grandparents. The whole shebang. Hellos all round, pats for Claude, me slightly sheepish as they clearly heard everything too.

'You know, miss,' says the mother. 'If you accepted Jesus into your heart, you would never get so angry. His loving ways would infuse into you like – like . . .' She is lost for words as she breathes in deeply like a yoga teacher. I look daggers at Dan.

'I'm sorry. What are you? Who do? Um?'

'Take one of our leaflets. We're from the local Alpha Christian church. These are our children, whom we teach at home, to protect them from harmful influences, from angry people like yourself. But we want to help.'

'Oh, thanks so much.' I turn on my heel and carry Claude towards the car. 'OK, Danny boy. Next time don't talk to strangers. You never know which nutters are out there.' I'm slightly livid, slam us in the car and drive off back to the Skyline Drive. B'Jazuz. Everyone I meet seems to be of some serious religious persuasion:

Grace: Christian Baptist missionary.
Her parents: Amish-Mennonite formerly Amish.

Dan: Episcopalian.
Good-looking family: Alphas – born-again Chrissy.
Me: Gucci.

A little calmer, we stop in a log cabin in the Shenandoah Park. Dan continues driving as he has to get back to Texas. He gives me his address in Victoria, Texas and invites me to drop in some time when I get there. I feel buoyed up by the human contact and hope he does too – or does he just think I'm a psychopath? 'Probably,' says a helpful Claude. We settle the bags in and go for a very light walk; no three-hour treks for us, oh no. I walk 100 metres down a path and Claudius follows sniffing the wildflowers among the oak and hickory trees and chewing the deep greenery, slowly, slowly, behind me. There are birds nesting around us: catbird and towhee, which we've never seen before, and warblers and thrushes. Claude wants to play at being wild, so I leave his food and water bowls outside on the porch for him.

Having a shower this morning, I hear a thump outside and dress to investigate. Hopping out on to the porch with a tin of cat food in hand, I round the corner and stifle a scream as I run face to face with a black bear wolfing Claudius's food down. It is huge. This is not Baby or Mummy Bear but looks very much like Papa Bear. With my adrenalin pumping, I notice how soft and black he looks. Claudius comes round the corner, sees Yogi eating his food and does a quick mental toss-up between my life and his pride. He settles firmly for the latter and decides on the most inappropriate course of action. He starts *hissing*, which in my opinion shows little or no knowledge of the natural order of things.

'Claudius, you happen to be further down the food chain, so I suggest you *shut up*,' I hiss back, but the bear has heard us, looks up and moves in our direction. I panic and throw my arm, cat food and all, out in his direction, to stop him scratching my Armani blue silk skirt. He gratefully starts lapping at the tin, and I cannot believe my good luck. I come over all Barbara Woodhouse and look around hoping that someone is watching just how bloody marvellous I am with animals. Someone *is* watching.

'Stop right there, miss.' It's the Park Ranger. 'I saw you deliberately feed that bear. We've been trying to migrate him back to the wild for a long time and I think you've just gone and blown it for us. They're attracted to the sugar in human food, you know.'

'This is cat food.'

'Feeding the bears is an offence –'

'I didn't know.'

'– punishable with a fine. And what's more, cats aren't allowed in the cabins.' $50 later – they assured me the money would go to the park's upkeep – I'm back in the cabin, feeling mighty peed orf.

Today we visit the Natural Bridge, another of Virginia's great beauties. I carry Claudius down to the creek to gawp up at the 215-foot-high bridge carved naturally out of stone, stretching way up above. I start to read him the history.

'Kitkat, this bridge was first discovered in 1749 when Colonel Peter Jefferson was hired to survey the trail running across the bridge. And guess who his assistant was?'

'George Washington.'

'Yes. How do you know?'

'I can see his initials carved in the wall.'

'Oh. Yes, I see.'

'And of course it wasn't first discovered in 1749. What about the Indians?'

'Um.'

'I think you'll find that they called it the Bridge of God.

That the Monocans prayed to the Great Spirit for a way of escape across the canyon from the pursuing Shawnee and Powhatans, and when they opened their eyes they saw this great natural wonder.'

Driving along, an enormous dinosaur out on Route 2 heralds the Enchanted Castle Studios, which specialises in making huge exterior fibreglass props to attract drivers' attention – *car culture!* We wander around the studio. They specialise in colourful cartoon-type characters: over-sized purple bugs, blue gorillas and giant pink turtles stand next to emaciated and bloody creatures from the crypt and horny-nosed witches. Claudius and I stand in the Enor-mous Feet exhibit and stick our heads through the painted screen of Munch's *The Scream* – his head is so much smaller than the human-sized circle, that the extra light around him looks like a halo. We giggle to ourselves and move on.

I decide to just bypass a bit of the Blue Ridge Parkway and bomb it down the I81 south for a bit. I don't realise that this is in fact taking me far away from the Parkway and only work this important fact out once I have missed a large section of it. As the day is wearing on, we find a motel with a pool up on a hill, with the interstate far below us. I choose it after seeing a woman walking a basset-hound the size of a large ram at the front. I assume the place is animal-friendly. In the office more evidence of animal-loving greets me: there are several sets of stuffed deer heads on the wall and a couple of stuffed black bears by the fireplace. There are two pictures of the owners' daughter Sheryl on the wall – a large framed photograph of a blonde with a crooked smile about to graduate and then a later version after she had been knocked up, her child and its very large square head on her knee – the child is on her knee not just its head, well of course its head is there but perched on top of its body, oh never mind. An even later real-life version is seated behind the counter.

'Hello, I'd like a room please.'

'Do you have any pets?'

(Hello? That's fishy – how come so soon? Maybe she knows I have a cat and they only allow dogs.)

'Yes, I have a dog.'

'What breed?'

'Burmese.'

'Colour?'

'Brown.'

'Name?'

'Claudius. Look. Have I checked into the vet by mistake? I just wanted a room for one night. Just me.'

'Oh sure. I'm sorry, it's just ah lurve animals. Gail does too. She's walking her dog outside. Can ah take a look at yours?'

'Oh no. I mean yes, but not right now. He's asleep in the car and I don't want to wake him.'

'But you'll have to wake him to put him in your room, and you'll wanna walk him, right? Oh go on let me see.

'No really, really, I'll show you later, maybe in the morning.'

'Well, ain't that your car?' She is already making her way round to the front door and before I know it is out rushing towards the passenger door.

Oh for crying out loud, I'm thinking inside but my demeanour is very meek and mild as she looks inside and sees a very much awake Claudius.

'Well, I ain't never . . . seen . . . a dog . . . that looked . . . so much like a . . . cat.'

'But he's a dog. Really. It's a special breed.' My spirit watching this scene from above, sipping a cocktail, stage-whispers, 'What are you doing? Just come clean, you fool,' but I can't. I've gone too far and somehow can't stop myself.

'Can I pet him?'

'Well, yes, help yourself.'

Claudius responds well, he clearly likes having his chin rubbed, and by some miracle makes no noise, not a whimper of a purr.

'Oh you sure are cute, aren't you?'

'You see, if he were a cat he'd purr. But he's not. He's a dog.'

'OK then, you go ahead to room 65 at the end.'

'Thanks.' I get in and whip off to the room thinking to myself, you utter *tool*.

I immediately go for a dip to cool my blushing cheeks and to ponder what has come over me recently. There's a tiny old pot-bellied couple by the pool, she half Chinese and already in the water, he American, a fat cigar hanging out of his mouth, a baseball cap on his head, videoing her while she screams, 'Come to me! Come to me!'

Half an hour later a knock on my door. Here's Gail with her basset-hound four times the size of any Hush Puppy I've ever seen.

'Oh hoi!' she cries. 'I'm Gayel. Sheryl told me about your strange dog. Can I take a look?'

Oh God not again.

'Be my guest.'

She takes one look and stops dead in her tracks.

'Oh hon, I hate to disappoint ya. That's no dog.'

I sit down shocked.

'Really?'

She comes and puts an arm around me.

'It's a cat.'

'Are you sure?'

'Sure I'm sure. How long have ya been thinking he's a dog?'

'Nineteen years.'

'*Nineteen years?* Are ya crazy?'

Pause. She eyes the cat litter in the bathroom.

'You're kidding, aren't you?'

'I am. Please don't look at me like I'm a lying hound. I just didn't want Sheryl to reject us. I'm tired of driving.'

We chat and I tell her my story.

'Ah lurve travelin', she tells me. 'So much to see and everything is sow beyootifowel.' She tells me about all the American cities she's lived in while Dogzilla slobbers over my hand. 'Grace! Yer all gunky. No one likes that – 'cept course fer me!' She even gives me contact numbers of friends in various spots around the States and promises to keep Claude's true species a secret.

Today we continue down the end of the Blue Ridge Parkway and pass places such as Blowing Rock and Sugar Mountain. I decide to treat us to something more than the cheapest motel I can find in spite of the recent strains on our kitty. The money kitty rather than the chocolate-coloured kitty that is. Methinks it would be nice to unwind a little after our recent run-ins. Hence the oddly named Pisgah Inn. I think a little relax and looky at mountains will do us good. It's expensive but worth it, I feel. When I've smuggled him into the room I lie next to Claudius on the bed. He stretches his paw out and curves his nails round my finger. The view from my room is pure white – it's raining and a thick mist has fallen over the valley. We are stuck way up in the clouds, and I can't see any mountains, let alone a view.

After a while Claudius goes over to the litter tray, placed as usual in the bathroom under the sink next to the loo. I lie on the bed waiting for the clouds to disperse. Then he gets off the litter tray. Then he gets back on. Then back off. Then back on. Off on off on off on. Panic and Terror immediately hit town. I bomb it to the front desk to admit that in spite of their large sign saying 'No Pets In Rooms', indeed I do have a pet in the room, and that aforesaid pet is ill and maybe dying. We phone the nearest animal emergency clinic and I rush him there in floods of tears, all fear of being caught by police dashed to smithereens as I hurtle along the Blue Ridge Parkway at a daring 60mph. When the vet tells me that there is absolutely nothing wrong with him, I feel as Zelda Fitzgerald must have when checking into the nearby Highland Hospital Sanitarium. Barking mad. I pay the $50 and drive back slowly.

Back at the Inn, with Claude sleeping off the excitement on my bed, I go to the restaurant for dinner. I sit next to some bikers whose helmets are covered in stickers saying 'Sex instructor – first lesson free', 'If you see my ex, give her a big smack from me', 'My other toy has tits' and 'Injection is fine, but I prefer to be blown'. They make a nice contrast to the retired couples. At the next table sits a huge sad-mouthed woman named Martha with three rotund noisy kids aged between five and thirteen. She's doing a *When Harry Met Sally* on the waitress, ordering a dozen things from the menu, but slightly personalising them, so that the chef will have to redo most of the plates. The waitress doesn't bat a lid, she just keeps writing on her pad. Later I drop off to sleep with Claude whisper-purring under my arm, and dream of all the angry conversations I've ever had with bank managers, but this time they all say, 'Yes ma'am,' and jot my wishes down on a little piece of carbon paper.

On waking this morning, my eyeballs are fit to burst and I have a streaming cold, and yet I feel calmer somehow. The clouds have cleared to reveal a stormy green sea frozen into high mountain waves, each wave covered in a thick multi-green afro wig. The wigs go for miles in every direction. Claude enjoys the view for precisely ten minutes while I get up and pack up to check out.

I put everything into the boot of the car and shut it,

doing two things simultaneously: (i) breaking a nail and (ii) locking both sets of car keys inside. As I walk away I'm transfixed mid-stride, like a jointed action man, as I instantly feel that icy shower of dread when you know you've done something remarkably stupid. For a second I picture a tow-away truck hurling my brand-new car full of possessions down a ravine or city dump because these new cars are so 'fancily newfangled' that they're pretty damn impossible to break into.

'Oh don't worry!' chortles Kevin over the phone at the nearest auto locksmith – a good hour and a half away. 'There are plenty of idiots like you all over the place. No this happens all the time.'

'Oh good,' I laugh weakly. 'So you'll be here soon then?'

'Come when I can.' Which is three hours later. Thank God I haven't yet put Claude in the car. He smiles a half-smirk through half-closed eyes when I tell him the good news. When Kevin shows up, he breaks into the body of the car easily with some broken coat hangers, but getting into the 'trunk' as they say over here, involves taking the entire car apart and putting it back together again afterwards. Relieved of $80 we move on. Our stay at the Pisgah Inn has been, er, most relaxing.

Today we journey through Translyvania county and aptly named it is too. Spooky events include:

1 In an attempt to get things on the right road, as it were, I book into the Florida Room Beauty Parlor for an eyebrow-plucking session. My antennae ignore the telltale sign of the beautician's lack of eyebrows and red scabs where her eyelids should have been. I lie down and *pad pad whip*. She hands me the mirror. Two huge and uneven holes in the middle of each eyebrow confront me. I should have said: 'Please

ruin my looks as fast as possible in such a way
that they won't improve for months.' I do the
only sensible thing. Burst into tears. She coos and
soothes to no avail. My one treat has been ruined
and the day is back on its helter-skelter spiral to
Hell. I must have murdered someone in my past
life to have such bad karma.

2 After driving in the wrong direction on several
highways I finally locate the photolab I delivered
my rolls of film into last night. They have lost
one of the rolls – the one with Claude looking
through *The Scream*. I start scrummaging
through the bins with the pasty-skinned over-
pierced redhead who took the film in the first
place, when a fat assistant claims I am on
unauthorised soil behind the counter and must
get out. To cut a long story short I end up
battering my fists on his chest like Penelope
Pitstop. Security are called. I'm evicted from a
photolab in a mall in the middle of suburban
America. Mayhem.

It turns out there's a name for what I'm going through:
insanity.

We drive for hours and hours and miles and miles and
finally arrive in Asheville, which is strange because on the
map Pisgah National Forest and Asheville are not very far
from each other at all. It seems to be a feature that
everywhere is much further than you think. And then I
used to consider a three-hour drive to Manchester exhausting and a seven-hour drive to Edinburgh absolutely
outrageous. Well, the drive was pretty at least. The land is
one of rolling green hills. Great plains ahead interspersed
with forested mountains stretching for miles. I'm often the
only car on the interstate, which means I can veer all over

the road looking at the views from every window, listening to Marianne Faithfull singing 'The Ballad of Lucy Jordan', even having a bit of a fiddle when really bored. Well it's not as though my driving skills are needed. The cruise control means I can cross my legs and one finger is all the power steering wheel needs.

I have the fear and am unable to get a grip. For some reason I am making a complete tit of myself in every situation I find myself in. I wonder if it's going to be like this all the way, in which I case I wish America were somewhat smaller than it is. I feel totally at sea. Claudius of course picks up on my moods and is unsettled too, which only makes me worse because I know it is my mood that dictates his. I lie awake at night listening to his rhythmed breathing. He eats, drinks, pees and poos with alacrity but he doesn't sleep in my arms any more. He doesn't make a fuss but I think he has started to wonder why I am putting us through this if I'm not going to enjoy it and I wonder the same. His lack of affection makes me scared that by the end of the trip, he will no longer love me. I know that the journey is meant to be me breaking away from my former life, but even when you're not that enamoured of aforesaid life, it seems not such an easy thing to do. I know what I should really do is live in the moment, but I've never been that good at it. It's not that I feel alone, it's the thought of endlessly packing up before midday, moving on to find a new place to rest and sneaking Claudius into endless motels each night that seems a little irksome. I'd like to be somewhere where he could roam freely. Where we could relax. It is so weird to be out here, so very out there. I wonder if I'll have fun again. Ever. Anywhere.

Chapter Seven

Speed

Cherokee,
North Carolina – Nashville, Tennessee

Today we move through true Bible-bashing country in the pissing pouring rain. There are more churches than houses, the Baptist Church, the Episcopal Church, the Church of Jesu the Nazarene, the Church of Bette the Davis. We end up in Maggie Valley, quite a contrast from the rolling green hills we've just passed through. It consists of long straight roads of motels and brightly lit diners. For most of the journey Claude sits across my lap like a thick chocolate sausage, now and then hopping to his litter tray. I drive slowly so as to be able to tell him about everything on offer: Santaland, an all-year Christmas binge; Ghost Town in the Sky with themepark rides, fake shoot-outs, saloons with girls dancing the can-can, arcade games and Indian dances, in fact everything but a ghost town, and so on and so forth.

Claudius considers and then pronounces roller-coasters undignified so we don't stop but carry on to Cherokee, excited to see the Indians. He reads to me from a guidebook: ' "25,000 peaceful and unified Cherokee existed side by side with white settlers for years but little by little their 135,000 square miles of land was whittled away by misleading treaties. In 1830 Andrew Jackson signed the 'Removal Treaty' although his life had been saved by a Cherokee Chief at the Battle of Horseshoe Bend in 1812.

From spring 1837 to autumn 1838, 15,000 Cherokees were rounded up and moved, mainly on foot, to Oklahoma, 1,200 miles away. Lack of food and frigid weather – that winter saw ice storms and torrential rains – resulted in 4,000 people dying. The US army wouldn't allow any breaks in the move to allow the ill to recover, so many were just left to die by the roadside." ' I almost start my own Trail of Tears when I hear this.

We drive through town to the Oconaluftee Motel, which allows animals. It's only just on the Cherokee Indian Reservation, which is not strictly speaking a Reservation, as that implies the Indians were relocated here which they weren't. The motel has 70s swirly carpets and curtains, the walls seem thin and the TV was designed in the Ice Age, but it's very cheap, and Johny and Melba, the retired couple who run it, are very sweet. Johny is a retired mechanic and often tinkers with his 1940s Ford. Melba used to work in a factory making machines that navigate spaceships to the moon. They invite me to join them for pizza on a large squishy brown sofa in their sitting room and we watch the news. Reports of Gay Day at Disneyland where pro-life campaigners shout 'Choose Jesus not Mickey Mouse'.

This morning, I suggest a minor trip to Claude:

'Kitkat I'm thinking of visiting –'

' "– Well it was Gatlinburg in mid July, I'd just hit town and my throat was dry, I thought I'd stop and have myself a brew . . ." '

'Yes – how did you know?'

'Because I have a vague knowledge of both geography and your psyche. We are on one side of the Cherokee mountains and I believe that on the other is an adult amusement park-cum-holiday village-type place, full of bright lights and fast ideas, perfect for someone who has no desire to face the void.'

He turns away and then blinks back.

'My dear I'd love to, but I must stay for the end of *Born Free*.'

Fair enough. So I drive (badly, but enjoying not having to worry about jerking Claude off the seat) to Gatlinburg. My first stop is Ripley's Believe it or Not! Museum, full of ridiculous exhibits, most of them pictures or plaster dummies, making it much easier to Not! than Believe it! A cow with two heads, a shrunken head, a woman with a beard, a man with two pupils in each eye, etc etc. Then the Scary Bit of the museum. One exhibit asks me to pull a lever first Off then On so I do, only to watch a dummy screaming and jerking as it demonstrates electrocution. A father with his two very young boys follows me, pulls the lever and laughs his head off as I wipe away tears of fear. Then on to a skylift which promises a spectacular view at the top, but in fact just shepherds us to a stand of souvenirs. I attempt to drive like a maniac back through the parkway, but am stuck behind several cars burning along at 30mph.

Today the Claude and I take a little wander through town. The usual very slow pace when Claude is walking and smelling all the new smells, and slightly faster meander when I carry him in my arms. It's all pretty touristy, souvenir shops with mini tepees Made in Taiwan and Indians posing for photographs with folks on the street. We pass one wearing huge Chief feathers head gear and standing outside a tepee.

'Strange.'

'What, kitkat?'

'I thought tepees were a feature of the Plains Indians and that the Cherokee Indians lived in log cabins. Never mind.'

I smuggle him in for a coke at the Tomahawk Diner, and then walk back past the TeePee Motel, the Big Chief Inn, the Mocassin Gift Shop, all of which seem to be run by whites.

*   *   *

This evening – surprise! – we watch TV: a talk show about bullies with a tall, female, cropped grey-haired doctor bullying the mothers of the bullies. 'Give them love and boundaries,' she shouts. 'It's your fault.' Then to a victim: 'Have faith in yourself. You're a marvellous young man.'

Switch off TV. Silence in unfamiliar blackness. Strange musty smells. Try to ignore them. Maybe I meant this trip to be a journey to the heart of my loneliness in the mistaken view that that would somehow cure it, as if by provoking it out into the open I could take a good long look at it. Well, here I am and it hasn't worked. If anything it just sits there staring back at me, like some Jabba the Hutt figure, splayed out in its debauched extravagance, making no attempt to disguise its vile layers.

This morning I still taste traces of it in my mouth. So I am a little over-eager to meet people. Just now a car pulled up to the motel and a young, happy, good-looking couple got out. Before they'd even made it to the motel office, I fantasised their noticing me, inviting me out for a drink, our burgeoning mutual interest developing into a fully blown friendship culminating in larks around the States, heads thrown back in white-teethed-smile-in-convertible-car-type thing. Or just a drink would have been nice. While I muse on these things, they take a look at the rooms and before I'm even back on planet earth they get back in the car and drive off for more comfortable climes.

The difficult thing is when you have to find your way around, get lost, don't know what's good, don't know the opening times of things – all that travel stuff which can take ages and be a real bore. So I have decided not to do it today. Instead I take Claudius to the supermarket in my rucksack, to explain to him the concept of obesity and how it can be attained. Row and row, aisle upon aisle of packaged foods with artificial additives. Industrial-sized bags of crisps. And the sweets. I just want a plain chocolate bar, but the Yorkie, which is always advertised using images of pure Americana, the truck driver, the long roads etc, is nowhere to be seen. You can get almonds covered in chocolate, juicy chewy things covered in chocolate, peanuts covered in juicy chewy, chocolate covered in almonds, but no plain milk chocolate. In fact no just plain anything. The Americans are obsessed with making things easier: every kind of sauce you would ever want comes in bottles, teriyaki, spaghetti, barbecue etc etc. The fruit juices are all made from concentrate and never just the juice. Grape juice, cranberry juice, love juice (no not really). The fat factor over here stretches the imagination as much as it stretches the skin; way beyond the call of duty. I have developed an obsession with not becoming the huge pulpy figures around me, which means I am half starving myself, in the fear that just breathing the American air will put weight on. So straight to the catfood section then. Claude chooses Sheba (naturally, it's the most expensive) and then from the depths of the bag 'yes', 'no'-es the various choices I sing out: duck yes, beef yes, tuna yes, mackerel God no, until an assistant comes up and asks if I want a Tylenol?

While Claude sleeps in the motel, I hoof it to Hannah's, the newly built, huge, colourfully lit Indian-owned casino in the middle of the Smokies. Here, row upon row of fat, white and grey-haired fiftysomethings in nondescript utility clothing are seated at machines feeding them dimes and quarters, unwittingly giving back to the Indians their most treasured possession: money. This has to be the best revenge the Indians could have possibly thought up. Well, they welcomed the settlers and helped them survive, only to watch them turn around, steal the land and turn it into – THIS! This conglomeration of fast-food chains, factory-outlet malls, chain motels, boulevards of choked-up cars, suburban apartment complexes, the odd controlled environment national park. Well done.

The casino is extremely high tech: even the blackjack tables have electronic dealers. When someone wins a substantial amount, a lightning sign lights up over their heads, so everyone knows whom to mug later. The whole place is run like clockwork too. A fatter version of Wind in His Hair herds us back to the parking lot when we have been fleeced from our last quarters. Since plenty of states have no gaming licences, the Reservations are the only place where people can gamble, so they have literally thousands of visitors from miles and miles around all the time. Someone must be making a killing, but not the average Indian from the look of the poverty-stricken Reservation.

Back at the motel a new car is pulled up next to mine. New guests at the inn! A couple of students: Walton, exceptionally pretty, with creamy skin, sparkling white teeth, green eyes and long thick curly brown hair, and Jesse, long straggly hair and a soft pubey beard thing on the end of a very long chin. We say hello, they are here for just one night before heading back home to Nashville tomorrow. That's where Claude and I are next heading. They give me their number there.

This morning we set off for Nashville. What is this vague sense of disappointment I feel with everything I see? What is this longing for men lounging on shack porches, endless roads streaming into the desert, old Chevrolets ploughing up the streets, cloudless skies, any American cliché I can find? Why the desire for old town America of the 50s and 60s, places I've never seen, times I'll never see? Why the disappointment when old shacks are pulled down to be replaced by fast-food chains? Why the irritation over the neatly organised tours of 'genuine' Indian villages, which have been specially created for tourists? Jaron in New York was right. I suppose people do want all this new stuff. Still, it's ruining the atmosphere of everything around. You don't really need to travel any more – everything's the same. There are no big culture shocks to be had. Or maybe my desire to see something that will astound me is merely another symptom of an addiction to excitement typical of a twentieth-century short attention span. Or maybe it's a desire to see something genuine – something original and natural that hasn't been spanked up to its newest most convenient consumerised form.

'It's all very well being self-righteous about the resource-consuming present,' says Claudius from the back ledge. 'But are you about to give up my swish comfortable new car and your penchant for leather Guccis?'

'I'm sorry. *Whose* car?'

'Are you going to do things *au naturel* like Wilfred Thesiger and only use the original methods of transport? I don't think so.' He turns back to watching the retreating scenery.

He's right. How to integrate my beliefs and my actions so that I am At One with myself?

I've no idea.

Our first view of the Nashville Skyline comes after a five-hour drive. This is our first sighting of a large city since New York and energy seems to vibrate up through the roof peaks along with the country tunes that make it the City of Music. Instinctively I can tell that a pair of purple cowboy boots is waiting for me somewhere in there. We check into a motel and Claude settles in – he wants to sleep he explains, because even though he seemed to be doing so in the car, he wasn't, actually he was just meditating.

I have a cracker of a headache but drive to the centre, too excited to stay and rest with him. I get lost time and time again. The concept of buying detailed maps has still not yet occurred to me. I wind down my window to ask the next-door driver.

'Where's the tourist centre?'

'Oh, it used to be over thayer, but the tornado blew it away,' she says before driving off.

Great. I drive around in a few more circles until I'm on Broadway. At the lights I ask a biker the same question.

'I don't know,' he says. 'But there's the Big River. Come along and I'll buy you a drink.'

I carry on looking for a while and then park the car and look for my biker. I find the Big River – but there's a convention with literally thousands of bikes and bikers everywhere – all convening for drinks, music, auctions and generally to admire each other's machine. There are bikes that have been turned into planes, bikes with engines big enough to run a camper van, bikes every colour under the sun, with brown-brown, big-titted blonde babes climbing off them.

I return to the parking lot and chat with one of the Somalian guys, name of Mustapha, running it. He takes me on a quick tour of the neighbourhood, then for a drink at Big River and then invites me to his home to stay if I need somewhere. I think 'wotthehell' like Mehitabel and follow him in his car a little way out of town to see his apartment. He drives very fast and switches lanes like wildfire. I wonder if this is such a good idea. After all, I've known him for a total of forty-five minutes. Back at his flat, whose shutters are all closed, another Somalian guy, Ali, with bright staring eyes of black fire, is watching telly. 'You can stay here as long as you want. Think about it,' says Mustapha. I return to the motel and think about it. I have decided to stay there because (a) my instincts say he's all right, (b) this motel is on Nashville Airport's flight path and I might lose my hearing if I stay any longer, (c) the couple next door almost killed each other just now and started throwing things out of the door so that I had to move the Buick in case it got caught in the firing line, and (d) Claudius isn't allowed here so we're back to espionage tricks.

We move in. Mustapha and Ali are incredibly sweet and very hospitable – in fact overly so, they are constantly offering me drinks, food, newspapers, everything I might need. At first I wonder whether they think it weird that I said yes to staying here and whether some huge rape fantasy is forming in their heads – but not at all. Ali is very religious and, being a Muslim, prays to Mecca five times a day. Mustapha is a former maths professor and is very into politics, which I am into myself, albeit simplified 'baddy' politics.

This morning at five I let Claude out for a walk. He loves this time because all the animals are out doing their business and the day is fresh and inspiring and not yet too hot. There is plenty of garden for him to roam as we are in a big apartment complex, though I have spoken to him sternly about avoiding the cars. I check up on him every five, then ten, then fifteen minutes. If I can't find him immediately, I imagine I am him and start walking in ever-increasing concentric circles as I am pretty sure this is how cats map out their territories. He does not always find his way home, because sometimes he gets confused and sits outside the wrong door after his stroll. When I fetch him he gives out a grateful 'Mew!'.

Wandering around with Claude today, who should I bump into but my biker? He is no longer on his bike, but in his brand-new Mustang whose paint changes from purple to green depending on the light. 'That's a bad un!' comments one of the many admirers who slow down to take a closer look. Some of these American cars are truly awesome. The best Mustangs have to be the 1966 versions, which are overgrown American versions of the Lancia Fulvia Coupe (sob) but this is the newest snazziest version.

'It looks like a Ford Escort,' says Claude. I don't mention this to Larry who has just offered to take us around the city in it. We hop in. First up we drive around the Warner parks, just near Belle Meade, the affluent part of Nashville, which is dotted with enormous mansions, huge white wedding cake things. Next we eat lunch at the Loveless Café. This is classic Americana, a low white house with swinging benches on the porch and a colourful neon sign. They don't allow animals in, so we have to park in the shade and leave the windows open. While we order we both panic. Me that Claudius will die from the heat (even though the windows are slightly open, it is still 90° outside) and Larry that the Mustang will get stolen. I'm ravenous and stuff southern-fried chicken, corn biscuits (scone-like things), white beans and hash brown casserole down my throat. Off his bike Larry is not the hardened living-life-on-the-edge type I imagined. He has worked in a factory for twenty-one years, supervising the machinery that makes glass window screens for cars, and hopes to retire early. He is polite and sweet. Not really looking for big love or big life, just a nice time. After lunch I rush back to the car with the keys while Larry settles the bill. Claude is in a ball on the floor. Oh my God he's dead. I open the door without using the key, thereby setting off the alarm.

'Bloody hell,' says Claude as he bounces into action. Which means peeing on the carpet.

'Claude! You're peeing on his new floor.'

'Well, you scared me.'

'I didn't mean to. I thought you were dead.'

'*What?* Of course I'm not dead. I was asleep.'

'What are we going to do?'

'Pour some scent on it.'

I flounce around my bag and pour some Chanel Cristalle on to the carpet. Larry ambles over and gets in.

'Hi. Smells kinda horny in here.'
Oh God.

We wander around downtown, looking for purple cowboy boots in Scooters' Boots, a shop whose front desk is
made from a pink Cadillac. With no luck. Larry keeps
trying to hold hands. I mention a need to get back and we
start to do this or so I think, except he keeps offering to
take me to new neighbourhoods. I don't really feel I can
say no, but it wouldn't matter even if I did, because he
drives speedily in that direction anyway. He gets lost as
well, which considering he's a Nashvillan is a little strange.
He keeps saying, 'Well I haven't had this much fun in a
long time,' and then continues bombing off in the wrong
direction. My cheeks are cracking from smile ache, due to
the stupid grin which has been plastered across my face for
a while now, making it difficult to relax. I'm feeling a tad
scared, and preparing to jump out of the moving car with
Claude in my arms if he doesn't turn around at the next
junction. Which would cure me of my cellulite because at
the speed we're going, the road would whip off most of my
leg. Just as my hand's on the door handle and I'm trying to
remember how James Dean does it in *Rebel Without a
Cause* Claude whispers:
    'Don't do that. Open the window instead.'
    I do and after a while Larry turns around and says:
    'What the hell is that smell?'
    The Chanel has been driven out by the air.
    'Um?'
    'Did your cat use this Speed Machine as a bathroom?'
    He spins the car around and takes us straight home. I
apologise the entire way. When we get back, I don't invite
him in, not really wanting him to know how I met
Mustapha or vice-versa, because unless you're living this
life, it's difficult to understand. I kiss him on each cheek
to which he says he'll walk me to the door, adding,

'. . . although I've had my . . .'. This embarrasses me. Did he expect something else from me? Was I meant to get on my knees and lick his lollipop?

Moseying around town today, Claudius and I drop into a bar on Broadway. A nine-year-old is singing 'Stand By Your Man' in the husky tones of a thirty-year-old. 'Sometimes it's hard to be a woman,' she moans, gyrating her hips, flicking her white-blonde hair from side to side as her delighted guitarist laughs at the audience, his eyebrows raised in 'Did ya see that?' astonishment.

'What would you know about it?' I heckle good-humouredly to angry 'Shhhh!' 'Quiet!'s from the audience who are on her side, what with her being but a child and all. So I button it.

Guess who lives in Murfreesboro just outside Nashville? The astronaut I once met who told me about the stars. I call him up and invite myself over – for coffee. A strange choice considering I haven't drunk any in seven years. Hoot (no seriously, that's his name) lives in a creamy, brand-new, Palladian mansion. Or at least that's where his immensely long drive leads. I knock on the door and it's opened by an old duck in shorts, flip-flops, his dyed hair slicked back behind his ears. He ushers me in. Boy, what a house. Huge bouquets of plastic flowers adorn every corner. Marble staircases, gold-leaf framed photos of graduation day, portraits of Austrian schlosses, Waterford crystal chandeliers, collections of dolls, bird-painted plates and miniature cars. The old boy gives me a guided tour and the story behind each purchase without asking me why I'm here, as though random tourists on his doorstep are an everyday occurrence. In spite of its size, the house has just two bedrooms, each the size of a cricket pitch. At the dining table, each place set has a glass bell with a porcelain bird on top, 'so that people can attract the entire table's attention if they need to talk'. The trinkets and ornaments in every space overload the kitsch portion of my brain until my eyes are staring in opposite directions, threatening to pop out. Then Hoot comes in with his four-year-old baby blonde daughter. I've just realised that Americans hug, and kiss once, if at all. This as the result of a hideous nose-crunching embrace when I made for both cheeks and he didn't. We both struggle to extricate ourselves, Hoot trying not to look repulsed while his daughter just stares.

He introduces me to his father-in-law and we sit down and chat politely about his space missions – he has flown Columbia, Atlantis, Challenger and Endeavour. Underneath I can sense he is slightly wondering why I'm here. He doesn't realise that as we've met once before, he's my best friend here. To wind up, he gives me a photo of the earth from outer space. He then offers me coffee and I don't like to say no, since it was my suggestion in the first place. As I leave we shake hands and I say, 'Well. I've had a hoot – Hoot,' and instantly regret it as his daughter gasps, clamps her hand over her mouth and runs off shouting, 'Mommy! Mommy!' As for the coffee, I drank two cups and haven't slept since. That was two days ago.

This evening I phone Walton and Jesse. They pick me up with some friends, Joel and Jean (male). All the guys sport Colonel Sanders goatee beards and smoke pipes – they're philosophy students. We eat barbecue chicken and fries in an old diner. Walton is addicted to Dr Pepper and drinks *five* over the course of dinner. She seems agitated and upset but when anyone shows concern, she blurts out, 'I'm fine. I'm fine,' as though wanting to be left alone. Still, it is impossible to ignore her with the amount of fidgeting she is doing, the pepper and salt are positively dancing between her fingers. I still have the über-jitters myself from my coffee injection two days ago, so to rid us of our excess, albeit nervous and neurotic, energy, I suggest a stint of line-dancing.

'You gotta be kidding!' the Philosophers holler, but seem game so we check out the Wild Horse Saloon, which promises 'boot-scootin' good times'. Being poverty-stricken students they can't afford the cover charge of $8, which perhaps is not such a shame considering the handful of Japs dressed in cowboy boots and large silver buckle-belted jeans lining up for their lessons.

Instead we wander (actually Walton and I charge on ahead) around Nashville, along Printer's Alley, a formerly seedy lane with run-down bars which has now been cleared up for tourists (of course) but still features broke musicians trying to break into the Big Time. Stars such as Hank Williams, Chet Atkins and Dottie West played here before they were Big. Different types of music sing out from every doorway, country here, rock there, reggae here, blues there. We pass a huge black guy sitting on a tiny stool, like an elephant on a matchstick bike, playing the guitar on the sidewalk. He sings of fat-legged women with great big butts, his blue eyes swinging around the street, his toothless mouth blubbing and vibrating to produce guttural sounds now deep now lightly caressing. As we move we moan that the tornado didn't blow away the Planet Hollywoods and Hard Rock Cafés. 'Tornados have no taste,' says Jesse. Again that strange nostalgia for atmosphere. We ponder this over a few beers.

Then we hit The Idle Hour, a low-down dive on a backstreet, for more beer. I forget that I'm in the presence of teenagers and we all get ID-ed. I'm thrilled that the guy thinks I'm younger than twenty-one, but have no ID being (a) a Brit, and (b) unused to people thinking I look anything other than a worn-out old hag. So we're chucked out and do that student thing of hanging around outside wondering what to do, while no one takes charge or makes decisions. Instead we discuss Joel's three nipples.

And the fact that Jean has a girl's name. And that he started life in Hawaii before moving to Illinois ('the descent of man to a State of Hellaciousness') and then watched his house burn down rather than call the fire brigade, so addled was his brain by the move.

Meanwhile Walton can't keep still. Neither can I for that matter. She paces up the street in one direction while I charge off in the other – she wants to be alone. I think.

'Is it wearing off yet?' I shout over.

'No,' she hollers back. 'I'm Alive. Alert. In control. How 'bout you?'

'Buzzing. You feel in control?'

'Yes. No surprises now.'

I turn and join her. 'Surprises?'

'Of the type I've had recently. My father just died.'

I stop. 'I'm so sorry.'

So does she. 'Don't be. I hated him.' She pounds the pavement again.

'For dying?'

'For having an entirely separate family from ours. Which I've also just found out about.'

'Oh God, how awful.'

'Yes. I only found out about them because he left everything to them. Including the house my mom is living in.'

'*What?*'

'Yes. So. How 'bout you? In control?'

'Er, not as such, no. But I don't mind any more.'

'Why not?'

'Because I tried once and I felt I was banging my head against a brick wall. I couldn't control anything, least of all everything.'

'Why did you try?'

'My mother died.'

She stops. 'What happened to you?'

'Nothing as dramatic. I retreated into silence in my flat

with my cat for two years.' Her shoulders relax down from her ears. So do mine and we wander back to the others.

Who have decided to hit the Station Inn for some bluegrass music. We enter a large school-hall-like room with a stage down one side and simple iron chairs and tables down the other, with huge pitchers of beer on. The walls are montaged with photos of people having a good time over the years, and home-made posters and T-shirts advertise local players. The folks in the band play twangy twangy foot tappy stuff for us folks, and our mutual enjoyment of it connects everyone in the room to each other. There is nothing starry or ambitious about them and during their break the musicians come over and talk to us and other members of the audience. During the set, they talk with each other and their friends, in-jokes between the crowd and the singers. One guy there to enjoy the music with his glass of beer, by himself, chewing a piece of towbaccy, a baseball cap flipped back on his head, shouts out his appreciation, 'Ah enjoyed it,' at the end of each song. My cynical thoughts ('that fiddle player looks like he's had his head clamped') are out of place – and are fast disappearing. People are so friendly, open and unjudgemental.

Late, when Walton and I are happily mellowed, the Philosophers drive me home and play classic old country songs: Johnny Cash's 'A Boy Named Sue' – the story of a boy who searches for his father and finds him in 'Gatlinburg in mid-July . . .'

Chapter Eight

The King and I

Memphis, Tennessee – Oxford, Mississippi – the Delta, Mississippi

Moving to Memphis, home of the Blues, from Nashville on the I40, the Buick buzzes along happily. It's deeply relaxing having a new car that I need never worry about. Claudius loves the Johnny Cash tape I've just bought. He particularly likes 'Jackson' and keeps pressing the rewind button, listening to it again and again until I stare over with a 'Do that again . . .' look on my face. He looks away and stands his front paws on the inside door handle to watch the world roll past.

We drive for four hours. My thoughts revolve around a particularly satisfying funeral fantasy. Soon I'm sobbing over the eulogies and tears of my incredibly good-looking husband and the woebegone beautiful sprogs I've left behind. There are even a few stars I've made friends with along the way, Richard Gere *heartbroken*, Jimmy Page *speechless* with grief-induced rage, Adam Ant (*Adam Ant?*) mouthing, 'What am I *doing* here?'

During my usual preliminary recce while Claude naps in the motel, I wander into a honky-tonk, the Rum Boogie bar, on Beale Street, the main music street, where a huge black woman with long straight shiny molasses hair, a gold skirt and huge gold bikini top, thick fat layers rolling between the two, with a gold sequin bowler hat, takes the microphone outside and sings to the passers-by in the street. She then passes a bucket around which people vie to put a dollar into, just to hear her call their names out – *celebrity!* 'We have CarolAnn from Atlanta, Georgia in the house. Put yo hands togethah.' At first I feel funky and tough for having chosen a happening place (and finally venturing out by myself at night, rather than staying in and watching telly with Claude), but when my fear abates a little and allows me to look around, I see unfriendly, half-pretty girls propping up the bar, and drunken, bald sales convention reps lunging drunkenly towards them to haul one or the other off to dance.

A stroll down the street. A whole mêlée of people: a drunken woman begging, her cowboy hat and Elvis specs sliding down her bonce, old men shuffling along in black leather slippers flicking fag butts off to the side, black girls heading great towering sheets of lacquered hair with tiny curlicues falling down each side, 'hey'ing each other, their hands up to give five, their nails long, curved, painted with intricate tiny stars and angel figures. Wrapped in metallic-blue tubes, their feet shod in high strappy platforms, they dance in the street to the music coming from all directions, their bums sticking out, jigging and turning in time, their arms, proud and unshy, reaching above their heads.

Back at the motel, Claude is flicking channels in a bored manner. He's pleased to see me and purrs contentedly for a while. We sleep and I dream of our home in London, but all the colours in the flat are faded. I have been placed there very quickly, have no idea why I'm home so soon and yet feel guiltily grateful.

No excuses from Claudius this morning. He hops in the rucksack eager to see Elvis's neo-Palladian mansion, Graceland.

The place is divided into two parts, the mansion on one side of the road and a strip mall with various attractions on the other. Claude and I start with the mall. Briefly we inspect Elvis's fantastic car collection (which includes a purple 1956 Cadillac convertible and a 1955 pink Cadillac) before checking out the gold-plated seat-belts and televisions in his customised airplane, the Lisa Marie jet.

'I don't think much of this bag,' sighs Claudius so to make up for it I buy him a purple Graceland mug to drink his water from at night. Before we tour the house, they give me a headset with a tape of Priscilla's soft tones talking about carefully chosen personal nuggets like 'Elvis loved to have jamming sessions till early in the morning. He loved to go horse riding with his friends. He loved to joke too!' designed to make you feel one of the Presley in-crowd yet giving no real information at all. Claudius, who is absolutely forbidden in here and therefore hiding grumpily in the bag, keeps saying, 'What's she saying?' and I tell him, prompting people behind and in front to ask why I am talking into my rucksack. I just smile like a loon and walk on.

At first glance we're quite surprised by how vaguely dreary it seems, but the décor is as Elvis left it, i.e., total 70s kitsch. When no one's looking, Claudius pops his head out to see the gold-fringed cobalt-blue curtains, white carpet, huge white sofa, crystal chandeliers, peacock-feather stained glass, mirrors and ornate mouldings of the dining room and living room.

'I bet this is where he used to practise his karate kicks,' I whisper.

'What, in the dining room? And kick those glass cabinets full of knickety-knacks?' he whispers back.

Downstairs the TV room is more 60s than 'The Avengers'. The walls are navy and yellow, as are the leather sofas, the ceiling is mirrored, and the carpet is shag! Bright yellow shag! There are three TV screens next to each other.

'Not even I can watch three tellies at once,' I murmur.

'Power. Powerful people do it,' says Claude.

Right.

As for the jungle room, the ceiling is shag! Green shag! On the ceiling! It has a full-wall stone waterfall, the sound of which reminds Claudius of nature.

'I need to pee.'

'No way.'

'I want a look at that fake fur-upholstered furniture.'

'Absolutely not.'

'Let me out now.'

'No.'

We then shuffle along like sheep with the other hordes of fans to the Hall of Gold, at the back of the house, where all Elvis's trophies, Grammies, gold discs and awards are kept. There are also chocolate-boxy life-size portraits, letters from presidents, guns, video clips and costumes from his concerts and films. Nowhere are there any images of him in his bloated fatty stage. The public has been protected from any image of Elvis that might hint of the excesses of fame and fortune. He has been enshrined in a for ever slim and gorgeous form. 'No wonder, he's the King!' whispers Claudius.

A deep silence pervades the Meditation Garden where Elvis is laid to rest between his parents and grandparents. Until a fruity snore vibrates up from the depths of the bag causing my neighbours to stare at me and me to stare back at them. To cover up I start to make my own snoring noises which are interpreted as deeply irreverent by a couple of the tearful accolytes standing by. I see them approaching a member of staff. I scuttle off back to the car.

Today Claudius and I drive just an hour from Memphis into Mississippi to visit the university town of Oxford, William Faulkner's former home. The town square consists of select boutiques and eateries surrounding a white Italianate town hall with clock tower.

Carrying Claude for a look at the shops and how the land lies, I meet Mary Love (yes that's her name) Taylor.

'What a beautiful cat.'

'Thanks.'

'What are you doing?'

'We're travelling around the States in my car.'

'I'm the president of the local Humane Society.'

'Ohh. Greeeeaaat.'

Instead of taking me to task me she invites me to stay at her home – bingo.

Her home is tall, turreted and wooden, a happier, hippier version of the *Psycho* house. Inside it's all cushioned-up, in a mahogany antiquey way. Old packets of musty French cigarettes among the piles of magazines and books. High ceilings, four-poster bed in the spare room, lacy table cloths, a Victorian bathroom with 1920s sweet boxes, a double washbasin and a screen with wisteria painted on it to hide the loo. In true southern style she has painted the ceilings blue, to fool the mosquitos into thinking it is the sky. Splat. She has a cat that is bloody fat. I've seen smaller goats. Still, she's docile and friendly. Claude and I settle in.

Mary Love and I are getting hammered at the local bar. There are lots of pretty girls around us – too many for my liking – and preppy boys. The scene is white (New York and Memphis have been the only places where blacks and whites mix socially so far) though there's one black girl who looks like one of the Supremes, dancing with a drink in her hand, being whistled and clapped by a large group of students behind me. Mary Love looks all demure American, thick blonde hair, blue eyes, great toned bod, but she's wild. She flirts with her friends and has a laugh to crack crystal. After a while she lights up a huge cigar. 'This is the closest to a blow job till Sunday when John returns,' she shouts. Her friends join us. Tod, a huge fat black bald guy, camp and definitely gay, talks about wanting to do horizontal aerobics with me. Maybe not gay then? 'He's a ladies' man,' whispers Mary Love. What does that phrase mean? A man that lots of women want or a man that wants a lot of women because he hates them and only sees them as sex objects? Her other room mate, Kizzy, is over six feet tall, with enormous knockers, a former *Playboy* playmate. She's also a member of the Humane Society, a cat-nut and her T-shirt says: 'Don't stare at my kitties'. She reveals that she has 'pounded' more than a hundred men. Another girl, Brenda Lee, perfectly manicured and made-up, all southern belle composure, comes over to the table. They gossip and, as she walks away, Mary Love leans over. 'Her husband committed suicide on their porch in front of their dog, blew his brains out, while the police tried to talk him into putting the gun down.'

'No!'

'Yeah. Small towns hide a lot of skeletons.'

'Oh?'

'My family's pretty normal, though. My parents have been married for forty years.'

'Wow.'

'Yeah. Their marriage is probably kept alive by Dad's live-in girlfriend and their three-year-old boy.'

'Oh.'

'Yeah. I'd like kids some day. Not yet though. My sister's already got four and she's only twenty-five. Well what do you expect when you've married four times?'

'Ah.'

'I'd like to marry John – he's great. Still, I had to fight for him at first.'

'Oh?'

'He has a Svengali effect on women and when we first started, he was dating other women as well. I made friends with one of them, Mary Sue, and we used to goad each other on with stories of John's most recent hound-dog

lying antics. One night we were gettin' drunk, I gave her a
lift home, fell into a coma and woke to find her kissin' me
all over and headin' south.'

'Agh!'

'Yeah! I grabbed her by her mane and threw her out, let
me tell ya! So don't get any ideas just cos we're in the same
house!'

'NO!'

'Only kiddin'.'

Suddenly 'I Will Survive' by Gloria Gaynor comes on
the juke-box. Hordes of women rush to the dance floor,
their arms in the air, as though shouting after a thief who's
just run off with their bags. When the music is turned
down, a chorus of women sings every word of the Survival
song, a litany of heartbreak and wrong done, blasted out
in front of the perpetrators who took them there and
bought them the drinks that gave them the courage to sing
it in the first place.

Charlie, who has set up a local record label, is on my
right. His T-shirt says 'I only sleep with the best'. He finds
old blues players from all over the Delta, cuts them deals,
and funks up their music. He is small, very good-looking
and totally rock and roll. He mumbles so much I understand only 40 per cent of what he says. I dread being asked
questions in case he realises, but he talks about horses,
rodeoing, cow-handling, things I know nothing about. He
admires Monty Roberts and that's enough for me. 'Let's
split,' he says. 'Fine,' the three Budweisers, two red wines
and two Martinis with olives on sticks I've consumed
reply.

He drives his 1970s pick-up truck screechingly round
the few corners between the bar and his house. It is a
warehouse-cum-garage with crap everywhere, a few
household appliances casually standing about the room
like a junk yard. Dusty tapes, CDs, a book about Keith
Richards, broken cartons, glasses all over. We listen to Ike

and Tina: 'Nutbush City Limits'. He murmurs to me about selling old cars before the music business, and working in the soya fields before that and jail for five months before that. He never knew his dad but was brought up by his brother Joker, 6'7", who beat up the father of the 'trash whore' he was dating, because Charlie trashed the motorbike they were riding, and the father punched him in the face. 'Ahm gonna kill you and everyone you lurve,' said Joker before thumping the father into the ground.

'I feel bad about my home. It's a dump. Right?' He can sense I'm a princess.

'Don't feel bad. It's yours. Right?'

We then go to his office to pick up some music. 'Why not try Jesus?' one of the random stickers on his wall says. The carpet is encrusted with matches, split beer, old roaches, stale bits of tobacco. In the warehouse out back is a huge old 1971 Lincoln Continental, like the one JFK was shot in.

'Let's play JFK,' is my great idea. 'I'll be Jackie O.' I climb in the back. He climbs in next to me and sits very close.

'OK. You're JFK. You get shot. Bam.' I wack the side of his head with my hand – hard. Then start scrambling climbing out of the car, noting that in fact it is filthy, there is dust and mud all over it and I am ruining my outfit.

Then the booze kicks in and my head whispers, 'Take me home or I explode.' Charlie drives me home. 'I'll call you,' he says and then: 'Glad the police didn't stop me. I don't have a licence no more.'

I wake up this morning, feeling a lot more alien and a lot less beautiful than Lisa Marie in *Mars Attacks!*

Claude and I sat on the porch today, sweltering in the shade – it's 100° out there so too hot to budge – grateful that we don't have to pack up and move on immediately.

The journeying is hard. I don't mind moving on, in fact I like the promise of new faces, new voices, new skies, but it's a tiring process and, I'm not afraid to admit, a depressing one at times. Whether it's smuggling Claudius into dingy motels and fearing they'll discover us and chuck us out at eleven at night, or staying with friends and worrying that I'm impinging on their homes and time, I feel no security in my soul, no foundation on which to build. I don't even have the luxury of a time capsule, and then the comfort and promise of home, because I have no home to go to. To get there would mean putting Claudius through quarantine which I'm not prepared to do. I could come over all hippie and say that the road is my home but I don't want to put either of us through this for ever. I want him to be able to feel the same grass under his paws at the end of it all.

In spite of this uncertainty I love him without thought, without question, without reason and it is this that steadies me in the self-imposed set of current choices, otherwise known as my life. Is loving an animal that's dependent on you for food proper love? I suppose if I were really brave I would give him up and give this love to a human, someone who has the choice to leave me or not. Could Claude leave me? Could he just lie down and die?

Mary Love and I get dressed up – it's Friday night! – and she gives me a choice of the local bar or the mall. 'The mall!' my retail instincts shout, clamping their hands over my alcoholic ones. I slightly wish she had given me this choice before we got dressed, as we are dolled up as follows: her in a little black dress, me in my pedalpushers and black and white crossover top, with kitten-heel black sandals, both with enough cake on to feed Marie Antoinette's starving thousands. We're asking for trouble and sure enough it shows up in the form of three rednecks who whistle us through the mall, drawing everyone's attention to us, and generally making us look like whores. We're trying not to notice them, we're trying to hold our heads high, but the shops are disappointing and there's not much else to occupy our attention. Until we find the 'All for a Dollar' shop. The goofy girl behind the counter wearing a 'sunbrella' pipes up, 'How y'all doing tonight?' I buy nail-varnish for a dollar. A dollar! Red, too!

In spite of such excitement, there is something horribly disillusioning about the mall mentality. These are the folks who eat in McDonald's abroad, the people who support huge chains of faceless, characterless strips, which plough up the land and put small places out of business. What can the individual do when faced with such an attitude other than feel voiceless and powerless?

Charlie hasn't called. I wonder why.

Claudius woke me this morning at 4am. Something is wrong, but I can't tell what. He's doing all the things he's meant to be doing, peeing, pooing, but his fur is baby rabbit soft, a sign that he feels insecure or out of sorts. He is also moody. When he turns away from me, it's like being with a boyfriend who no longer loves you, but of whom you're too enamoured to turn away. Not that he will do the obvious thing and just tell me what is wrong, but my sixth sense warns me that things aren't all they could be. He has not purred for a day. Is it the travelling? Is it the heat? What is it?

It is this worry, this palpable fear of not having him around any more, that rockets me into psychotic melt-down faster than anything else. Then I doubt myself totally, wondering what on earth I am doing. And this is brought about just by the suspicion that something is wrong, before I have even verified the facts with the vet. The only way of taking my mind off things is to undertake some extensive retail therapy. A couple of hundred dollars lighter later, with a snazzy little white shorts and top outfit under my belt, I am ready yet again to face whatever life may throw at me. The shorts are just above the knee, the top is a sleeveless little 60s number, the material is snow white with blood-red cherries on it trimmed in black lace. Very Jackie O.

Today I drag myself kicking and screaming from the Hotel California effect of Oxford and its hot drowsy days, along Highway 6 for a day trip. I leave Claude sleeping soundly on my bed and head for Holly Springs because I've heard a juicy rumour that Robert Altman is shooting his new film there. Ever in search of excitement and glamour, I hop in the Buick and buzz over. Apparently the small town is simply heaving with stars at the moment. The road where they are filming is blocked off so I drive down another to try and get round the other side. A good-looking guy is standing outside a house with lights and a sign saying Graceland Too. Maybe this has something to do with the film?

I pull up and we shoot the breeze. He is from New Orleans and has come to see the legend that is Paul McLeod. *Who?* We knock on the door and Paul lets us into a musty-smelling room that has every square inch of ceiling and wall and floor covered in pictures and newspaper clippings of Elvis. Paul McLeod first set eyes on Elvis when he was thirteen and since then has been the 'World's Number Onemost Dedificated Elvis Fan'. So great have been his efforts at lauding the King that he has appeared on both Oprah and David Letterman – *celebrity!* Paul takes us on a tour of the ground floor of his house, and he speaks so fast and in such a strong southern accent that I pick up maybe 25 per cent of what he's saying. His speech is fascinating not only because of what he is saying but also because he has badly fitting false teeth which slip down into his mouth at least once every minute. The speed of his words produces a thick white paste of saliva that forms a sheet across his teeth, sometimes splitting up to form droplets that land on his lips, sometimes forming long thin white lines stretching in varying thicknesses between top and bottom rows of teeth.

Elvis is his life. It is his personal mission to catalogue every mention of the King on the radio, on TV, in newspapers and in films. His workload has doubled since the advent of the Internet. He works with his son, Elvis Aaron Presley McLeod, who by a lucky twist of fate also shares his father's obsession, and, if his school photograph is anything to go by, has done so since a very early age. Their obsession has weaved ever-increasing circles of work around the two, as, like a TV within a TV within a TV, they collect references to Elvis and then references of themselves referring to Elvis, so that now they barely sleep at night but always keep the eight TVs in the living room going at once, taking shifts to keep on the look-out. Their lack of sleep means they receive guests at all hours, even busloads of Japanese at three in the morning. They are greatly helped in their work by the fact that Paul has a developed sixth sense.

'Often ah jess know when they's a mention of Elvis. I say Elvis, channel 5 in five minutes. And sure enough . . .'

Paul is fascinating, not only because of his strange tales of winning Cadillacs in gambling sprees, black midgets, dogs with dyed fur and a speedy rendition of 'It's Now or Never' in Italian, but also because he is an Obsessed Person. I can't work out whether there's something weird about worshipping another human to this extent or not. Even if it is the King.

My burning question, which I ask repeatedly, is: 'Did you meet Elvis?' The first few goes Paul doesn't hear me, but finally he says, 'Yes sure, I knew his family.' And then to my persistent: 'But the King himself?' he replies, 'Yes, I knew his family.'

He carries on: 'Disney wants to buy us out but I said no. Graceland sent their lawyers to come and take a look but they loved what we're doing. They gave us a framed piece of the Jungle Room Shag Carpet. More American televisions were switched on to watch Elvis's 1973 *Aloha from Hawaii* than saw the first man on the moon. This is our hall of fame, where we have a picture of every person that's ever visited. Elvis Aaron remembers everyone even if they come just once. Five years from now he'll remember you. We were the first to send flowers to Elvis's grave. One lady visitor she asked me to sing for her, I placed her behind that curtain, and with this,' he pulls out a plastic orange-and-yellow karaoke microphone, 'I sang "Well bless my soul what's wrong with me?" and she peed her pants. Swear to God she jess stood there and peed all oer hersel.'

By this stage the good-looker, Jack, and I have bonded due to our mutual location in 'Outer Space Fruit' territory. He suggests we go to the Bette Davis Grocery together. 'I'll follow you,' I shout merrily as we take off back in the direction of Oxford, away from the stars and Robert Altman, me realising that yet again I'm following a complete stranger for no good reason. The Bette Davis Grocery turns out to be an old shack-like store serving barbecue from sweaty counters just outside Lafayette County. Its main claim to fame is that it sells beer on a Sunday which accounts for the steady stream of business to the friendly black girls inside. 'Have a nice day and be sure to come back,' they holler after us and everyone like us. We will, we will. Jack then invites me to a party that evening. 'Yes please,' is my slightly too speedy reply.

So I drive home to see how Claude is. He is still rather quiet, and eating a little less, though it might be because of the heat. He says it's still too hot for him to go out, and there are still no symptoms as such, other than my own neuroticism, so I doll up for the party: nothing fancy just black pedalpusher stuff again. Jack and I drive to the tiny town of Taylor, where Miss Clara Rule Cardine lives. She must be in her late forties, is beautiful, dignified, warm and open and lives in a large house overlooking cotton fields. Everyone is extremely friendly and interesting not just because of the 'Bloomer Droppers' Miss Clara Rule is feeding us: addictive nectar-like drinks, which apparently make you do just as their name implies. I down several in excited anticipation. I wander out to the back porch, past the sign on the backdoor which says: 'When you come in, wipe your feet and then rub mine' to sit on the swinging chairs to look out on to the low green cotton plants behind the house. I am joined by a couple of ghost slaves, formerly bent over in back-breaking sweaty pain to harvest the crop, now sipping mint juleps, the cracking whips for ever silent. They watch me intently before retreating to the shadows.

Back in the kitchen, Miss Clara Rule serves us day-lily salad, a bowl full of unopened flowers, which are delicious once you're over the fear of poisoning. The most beautiful girl in the room is undoubtedly the tall dark Morgan (why do all these southern belles have men's names?) who has just walked in. I feel annoyed by her beauty, get over it, get a grip, start talking to her. We bond over topics such as depression and how the rest of the world doesn't understand us. She tells me horror stories about her father neglecting her. While we talk we eat warm potato salad, sweet soya bean salad and huge pieces of chicken breast. 'Some of those are bigger than my titties,' points out Miss Clara Rule. Stuffed and slightly squiffy, we migrate outside to listen to the still and watch the stars.

Miss Clara Rule gets out her huge 50s convertible Cadillac and offers us rides. Eight of us pile in, some on the seats, some on the boot, as she drives us slowly around her cotton field, switching her headlights on and off, off and on, eventually off and we feel the wind in our hair and smell the warm scents from the trees and look up to the smiling stars above us and wish to be no other place than right where we are. Then when we are totally silent Miss Clara Rule turns on her music box and plays old country favourites. She suggests we go to the river. 'But,' she holds up her forefinger, 'no one can go until they have a hat.' We all race upstairs to her dressing-up box to choose from an extraordinary array of old boaters, felt hats, baseball caps, top hats and more. I scruffle around until I find a purple one and a mink for my neck, Morgan has a bright pink feathery thing which contrasts with her black cocktail dress. We then admire Miss Clara Rule's dresses; civil war Scarlett hoop things, beaded tasselled 20s flapper dresses, tulle 50s cocktail dresses – all in bright colours and surrounded by an old mahogany wardrobe joined by a four-poster and a rocking chair, wrapped in a bright large room overlooking the cotton. We then run back to the car which speeds off. Down by the river Miss Clara Rule tells me about her daddy dying when she was fifteen. She gets slightly choked up and pats her chest gently with her fingertips.

We get back in the car and one of the boys says; 'Hell, this music makes me wanna dayence.'

'Did someone say dayence?' asks Miss Clara Rule, as she swerves the car over to the side of the road and turns the music up louder. We get out and Jack and I dance together as everyone else pairs up in the dust under the stars. I look over at Jack who is watching me. I watch back and he kisses my mouth as the warm wind shoots through us and the cicadas bleat out a midnight song. Then we drive to the cemetery, drive right in and park among the stones. Miss Clara Rule wanders off into the distance, her vague white form getting smaller and smaller. I follow her – propelled by my schoolgirl crush – but have trouble keeping up so take off the kitten heels, which are covered in dust and mud, and find her looking at friends' graves, a few quiet tears slicking her cheeks. As we wander back I realise I am sick-drunk and have to either stop drinking or hit my bed very soon. We drive back to the house and eat the remains of the dinner before setting off for home – it's six in the morning.

Jack insists that my excess of alcohol makes me a danger on the road and wants to drive, but he has in fact drunk as much as me if not more, so I refuse on the grounds that the car is not insured. I roar off at a terrific lick. In spite of his concerns for our safety he kisses my back and neck as I hum the car along, bites me a couple of times (ow!), rubs his hands roughly all over me, and finally grabs my hand and plumps it on his rocket which is very much on the launch pad. For a millisecond I think what strange jeans – so plasticky and clammy – until my senses take over and I realise he has stuffed my hand *into* his knicks and not just placed it on his trousers, as might befit a first-night kiss. His one-eyed sea monster is rearing up and swaying from a bed of wiry seaweed. Aarrrgh! I fiddle for a few moments – it seems only polite – but then quietly put my hand back on the wheel. 'Sorry,' he muffles. 'I don't normally do that.' We both laugh a little nervously.

When I get home Claude is pottering around downstairs – so we go for a walk in Oxford's graveyard. The sun is rising among some sand-rippled clouds way up in the distance. The air is almost cool, the threat of unrelenting heat momentarily hidden. No cars at all. Peace.

Claude and I spend a calm day together – he seems OK. Much later that day I wander in a hungoverly fashion to the town square and find Jack in the bar having a drink with Morgan. Instinctively I know he prefers her to me and feel a pang of jelly babies. He is about to return to New Orleans and invites me to stay with him. I like him very much, in spite of our strange run-in this morning, so I gratefully accept and say goodbye.

Morgan and I wander back to her house (via mine, which is only a block away, so as to pick up Claude) where Scott is preparing us dinner – a very unAmerican dinner of grilled meat and vegetables which I am greatly looking forward to. I am glad to be out of my place, because John is back and Mary Love and he are humping and pumping the house down. We eat on the porch drinking large glasses of sweet red wine, smoking cigarettes, taking things slowly because the summer night is just as hot as the day.

I chop up little mouthfuls of meat for Claude but he doesn't touch it and looks peeky, walking stiffly, his back legs threatening to give out at any moment. I can't bear it. Morgan suggests a speedy trip to the emergency vet and drives us there.

They do blood tests, shaving one of his front legs to do so, take X-rays, and finally suggest I leave him in the hospital for two days' worth of intravenous liquids, to flush out his kidneys which they suspect are old and not functioning properly. I can't bear to leave him there all alone but know I have no choice. Morgan suggests I visit her mother in the Delta for a couple of days to take my mind off things.

Driving away, I have no idea what lies in store for me. The lack of control is terrifying. I don't know whether Claudius will live or die. I have tried to look at it from every angle – am I clinging on, is he in pain, does he want to die, is he trying to tell me something?

I need to make the best decision for both of us. Is it the travelling that's making him ill? Should I fly him back to Janie's and let him enjoy the stability of Connecticut while I carry on? Or carry on together as we are meant to be, though worrying about his state of health?

When things are hard should I battle through, as with a marriage, or give up and try something new? My instinct is that I should carry on, stick at it just to see what happens:

like reading a difficult book you're not into. I have an inkling that the easiest way is not the one to take as the learning curve will not be as steep.

Decisions. I am stuck in some sort of lethargy – swamped in my own quagmire of indecision. Why did I think that life was going to be a bed of roses? Why in the back of my mind do I think that I should be happy because I am travelling and doing what I want to do? Why isn't it easy even when you feel you are on the right path? Why does the right path so often and so quickly become the wrong path? Hello? Is there anyone out there?

Driving through the Delta. The cotton doesn't grow very high, so the land is flat for miles and miles, but green, so green. The sun is so intense it burns all colour from the sky to create a misty grey rather than the cloudless blue you'd expect from a summer's day. The sun then turns its attention to the road, burning pockets of shining tar. The odd run-down bungalow shack with a huge rusty boxy ship car outside dots Highway 1, the Great River Road – which follows the line of the Mississippi. I'm on my way to Leland, better known as birthplace of Kermit the Frog – there's even a shrine to him – listening to Muddy Waters in an attempt to drown in his sorrows rather than my own.

First I stop at Clarksdale, the heart of the Blues, and 'do' the Delta Blues Museum. I leave somewhat confused because I manage to 'do' it backwards and don't realise until the very end when I notice the dates are earlier than when I started. I look for somewhere to eat, slowly, because standing outside is like being under a giant's magnifying glass with the sun concentrated on your head. Most of the places mentioned in the guidebook are closed or long 'gone to Kansas'. A trifle frustrating.

I make it to Holly, Morgan's mother's home, which is an elegant large lemon-coloured one-storey house decorated with remnants of a formerly grand southern home, old portraits, silver, antiques. She gives me a tour of the neighbourhood, and we drive to Doe's, an eatery so famous that even Bill has eaten here. The front door leads to the kitchen where the owner is frying up steaks the size of lawns, and preparing tamales. In the back room is an enormous central wooden table at which a fat woman with greasy make-up and tightly permed hair shoots us a 'hi darlin' as she vigorously tosses salad into eight wooden bowls and carries them all at once next door to a rickety table with eight laughing diners around. Nothing has changed since the 40s – neither the lino, the curtains nor the table seemingly – so it has a grimy charming yesteryear feel to it.

Then we drive through the black areas. Holly locks the doors. She explains that blacks and whites are still very segregated here, that they have little contact, they have their own shops and bars, and when blacks move into a street the whites start moving out or building very high wire fences around their property. All very friendly then. I can't understand this attitude of fear – or is it just residual guilt from the years of slavery? Fear that the blacks will rise up and take their revenge?

Back home we eat the tamales from Doe's. As we chat and I explain about Claudius I can't help crying. Holly hugs me. She runs me a bath and makes me herbal tea and generally fusses over me until I am tucked into bed. I sleep fitfully without the old kitkat near me.

Rather like Ma, Holly doesn't believe in moping and thinks I should be out and about today. She takes me to her brother's cotton farm and then the Catfish Museum – one of Mississippi's growing industries is the catfish – but the name reminds me of you know who, so I kiss her goodbye, thank her and start the drive back to Oxford.

Chapter Nine

What's Up, Doc?

New Orleans, Louisiana

I drive fast back to Oxford, excited to see my kitkat, and rush to the vet's. Claudius is no better, in fact he is terribly weak, but I pay the $300 bill even so. The vet gives me high-caloried liquid food to feed him from a syringe because Claude hasn't eaten anything all the time he's been there.

We speed towards New Orleans at 95mph. Sod the speed limit, I have to get this drive over with. Claudius is on the front passenger seat next to me, too weak to stand on the door handle to look at the huge cement bridges on stilts that carry us over the swamps as we approach New Orleans or the cudzoos that cover most of the vegetation in the marshes.

'Claudius I'm not sending you back to Connecticut. The whole point of this journey was to be together and I will never leave you. I respect your decision whatever it is. If you want to go you must go. Your behaviour has proven what I always knew, that you have an enormous spirit, but if you have had enough and don't wish to continue, well then I stand by you.'

Jack's flat is in the Garden District, the clean large white-housed neighbourhood where all the rich whites live. It is a tiny white apartment with a mosquito-net-covered terrace. I settle Claudius on the bed and think about what to do. I find the nearest vet in town and have a conference with a charming young female doctor. She gives me a list of things, appetite stimulants, stomach acid neutralisers, vitamins and liquids to give Claude at home under the skin. Another $100 later and I am on my way home to administer them. None of them work, if anything they make him worse. I am at a loss as to what to do.

Claudius lies on the bed, his only distraction the Talking Van in the street. This is clearly a cousin of the disco ambulance in New York. Either it talks or there is a rapper trapped inside. Each day it pipes up of its own accord: 'I know you want to take a look inside – but I suggest you move away from the ride', or: 'You too close to my perimeter. Get away from the scene or my alarm will get keen. You have been warned. Five, four, three, two, one. I'VE BEEN VIOLATED.'

Shame that I'm in the biggest party city in the world and really don't feel like partying. Tonight Jack takes me to a housewarming party, also in the Garden District. In the back yard are a few people drinking beers, smoking joints and sniffing in the choking fumes of a barbecue. 'Hi brother,' says Tommy, a Korean-American coming towards us. 'I'm Clare,' I say extending a hand. 'I'm a hugger,' he says enfolding me in chubby arms. I recoil slightly in terror but find the hug strangely relaxing. We sit cross-legged opposite each other in an intense jointy chat for hours. He talks of finding himself. I like the way Americans talk openly and proudly of spiritual quests, unlike the hushed tones embarrassed Brits use, almost apologising for their enlightened ways. Americans are so optimistic about it all. More and more I am having my English cynicism debilitated by the kindness and warmth of the people I am meeting. By the end of the night I'm almost 'I love you man!'.

On to Kelly, outrageously curvy in black. She is kind

when I start talking about Claudius, even though it is clear from what I am saying that I am an obsessive nutter. She suggests a foray into the French Quarter to take my mind off things. We walk down New Orleans' most famous party street, Bourbon Street. Neon-lit titty bars, themed clubs and pubs, drunken leering men stumbling out of them, touching any passing girl, spitting phlegm on to the street, tourists everywhere, rubbish all over the road. We jump the queue at the House of the Blues and eat po-boys stuffed with shrimp. Kelly invites me to meet her flatmate Stephanie next day, who may be able to help me deal with the Claudius situation.

Back home I fall fast asleep and dream about Ma. She is screaming at me, dripping poison and hatred from every word. I never loved you, she sneers. I am five years old and the emptiness these words produce is soon replaced by powerful self-hatred. I wake up depressed.

I feed Claudius his disgusting brown food, give him some liquids and settle him down, after which I go to meet Stephanie. She gives me an energy massage. I lie in the darkness with my eyes closed, listening to her tapes of dolphins burping, and feel nothing. Apparently she is massaging my aura to unblock energy, thereby making me stronger for Claudius, but she could be flinging her undies around the room for all I know. She could be picking her nose or performing some Indian dance, I'm just drifting, drifting.

My sister's cat Libby's pregnancy was planned. No midnight trysts with mogs for her. She was pretty much forced to fuck, or rather she was mounted by a Chocolate Burmese show cat. We watched her through her pregnancy and then one night my sister, who promised me whichever kitten I wanted, helped her deliver five tiny kittens. Only one, the first-born (mazal tov!), was the deep chocolate of his father. My ten-year-old eyes recognised a winner and pointed at the tiny thing: 'He's mine.' The next, his little sister, was a blue, and Ma chose her for herself because of her gentle nature, and because she and Claudius were never apart. The little thing was fed only raw steak once he was weaned, as we had high hopes for a show career for him – though a few white furs on his chest soon put an end to that. From the day he was born, Ma and I were racking our brains for a name. Eventually we took the typically middle-class route of naming him something grand and classical rather than Tom or Tiddles. After all, our labrador was Black Prince Hamlet.

The day he and Cleo first arrived at home, I ran home from school. My mother had painted the walls of our dining room a bright red – rather risqué for suburbia in the 70s – and the mahogany furniture and silver made for quite a flash effect. Claudius was not out of place, sitting on one of the chairs, his brown fur and green eyes contrasting with the red walls, attempting to look sure of himself, though still just a tiny ball of a fluff thing.

Cleo died a couple of years later from a car accident. Claudius wailed for days. From then on he and I became inseparable, brought up under Ma's vigilant eye. Every picture of me in my teens, going through various stages of self-conscious hideousness, features Claude as well. Whenever we went on holiday I sent him postcards. When I lost my virginity he was on the bed next to me, not watching, but protecting quietly. When I went to work, he stayed with Ma.

Whenever I could, I visited the two of them in Ma's cottage in Wandsworth. Often we stood around smoking and chatting, me at the table in the dining room with a drink, Ma in the hall with hers, her hand on the front door knob, opening it for Claudius, who had decided the cat-flap was no longer good enough, then closing it and waiting while he sauntered round the back of the house, came in through the garden doors and then padded down

to the front door again. She opens the door, he goes
through, and so on and so forth until she flips.

'Right, Claude, that's enough for today. You open it
yourself if you want or use the catflap like normal cats.'

A Streetcar named not Desire, but Charles, takes me to the
edge of the French Quarter where I wander around eating
beignets, very sweet crumbly icing-sugar-covered dough-
nut things. Lithe, athletic black hip hop dancers are
putting on a show just opposite Jackson Square, drawing
huge crowds. The two-storeyed coloured houses have
balconies with lacy black ironworks (cornstalk fences)
which drip with tropical plants whose spiky fronds fall
down like large green spiders. Almost every shop sells
purple, green and gold beads, the colours of the Mardi
Gras. There are lots of second-hand clothes shops selling
carnival costumes, glittery, colourful works of art and
feathery masks. The French market next to the river has
stalls of pretty bottles of spicy sauces, strings of purpling
garlic, huge stripy green watermelons. Black boys line the
streets and tap dance/shuffle. They have tacked bottle tops
on to their trainers, and dance for money.

'I know where you got them shoes,' a smily black guy
says to me.

'No you don't.' (They're Manolo Blahniks.)

'I'll bet ya I do.'

'How much?'

'Ten bucks.'

'That sounds fine to me.'

'You got them shoes on yo feet on Bourbon Street in
N'Awlins.'

'Oh for God's sake.'

Ah hands mah money ova.

Feeling slightly unnerved, I visit the Voodoo Museum,
deep in the French Quarter. Voodoo was brought to New

Orleans and its environs by the slaves shipped over to work the plantations. They tried to hold on to their culture and beliefs through their faith, but the religion was much misunderstood and forbidden. The museum attempts to undo its spooky image. So no dolls and pins then.

Staring at the Burmese Python in the Altar Room, name (and attitude) of Zombi, it occurs to me that Claudius could do with some Voodoo healing. The Voodoo shops, of which there are plenty around, sell brightly coloured potions, talismans, masks and juju dolls. Tourists swarm into them looking for love potions, but I swarm in looking for a cure for Claudius. I get a health potion which I have to rub on his forehead, his third eye. I also get a gris-gris (mojo) bag and Voodoo doll.

I get to work with the Voodoo equipment. I anoint Claude's third eye, the bag and doll with the potion and then incant from my heart: 'I, Clare, invoke the assistance of Almighty God, The Divine Good Forces, My Guardian Spirit, My Ancestors in the Spirit World and My Spirit Guides. I wish Claudius to be well and happy again.' I have to do this for nine days in a row. In spite of his state, Claude is still able to give me a 'What *are* you doing?' look. I also give him a shot of antibiotics. Then I feed him this revolting stuff packed full of vitamins. He is not at all amused by this process and often spits it back out, all over my purple silk skirt bang in the crotch area.

While waiting for everything to take effect, I decide to go on a walking tour of the Garden District. A group of the usual touristy types meets in the lobby of a hotel. We have chosen the most irritating tour guide imaginable. His speeches are a series of dullard facts, delivered in a slow monotone. He often stops mid-sentence and wanders off, leaving his group bemused and confused behind him. After a while people start dropping out, at first one or two slip off as he turns a corner, but after a while the group gets angrier and bolder and small splinters just bugger off in the middle of a speech. The best part takes place as we cross one of the Garden District's major streets, dotted with large white houses, some with Grecian columns and turrets and bay windows. Tour Guide momentarily forgets that a dwindling group of ten people is behind him, starts crossing the road against the lights and keeps going, in spite of the mayhem that ensues. Everyone just follows like lemmings and soon the road is covered with fat, sweat-panted, sneaker-clad tourists running in all directions screaming. Some are stranded like rabbits in the centre, others are making a wobbly run for it. The whole scene is carnage and most amusing.

Jack is peeved and we are driving home in silence. I have just disgraced us at a swish do his tutor held for all the young doctors in his class. It was an upmarket version of 'barbie by pool', proper cutlery not plastic, chilled glasses of Chardonnay or salted beakers of mint julep. I was by the pool in my cherry outfit and beige candies, downing the jules like nobody's business and generally flirting with anything that moved. I was making very little headway with a particularly good-looking young doctor who wasn't listening to a word I said.

'So you're travelling around America?'

'Yes indeed.'

'How?'

'Pogo stick.'

'Hmm?'

'Pontiac.'

'Uh-haah.' Eyes veering off over my shoulder.

Important tutor is walking in our direction and Jack is blushing up, ready to make a few respectful, incisive and witty comments, thereby drawing Big Cheese's attention to him, when an enormous spider, we're talking gargan-tuan tarantulan proportions, chooses this moment to introduce himself to my candies. I fucking freak, but big time, and start getting out of the way as fast as I can. Which is across Big Cheese's path, but not on the pool side, that's where he is. Basically the force of my velocity times my direction times my energy equals Big Cheese in pool, who then proceeds to flip out in the most ugly angry way. And Jack is in silence all the way home.

What with Claude having a daily flirt with Death and Jack angry with me, I try to ward off the Depression I can feel tiptoeing up behind me by downing huge handfuls of pills each morning – St John's Wort rather than the real thing, because I've tried them in the past and find the numbed woozy effect totally addictive. Then at night in order to get some sleep rather than lie awake wrestling with my demons, which choose that time to spill their venom into my guts, I chomp on some American sleep-inducers, buy-able over the counter, but strong enough to kill a horse. In spite of these I still have to fly United (wear an eye mask) or the tiniest hint of light through the curtains, even a flicker of dawn, still musty and foggy from the night, is enough to blind my sensitive 'I'm a *real* Princess' eyes and wake me up.

This morning at daybreak Claudius crawls into my arms and sleeps twitchily for twenty minutes. I don't move a muscle even though I'm in a horrid crampy position because I'm so happy to have him there. Then he gets up and for the first time in two weeks eats a few bites of his food by himself. He then licks his chops looking extremely grumpy. But it's a start, right?

Jeremy, a Friend From Home, is paying me a much-needed visit. He's a writer and producer, on his way back from the film festivals in Los Angeles and San Francisco, where he was showing his first film. He enjoyed a howling success, although the film, as I had predicted, was received as a broad comedy rather than the tear-jerking tragic mystery drama he had intended it to be.

He has known Claudius for years and is concerned to see him looking so thin. He can see the same fight in Claude's eyes that I can but says I should give it a specified amount of time, such as a week, and if he's not improved, then put him down. *Put him down?* His words are like a lightning bolt of grief.

Jeremy wants his film screened here so we make for the Zeitgeist Alternative Theater round the corner – a gay cinema showing short films. Herve, who owns it, has made three of his own films, autobiographical pieces about being fat and gay. He is indeed both fat and gay, and wears thick 50s top-only-rimmed specs, his head shaved apart from a tuft on his crown which wobbles as he speaks. They discuss business, and we stalk off.

Claudius is improving! The Voodoo has worked. He is eating a little by himself, showing interest in his environment and is pleased to see me. He is purring again.

And this morning he talked to Jeremy for the first time. The portentous moment took place at six when Jeremy took a freezing shower in an attempt to 'cool orf'. As he passes through my room he notices Claudius sitting up in bed looking at me.

'Is everything OK, Claw Claw?' he asks.

Claude cocks his head in my direction and utters one word:

'Wind.'

I am still trying to make up for the pool fiasco: buying Jack sushi, cleaning the flat within an inch of its life (even though he's house-sitting for a friend), offering foot massages etc, but he's stony. He makes it clear that the only way forward is a proper apology, face-to-face with the tutor. So I drive out to his home, off the Great River Road in the countryside surrounding N'Awlins. He lives in one of those great plantation houses, complete with ornate white grillework on the windows, porches all the way around and sugar fields visible from every room. The gardens abound in azaleas, magnolia and crepe myrtles but the trees dotting the drive are covered in Spanish moss, a particularly spooky grey dust string of a plant that hangs dead down from all the trees in the area. His family probably had this when slave boys whistled the food from the stone kitchens before fanning the ladies at table and setting glass globes containing molasses and sugar water to keep the flies off. I knock on the door and a good-looking black guy, muscled up in a tight T-shirt and lacy boxers (*lacy boxers!*) opens the door. He is followed by speedy footsteps and then seems to disappear. The tutor is standing there. Suddenly I feel very foolish for having driven all this way. I hold out a box of chocolates and apologise profusely for the other day. He seems embarrassed and shy and says not to mention it and then pretty much slams the door in my face.

Very strange. Still, Jack should be happy.

While chopping up tiny bite-size pieces of Gruyère for Claude:

'It was one of those houses that would have had sixty wooden shacks out back, each housing two entire slave families. I don't know how people could have lived in such splendour when they just had to look out of their back windows to see that dire contrast. No wonder the women, with too much time on their hands, spent a lot of it swimming in the mint julep jug.'

'I don't think they worried too much about it.'

'But I've heard horrific slave stories, of branding and babies being sold from their wailing mothers. How can people do that?'

'It is generally accepted that, the further apart the

owners and slaves are in race and religion, the worse are the abuses the slave suffers. In Rome, both owner and slave were white, and slaves often bought their freedom or rose to positions of authority in the household. In Africa, slaves and owners were both black and therefore the slaves were often included in social activities. But in the old South, where white man owned black, the African was seen as uneducable, lazy filth, and hence was treated for the most part with contempt. And it still goes on today. I'm the colour of chocolate so you think it perfectly all right to force-feed me disgusting liquids . . .'

'Which gave you the strength to get better. And considering you haven't driven once or carried one suitcase I think I know who's the slave around here. I assume nourishment by Gruyère is not on your list of Feline Rights Abuses?'

Claude is even perky enough to have a wander around the neighbour's garden for a couple of hours. Of course he refuses to return when I call, gently squinting his greens at me as I scale the neighbour's high fence, risk getting shot, pick him up and bring him back. After which he wanders off to squirm back under the fence: an outdoors version of Ma's front-door and catflap routine.

I am in the kitchen, sweating profusely, pouring pistachios into a bowl and opening Mexican beers all at the same time (well what did you expect? I'm a Woman, a W-O-M-A-N, I'll say it again) to take out to Jeremy and Claude on the balcony. Through the open windows I hear Jeremy discussing his latest play, a showpiece for Claudius called *Gay Cat from Outer Space*. Claude is replying through his whiskers that he is in the twilight of his career and not sure he can take on such a demanding role.

'Well how about a few poetry readings then?' says Jeremy.

'How about his getting one hundred per cent better before carting him off to humiliate himself in suburban rep performances?' I holler, my hands on hips from the doorway.

'Spoil-sport,' mutters Jeremy.

'Jealous,' whispers Claude.

Jeremy is still trying to get his film screened here, so far without much success. He calls Herve who suggests a midnight tryst at Roundup, a local bar. Jeremy insists I go along too though I am pretty sure this is not what Herve would want. As we arrive a drag queen in a peroxide wig is hosting a best stripper/dancer competition. Guys take it in turns to strip down to their thongs, get up on the central circular bar and gyrate in pseudo confidence (these are not professionals) before a baying crowd that occasionally sticks dollar bills down the thong, if they're any good. The guy then plays out his stripper fantasy by doing a bit of frontal gyration. Next to me two fat sweaty middle-management types are shoving money down a young guy's pants and taking the opportunity to have a really good feel as they do so. The boy isn't at all shaken by this, but neither is he stirred. No oestrogen anywhere. My presence seems no threat, however, as plenty of guys smile as they walk past. One across the bar is Versace-ad good-looking. We exchange meaningful looks and I wonder if tonight is the night that I get very, very lucky indeed. Eventually he saunters over. I say saunter, but actually he trips and galumphs because the place is heaving. He finally arrives, we smile at each other and I am just about to say something witty and beguiling like, 'D'ya come 'ere often?' when he grabs me roughly in the crotch. I scream. He does too, rather undercutting the effect of mine.

'You're a girl!'

'Yes, what did you think?' I reply, simultaneously hurt and horrified. There are disgusted tuts setting off like firecrackers around me.

Actually this has happened to me before but I was twelve at the time so it was a bit more understandable. My mother was filling up at a petrol station in Norwood, the ghastly south London suburb I went to school in (my English compositions here already peppered with tales of escape to sexier climes). In spite of her posh accent, my mother still liked to 'Dot Cotton' it up now and then, so she told me to go and buy her some fags. Back in those days, the heady atmosphere of trust that pervaded suburbia, was due to the unadulterated bliss and comfort we were all living in – well we were driving a brand-new Lada. Kiddies could buy their parents cigarettes because no one thought for a second they'd break them up, roll them into joints and then sell them to their twelve-year-old buddies – or even just smoke them themselves. Anyway, I'm on my way into the shop when the guy at the counter hands over the booty and pipes up: 'Are you a boy or a girl?' I'm fine. No really. It only cost a few thousand pounds to sort this incident out in therapy. And I remember running home, sobbing the story into Claude's fur and then listening to him cackle with laughter for half an hour.

Herve does not show and Jeremy checks for messages. We try another bar. While waiting for Herve, Jeremy makes friends with Scott, a rigger, one of those people who work on the Mississippi for days and days without a break. He tells me to be careful in Texas, my next destination, lots of women are getting raped there. Yadda yadda yadda, I think, bored with travel-scare stories people keep laying on me, but vaguely grateful that he realises I'm female. Still no Herve.

July 4th. Where is everybody? The streets are deserted and Jeremy and I have the distinct impression that everyone is at a groundbreaking party we have not been invited to. We cheer ourselves up by buying a huge picnic and set off to sunbathe in Audubon Park with Claude – his first outing in days. The grass is deliciously smooth, flat and comfy. The temperature is 97°. Mad cats and Englishwomen. Claude refuses to settle in the place we have chosen, instead staying under a tree about fifty yards away. He won't be persuaded so I leave him there, stretched out like a panther, and keep an eye on him from the luxury grass. I'm in my stars and stripes bikini, Jeremy in his grey shorts, and we're eating cherries, pieces of baked chicken, angel cakes, coconut ice creams and tomatoes all at once. Then we lie down to sunbathe. The sweat has just started to pour when I hear a strange buzzing. I feel that we are not alone. I lift my head and see two things:

a)   a little cart with a very fat man in it whizzing close by and

b)   a golf ball making its way at lightning speed towards my eyes.

Pandemonium ensues as Jeremy and I gather our clothes, food bags, rubbish, books, suntan lotion and speed off to join a slightly smug Claude under the tree.

Later, Claudius, Jeremy and I are sitting on the balcony enjoying the evening breeze, which you might think is cool and refreshing after the day's heat but in fact is nothing of the kind. Later still we head off to the river surrounded by young preppy things dressed in sequinned striped top hats with stars bouncing on wire stalks and thousands of other New Orleanians to watch the fireworks: giant spiders of red, blue, green, pink, purple and white light thread the sky to the sounds of 'God Bless America' on huge speakers. Claudius clings to my shoulder as he looks up. Luckily his deafness prevents the fireworks' cackle and hiss from being a scary experience. Back to our balcony to watch the night. The street, normally so clean, American and residential has taken on a carnival atmosphere. We smell other people's joints and spy on the couple over the road who are seemingly sitting on the sidewalk, she on his lap, but whose rhythmic movements tell a different story.

Jeremy wants to see the swamps so we leave early to avoid the heat but by ten it is already stifling. Claude stays in the cool of the apartment. He waves us off.

'Cats love heat but this is ridiculous.'

We take a boat trip. This means tooling up and down the bayou looking at the cypress trees dripping with Spanish moss, watching some river guys spraying deadly chemicals on the lilies and looking out for egrets and gators. A woman from Texas (accompanied by a younger son/friend/gigolo, both with identical long brown straggly pony-tails, wearing khaki and friendship bracelets among silver jewellery) throws them marshmallows. How disappointed they must be to open those huge jaws, snap! and then taste a momentary soft sugariness before it disappears totally. Hardly a lump of raw chicken. The scrawny white guy in a baseball cap driving the boat has a nasal Louisiana accent. 'Dem alligators – dey sho wants yo mushmallus.'

The final leg of the tour is a small murky pond in which there are turtles and one alligator turtle, which, on particularly grumpy days, likes to eat its neighbours. The driver fishes out this horrific little prehistoric creature on a stick, to show us its muddy green-finned back, its gaping, snapping beak-like mouth, its seemingly eyeless face. The stuff of nightmares.

It's Jeremy's last evening and we feel like Thai so we go to Lucky Cheng's.

A very thin black girl with huge tits and extraordinary cheekbones does a Marilyn 'Happy Birthday Mr President' for her table. They clap and she walks away, diva-esque, swinging her hips so much that they almost touch the walls with each beat.

Our server is Asian, pretty, great legs. Her accent is Asian Louisiana, the combination of which almost produces an entirely new language. After some polite chit chat, hi how ya doin' sorta stuff, I order. Literally in the middle of 'green curry for two . . .' she leans over, flashing her cleavage and says:

'So, what's your preference?'

'I'm sorry?'

'Boys or girls?'

'Um, boys for both of us. You?' with an '*Is this normal?*' look to Jeremy.

'Men now, though women when I was a boy.'

'When you were . . . oh I see. Are you all like this?'

'Trannies? Yus.' (So when she was a boy she fancied women and now she's a girl she fancies men . . .)

'Do you, ahem, have a toolbox, so to speak?'

'Oh my God' – this from Jeremy, shy and retiring for the first time in his life and now enacting various states of lockjaw.

'Yes I do.' She blinks and looks down, an Asian transvestite version of Prinny Di in her coy days. 'But I took the pills to make my breasts grow.'

'Which pill?' I ask excitedly. Then more soberly: 'Do you have a boyfriend?'

'Yes I do. He's attracted to supermodels.' Yes, my dear, but are they attracted to him? I want to say. Is this an inverted compliment to herself or does it mean her boyfriend is a total trophy-woman-objectifying arse? I'm not sure.

'But he's not attracted to men.'

'Oh no? So you don't have sex then?'

'After two years together? Of course we do!'

'So has he not noticed your um . . .??'

'Yes he has. He doesn't want me to have the full change but I do. You know you have to go to a psychiatrist for a year before and if they say no, you can never apply again.

One guy murdered his psychiatrist when he said no. I'll get your cocktails . . .'

'Oh. Great.'

This conversation has muffled my timidity, so in the loos I ask one of the older girls – big blonde hair, a rhinestone top and lots of make-up – how she decides which bathroom to use? Does she alternate to make it more fun, as strictly speaking she can use both? She gives me a filthy look and exits. I go back to Jeremy and the margaritas – he is bemoaning the lack of screening for his film into one of them. I scan the restaurant and notice the woman at one of the corner tables with a fat mafioso type. At the next table is someone vaguely familiar. She's gorgeous, very made-up, designered up, gold hoops in ears, high high stilettos. She's with a beautiful black girl, very tall, quite broad. Ridiculously tall in fact, and now I look closer, yes definitely, a man. Who are they?

'Oh my God.'

'What?' says Jeremy, sucking up noodles and splashing both of us in the eye in the process.

'Jack's tutor is over there with the black guy I told you about.'

'Where?'

'In the diamanté jumpsuit.'

I hop over excitedly.

'Hello! How are you!'

He stares into his soup. After a pause:

'Miss Clare, whenever we meet, you make things awkward for me. Is there any way of ensuring this meeting is our last and that the knowledge of it remains between us?'

How unfriendly.

'Yes of course. I'll keep out of your way from now on. I didn't mean to embarrass you.' Then a flash of inspiration. 'I just wanted to ask you if you knew any way we could get my friend's film screened? It's about a couple's struggle with society when they come out.'

He carefully removes a card from his handbag and writes a name on the back.

'Call my friend. He'll do it for you.'

'But this is Herve. We've tried him without much luck.'

'I said he'll do it for you. Goodbye.'

'Goodbye for ever then.'

He looks down and away.

Back at the table.

'Jackpot. We have a screening. And Herve will appear this time.'

'Just one problem. I'm on a flight tomorrow morning. This is my last evening.'

'Oh bugger. I didn't think of that.'

'Never mind. Thanks for trying anyway.'

'Don't you think it damn weird to be ashamed of being gay and a tranny in America's most liberal city?'

Jeremy and I then obsess over our mothers' deaths – his died of the same disease exactly three months after mine. Not for the first time, I tell him of the zipper bag routine, he tells me about not letting the body go until it smelt. Each of us furtively revealing our scabby wounds to the other, marvelling how all that pain is now an ordinary part of our everyday lives.

A couple more vodkas hide the bitterness in our mouths, though do nothing for the pinched lines at the sides of them. To cheer up, we drive to the Maple Leaf at the other end of town, to hear some music. A black brass band, Rebirth, is playing.

The place has two rooms, one taken up by a long bar, the other by a large dance area and small stage. There are no lights on in the dance room so the band is invisible apart from their instruments glinting in the dark. There are ten people up on that tiny stage with maybe forty watching from the floor. The scene is both black and white for a change – the black girls dance and laugh at how badly the white guys move. The atmosphere is friendly and relaxed – not the usual competitive smell in the air when a bunch of strangers find themselves in a party situation. The music is like an infusion or intravenously applied pleasure pill. It is pure New Orleans jazz, very loud with a stomping beat. Jeremy and I dance until our hair is completely down.

This morning I see Jeremy off at the airport. We say goodbye and the loneliness sears through my heart which is already heavy with *miss*.

Claudius and I have been in Jack's flat in New Orleans for two weeks. Claude is better and it's time to move on in the direction of Texas. I pray his health holds up once we're back on the road. It'll be positive proof as to whether it's the journeying that makes him ill or not. I know it's a risk but I can't stay here for ever. And the road beckons.

Chapter Ten

Working Girl

Breaux Bridge, Louisiana – Galveston, Victoria, Austin, Texas

It is a long way to Texas, about eight hours to Victoria from New Orleans. We chicken out after three hours of heading west and stop at Breaux Bridge, in Louisiana.

Staying awake on the road is a problem. In spite of jagged and interrupted sleep patterns at night, in the car during the day I am like a baby. I have invented a method of dealing with this which is to keep the air conditioning on at the lowest temperature. The only disadvantage is that I can't stroke Claude because my hands are totally frozen and he asks me to stop whenever I try.

We stop at the Bayou Boudin Cracklin run by Ricky Sonnier, the Cracklin King of Louisiana, so titled after winning various cook-offs. As a welcome present I am given a 'lagniappe' sampling of boudin, cracklin', hoghead cheese, some praline and a glass of root beer. It's a delicious if fat-ridden snack. Claude and I mooch around with Ricky's pretty children, who are unfamiliar with the concept of seven human years to one animal year. They are fascinated by Claude's age but think I'm 133 too.

The cabins we are staying in are built on stilts with their own little porch and rocking chairs on which to smoke cigarettes and look out to the bayou beyond the land. Claude likes the gardens immediately and has a good long nose around, especially under the stilts and near the edge of the water. There are plenty of other cats around and several kittens, who all recognise wisdom and demeanour when they see it. They let Claude on his way to smell all the best plants first. I somewhat cut his street cred when I whisk him up from the side of the bayou. There is a sign saying *Aggressive Alligators Nesting*. Juicy brown cats are no different in their eyes from whole raw chicken. They don't stop and say, 'Hell now, thes a pedigree Burmese cat, advanced in wisdom and age. Ah guess ah'll jess look elsewhere for mah supper.' Nope. It's snap and 'Mmmm' when chocolate-coloured kitkats potter by.

I have a look for the gators. A couple of nutria are swimming around the edges of the swampy mushy water. Halfway down the bayou I lose my nerve and start tiptoeing in fear of being eaten. Apparently if you want to escape a gator you run in zigzags because they can only run straight, but they do it fast, and so are likely to snap at your legs in cartoon fashion if you're not careful. I practise a few zigzag runs, knees high in Joyce Grenfell from *St Trinian's* fashion.

I stop when I notice a man and his son in a wheelchair watching. We exchange hellos.

'I'm Bird. This is my son Clit.'

'Clit? *Clit?*'

'Yip. Thes raght. And you?'

'Clare.'

'Carl?'

'Clare.'

'Carol?'

'Clare.'

'Karen?'

'Yes, that's right.'

'Have you been to Mulate's?' (Pron. Moolatz.) 'They play some good Cajun music there.'

'No,' I reply. 'Are you thinking of going?'

'Well, I guess we could go – you can come with us if you like, Karen.'

'I'd love to. Just wait a sec while I change out of my dirty day clothes.'

I skip off, excited about an evening of good music and some chit chat with the locals, getting the true colour of the surrounding scene. Maybe a few jokes. Maybe a few beers. Maybe a little dance. Although Clit's wheelchair might be painful on the toes if he's not careful. Ten minutes later, after a shower humming a sort of 'That's just me. Making friends where'er I go'-type tune, I saunter back out, cool as you like, a little mascara blackening my lashes, a little rouge burning my cheeks, a little lippy on my kissers, my kitkat under my arm ready for a brief evening stroll. I'm preeetty sure my Gucci mini skirt will impress the folks, and that I'll get used to the steel stilettos on these high shoes any minute now.

'Yo cen tek yo cat to Moolatz,' says Bird.

'No, I know, I'm just walking him briefly.'

'I gotta take Clit home. He needs his medicine.'

'What?' says Clit.

'Yo need yo medicine.' Accompanied by a wink.

Clit looks blank.

'Really, you can't come for just one drink?' I beg.

I don't know what I said or did but all of a sudden I'm going to Moolatz by myself. Oh fuck it, I don't need you, I'll go alone.

Mulate's is by no means heaving with fun-seekers. It is very quiet tonight, understates the woman behind the bar. There is one other woman propping up some beers and fags, her face in the Droopy position. She stares at the same spot ten inches ahead of her on the bar until a man from the dance floor comes over. They say not a word to each other but she follows him to the dance floor, her head in the same position. They waltz at arms' length, their eyes unmeeting, her face unchanging until the end of the song, when without a word she turns on her heel and makes her way back to the barstool to resume her miserable vigil.

A patchwork of thousands of business cards adorns the ceiling, leftovers from twenty years' worth of visitors. The tables have red check table cloths, the floors are dark wood. A Cajun band plays toe-tapping thigh-slapping toons such as 'Waltz You to Texas'. The dancers cover all age ranges, crumblies to teenagers. They are nimble, in time and synch with each other. One moustachioed guy, slightly overweight – juh right! I think we mean a porker – wearing large square specs, an orange beret and Dr Scholl shoes shimmies his partner on to the dance floor. He keeps his upper body totally still as his legs and feet slip out here there and everywhere. An older couple, in matching clothes like grown twins, red check shirts and denim, she in skirt he in jeans, are bouncing up and down, seemingly stuck at the chest.

In spite of the lack of company, it is friendly and fun, however I am starting to feel a bit like a lemon. I accost one half of a couple, the guy, who has come to the bar, after being particularly proficient on the dance floor.

'Are you professionals?'

'Nope.'

'Because you dance so well.'

'Yip.'

'Where did you learn?'

'Texas.'

'Is that where you live?'

'Yip.'

'So you're visiting?'

'Yip.'

'Me too.'

'Uh.'

'How do you find it here?'

'Hot.'

'Me too. Well, nice talking to you.'

'Yip.'

I slink out, grateful for the invention of cigarettes and

booze, otherwise what would I have done with my hands for the last hour?

Anyway, I need an early night. It's a long way to Victoria, tomorrow. Yes indeed.

As I check out next morning, Ricky hands me my change and says, 'Hope you enjoyed your stay. I saw you talking with Bud and Clint last night.'

'Who?' I reply and then, 'Oh. Oh yes.'

'Nice folks huh? Real frenny.'

'Yes. Very friendly.'

I've developed a great new way of driving. It involves sneaking up to other cars and refusing to get off their tail until they move over. If they refuse, which is often, I swing out violently *à la* 'Dukes of Hazzard', overtake on the inside and clip back in front of them within an inch of their life. Scary at first but this becomes second nature, addictive even, within a short space of time. I forget about the danger I am putting us both in. Live young, die fast. Luckily Claude can't see how I'm driving because he's either on the floor, his paws pushing against my feet in a softly padded way, or he's a snoring velvet furball on my lap.

We know when we're in Texas because the signs say El Paso, 827 miles. *827 miles*. We whizz past Houston, its menacing skyscrapers glinting in the distance. The roads seem huge, wide, empty. I edge up to 100mph. The sun, which is white, is pouring itself into the car in a blindsome way. We're heading for a few days by the sea, in Galveston, the seaside island resort. ' "We'll be drinking margaritas by the sea, Momacita!" ' Claude purrs excitedly as we whizz past billboards screaming *Microsurgical Vasectomy Reversal*. We are greatly looking forward to our beachside retreat, but the motel I have booked us into smells bad and the sea view we were promised consists of a thin navy-blue line in the distance, several buildings and a road in the foreground. Claude roams the concrete corridors before settling on our bed for a nap. I go to the beach looking out to the Gulf of Mexico, but the sea has a strong undertow, and is muddy sand for miles out – it takes ages to wade to anywhere deeper than thigh-tickling. It's also warm and on emerging I feel very unlike Venus – sticky, dirty and still hot.

Houston is just an hour away so I suggest to Claude a trip to the Houston Space Center with a Cats in Space theme. He says the idea is out of this world and promptly dozes off. Instead we move on to Dan's in Victoria.

I have searched for Victoria in the Texas guidebooks and found nothing. This is because it is a large no-town. People sleep here but work elsewhere. There are absolutely no sites of interest in or around the area. There are three large supermarkets: Dick's, Weiner's and HE Butt's. No, seriously.

I am very excited to see Dan, even though we barely know each other. But compared to everyone else, he's an old, old friend. My first night in Victoria, Dan says we should go to Bud's Deli, which is close so we *walk* to it. How totally weird. We sit at the bar and drink beers and talk to the girl serving, whose long thick hair is in a plait that tickles her bum. Every finger has a gold ring on, even her thumbs, her small blue eyes are stitched in and she has a sweet chipmunk smile. I feel like trying a Texan jalapeño pickle. I bite into one and within seconds can no longer feel my legs. It has released my sinuses but tensed my shoulders. Six of one and half a dozen of the other.

'They're hot,' she says.

'Thanks.'

'They make your breath smell none too good neither. But they numb your pain. I ate them throughout my pregnancy, and my labour only took two hours!' she chortles. 'My little girl just whipped out, thanks to them pickles.'

*   *   *

Claude is back to his old self, off all medicine, thank God. He spent today wandering in Dan's garden, chewing the long grass, biting it at the bottom and sucking on it all the way to the top of the stalk before shaking his head right to left in an attempt to tear it from its root. He has developed a penchant for Kentucky Fried Chicken and now refuses to eat anything else – er, apart from grass, that is. I try putting out normal catfood for him but he won't eat it and I am too weak-willed, and too wary after his recent illness, to make him wait until he is so hungry that he eats what I want him to. It's a battle of wills – he knows it and wins hands down. The result is it now costs $4.50 to feed him a day rather than the 55 cents his catfood costs.

He also scratches the front door every morning at 5am just as it is getting light, insisting that I get up and let him out. This morning just as I'm getting back into bed I notice an armadillo in the garden in the direction Claude is heading. I streak outside – literally, it is too hot to wear anything at night – ow! ouch! over the rain-starved spiky grass and whisk him up into safety – Claude not the armadillo, though after the bear incident in Shenandoah I realise it's the armadillo who's in danger. Of course a truckload of cowboys is driving past at the very moment.

Tonight Dan takes me dancing at the local dance hall – about thirty miles away in the middle of nowhere, stuck out in the sticks. As we arrive there are hundreds of pick-up trucks parked around – which I find exciting and intimidating at the same time. This means there are cowboys in there. Red-blooded cowboys who will tip their hat and say, 'Yes ma'am,' when they say hello, but will tip you over their shoulder and give you a damn good spanking if you're out of line. God I can't wait. As we walk in, a woman in a grubby yellow booth, with a faded newspaper picture of a Japanese musician pinned lonelily above her head, who has not changed her dress or hair style since the

50s, stamps our hands and staples (yes, *staples*) an 'admit one' ticket to our clothes. I am wearing a DKNY T-shirt and am none too impressed by this habit, but she is none too impressed by my 'fussin' ' about a T-shirt neither. The ceiling is covered in gold and silver foil fringing and the huge dance floor is rather empty, but there are plenty of lookers-on drinking beer around it. This is not how I want my first foray into cowboy dancing to be – I want lots of bodies hiding mine. As I step on Dan's toes and throw us both off balance.

The band plays songs such as 'All My Exes Live In Texas' and 'I Need a Lover Who Won't Do My Head In' and the couples take to the floor. All the men have cowboy boots, big silver-buckled jeans and hats on. The women wear short shorts, white socks and sneakers, or pretty dresses. All have big hair and lots of shiny make-up. I stick out like a sore thumb, just for a change. They dance either waltzes or two-steps or polkas. We sip our beers from the bottle and watch. I strike up a conversation with the woman next to me who has been married to her 'honey' for nineteen years, and they are still kissing and cuddling like teenagers. She says that 'Texan women don't take no guff'. Her husband leans over and tells me a joke:

'Where is the best place to warm your hands?'

'Oh now Micky, really . . .' hoots his wife.

'Between your butt cheeks,' he replies straight-faced without waiting for my reaction and immediately turns back to his beer. I look at Dan and smile a 'Scuse me?' smile. He insists we get out there and very self-consciously I stick-insect my way around the dance floor. He is quite shy too and holds me at some distance as though I smell. So far so good, however, as great howls of laughter haven't set up from the audience. Anyway, one guy is diverting people's attention from us. He is old, skinny and dances alone. He wears traditional garb, hat, boots etc, but has added aviator sunspecs which look great under the coloured lights. According to the music, he either does an imitation of Keith Richards or he waltzes/two-steps round the edge of the floor, his face always to his audience, grinning in a Lancashire mug, his arms clasped around an imaginary partner. I can't help giggling, but everyone else lets him do his thing, without judgement. The place gets more and more crowded and I am hoping for some line-dancing but none happens. 'That's just in the films,' says Dan. 'Or the cities.' After a while the band starts to murder 'Back Street Boys' and the crowd stops dancing in the charming couple way and starts to boogie self-consciously. After a while the loon dances by with a very pretty blonde girl in his arms. He looks thrilled to bits to have found someone to put those tight arms around, and slightly shy too. At 12.30 Dan says we have to leave because the fights break out around 1am. Ohhh, I think plaintively.

'The chivalry of the cowboy on the dance floor thinly disguises a thirst for violence in the parking lot,' explains Dan, but looking at the crowd tonight it seems unlikely to me. This is very much a family affair. Just then a couple of boys come up. I think they want to dance with me.

'Howdy!' they holler. 'Didn't recognise ya with ya clothes on.'

Oh God. Maybe now is a good time to leave after all. We drive back through the blackened night, along dusty empty roads, the wind hot on our faces.

Next day Claudius sausages across my lap on the long white-light road to Austin. We are going to stay with Jenny, the best friend of a friend in England. Austin's landscape is not typically Texan. For a start there are hills (known as Silicon Hills, because of Austin's thriving technology industry), which are wooded with pungently sweet cedars and filled with the sound of summer, cicadas. We drive past willows, sycamores and cotton-woods as we wend our way around the city.

At Jenny's office she immediately ushers Claude and I into a brain-storming with her two bosses. They are looking for a name for their new Virtual Office. 'Why not call it Orifice?' suggests Claude, smelling the glass windows, gazing wistfully on to the large lawns in front of their office. 'Why not call it Orifice?' I pipe up in a rerun of one of the most irritating episodes of my childhood. My first school was run by Catholic nuns. Sister Bernadette, a first cousin of the hunchback of Notre Dame, had just asked us which book of the Bible contained the story of the visitation of the Holy Ghost (since renamed Spirit to preclude any spooky connections). In a moment of since-unrepeated enlightened genius, considering I had never picked up the Bible, I involuntarily murmured, 'Acts.' Mary sitting to my right heard this, promptly shouted out, 'Acts,' and got rewarded with a gold star. I've never quite forgotten it.

'It's an opening and an office, and has vaguely smutty undertones to keep the childish among us happy,' I fully develop Claude's idea. They look at me indulgently and then move on to other matters.

Jenny moved here from London because of her job. Like me she's glad to see a familiar English face, even if strictly speaking it's not familiar, as we've never met before. Be that as it may, we know so many people in common that it is very easy to slip into feeling close.

Today Claude and I stay by the pool. He sunbathes, I angst.

'What if we don't make it to the other side of the States? What if you get ill again? Where are we going to settle afterwards?'

'Stop worrying and live in the moment,' he purrs.

Claudius decides to sleep on Jenny's bed at night, which irritates the hell out of me, but I have to hide it from him, to save him the satisfaction, as I can tell from his sideways glance, he's wondering whether I am affected.

Supper with friends of Mary Love's, middle-of-the-road, friendly charming folk. We meet at Chuy's, a famous Tex-Mex place. The restaurant is a fun, plasticky kind of joint, with pink and yellow walls decorated with Cadillac tail-fins, huge brightly coloured glass bubbles and psychedelic shapes. I down two lethal margaritas through their straws. Darlene – finally I meet someone called Darlene – has turned up with her husband James, their son and son's friend. I turn my attention to the boys. They are eighteen-year-old beach-blond California surf types. We smirk at each other across the table and I eye them up as much as I can without being rude. I crack the one and only joke I've ever cracked, the response to which is a thunderous silence.

ME: What do you do?
JAMES: I'm a podiatrist.
ME: Ah, so you molest young children.
JAMES: No. No I don't.
ME: Only joking. (*Very little voice.*)

Later I drive Claude to Congress Bridge to see the bats. This is the huge bridge that leads up to the State Capitol which was modelled on St Paul's. The bridge was built with inch rivulets underneath, which are perfect for bats to nest in. Millions have gathered there over the last few years, all leaving every night at dusk to forage for insects. There is quite a gathering under the bridge as they are something of a tourist and kiddy attraction. A girl wearing a T-shirt that says 'Ask Me About Bats' enthusiastically hands out leaflets, educating us as to the real nature of these flying mammals. The leaflet features Batricia High-flier, which elicits a little margarita-soaked guffaw from me. They are not the spooky things vampires would have us believe. They are great pest controllers, eating their body weight in pests every night. A fat woman with a little-girl voice asks the volunteer:

'Did they build the bridge specially for the bats?'

'Yes dear,' she replies. 'The city legislators thought the bats needed somewhere to live and spent millions on constructing this bridge which cleverly doubles up as a means for cars to get across the river as well.'

'Oh! You're kidding, right?'

'Right!'

Claudius and I settle down to wait for the sun to go down. Sitting right next to us is one of Jenny's bosses with his two kids.

'Hi!'

'Hi, howya doin? Lucky you're here. We wanted to get in touch with you. We have a proposal for you.'

Whereupon they offer me a job. A job! With money! Plenty of it! Marketing and general fiddling on the Internet for them. I thank them and say I'll think about it. They stroke Claude until the bats swoop out, first a few then more and more until the dark blue sky is filled with a plague of locusts or jumping frogs, so fast and small are they. As the sky darkens we can see less and less but the air is filled with a tuneless quiet buzzing.

Claude and I could settle down here, I could support us, the weather is nice, and I already have a friend. What more could I want? While deciding I visit the Hill Country whose serpentine roads only allow speeds of 15mph, or you career headlong off the hills. The crests have magnificent views of trees and the valleys of creeks of clear-running streams.

I stop at Fredericksburg, one of the German towns in the middle of Texas. The houses are old (well, 1860) Wild West saloon-type things. In spite of the odd schnitzel-adorned poster, there isn't a lederhosen in sight, and no one speaks German any more – that was the last generation. I buy a cowboy hat. I've wanted one ever since I saw Dala's in New York. It is slightly incongruous with my blue checked skirt from Gap, blue T-shirt and running shoes. In fact I look like a Class-A Idiot Tourist, but am so happy to have it that I don't mind the sniggers.

I wander into the local Cowboy Museum. It's a musty backroom affair with badly taxidermied animals whose gums still seem to be bleeding and fur moth-eaten and patchy. There are newspaper cuttings about Bonnie & Clyde's death including pictures of Bonnie's corpse, not pleasant, saloon doors, old guns, and a jackalope. This is a large bunny-cum-kangaroo-type thing, all saddled up and ready to go. The only other visitor is a cowboy named Harry, who lives in Austin. We chat and he explains how the cowboys drove cattle from south Texas to the railheads in the north over a ten-year period after the civil war from 1865–1875. By 1875 the land was no longer open, it had all been sold and fenced in with barbed wire, and by that time the railroads extended further down south anyway. Texas is 97 per cent privately owned. On the way out I look at the gifts which include brightly coloured onyx eggs.

'What are these doing here?' I ask the crusty old cowboy, complete with long droopy moustache, at the desk.

'Oh we have a few cowboys who lay those,' he says deadpan. He thrusts his arm out, grabs mine near the wrist and squeezes it, saying, 'Ah'm jess bein' humorous, ma'am.'

On my way out Harry asks me to eat Tex-Mex with him. For perhaps the first time in my life I manage to resist the margaritas. I have a piña colada instead. I sing various Barry Manilow songs in my head as I do. Actually, looking back, I wonder if I may have been singing them out loud as Harry was laughing and passers-by were shushing. Anyway.

Afterwards Harry asks me on another date. I drive back to Austin, my heart aching to be back with Claude. I'm feeling calm and steady enough to commit to a job. I'm going to do it. Settle down for a while. When Claude is purring in my arms I tell him what I have decided. He jumps down from my lap and hops up on to Jenny's.

That night I do not sleep very well because Claudius laps water from the Graceland mug next to my ear all night. I resolve to catch up on my sleep all day tomorrow – Sunday. The morning comes and I let him out for his usual early saunter. He comes back after about ten minutes wanting some more water – it's already hot out there. He goes out for another stroll. About half an hour later he has not yet returned so I go to look for him – our usual routine. I search his favourite places: the front door mats of the neighbouring apartments, under the stairs, his sniffing place at the corner of the building just where the woods start. He is nowhere. I start to panic because it is very unlike him to wander far. I start to search seriously, in every nook and cranny, under every bush, behind every car, in every building. After a while I take the car out and drive further afield, not that I think I am doing anything useful.

I am now horribly worried because the heat is intense. If he doesn't drink soon he'll die of dehydration. Horror thoughts invade my consciousness. What if he has been stolen? After all he is a Burmese and they're rare in the States. Not only is he brown, an unheard-of cat colour over here, but he's exceptionally beautiful. What if he's been run over? I start to search the bins for broken brown cats. What if he's been chased off by some of Austin's notorious wild cats? I start blubbing, rushing from one building to another, calling him. I have to hurry because the day is getting hotter and hotter – it is already 95° and it's boiling even in the shade. I smoke more and more cigarettes, down more and more Coke (a cola, you fool).

Jenny helps me look. We type out a message together: Has anyone seen my Burmese cat? He's ancient, toothless, deaf, etc etc. Jenny takes my favourite photo of Claude, looking most aristocratic, and she goes to her office to make copies. Armed with Sellotape, we start putting them up all over her apartment complex. I am very touched that she gives up, or rather I have buggered up, her Sunday and she utters not one complaint. We attach the signs to every door-post, to the mail room, to the pool and outside the laundry.

I feel utterly doomed. It has now been five hours and Claudius has never done this before. Is this the way our travels are meant to end? Is this how he is meant to die? Away from me, alone? With this horrid lack of closure? Me having no idea what happened? Constantly plagued by wondering and wanting to know the truth? Maybe he went off to die. He drank a lot of water last night so maybe his kidneys??? No he wasn't ill this morning – I would have known. I try to tune into him, knowing that he may be panicking and that if I am panicking too, any vibes he is sending me will get lost. I can't though because my mind is whirring and whirling around in hideous psychedelic vortices. I start looking in the same places as before, searching the same bush over and over as if the mere repetition will bring him into sight. By this time Jenny and I are maroon from sunburn. She goes inside and I look a last time under the concrete stairs outside. She starts screaming:

'Clare! Clare!'

My heart races as I'm terrified she's found his dead body. I run to her and there he is, lying cool as a cucumber on the mat outside her terrace. I pick him up and burst into childish heaving sobs, hugging him tight, kissing him over and over.

'Easy, tiger,' he murmurs through his whiskers. I hand him to her and she does the same.

He looks at us both as though we are off our trolleys. We immediately crack open the Bloody Marys. I make them so strong they can stand up without the aid of a glass. Claudius purrs loudly at the attention.

'I'm very cross with you. You're a bad bad kitten. Where have you been? Your aunt and I were having heart attacks. This is no laughing matter.'

'You're quite right. The way you're behaving is embarrassing.'

'Don't be so lippy.'

'Erm, I'm not,' says Jenny, slightly confused.

'Not you. Him.'

'Right.' She frowns.

Swaying from the drinks, we drive to Barton Springs to immerse our sunburned bodies in the freezing water. Claude stays at home to sleep off the excitement. Then we drink mango margaritas in more celebration overlooking Lake Austin. Just as I am about to order some more, I notice to my horror that I am in my pyjamas. The day has been so taken over by Claudius that I searched the apartments in my pyjamas, and set out for the swim and the bar in pyjamas also. Yes it is boiling hot and usually no sleep wear should be sported at all, but after the armadillo incident at Dan's, I feel nudity is not appropriate in friends' houses. When the horrid realisation takes place Jenny and I confab on what to do in slighty angry whispers, me a little peeved that she's let me out in them in the first place, she that after the day we've had, she's meant to be concerned with my appearance too.

In the end there is little to do as I'm hardly going to walk away from the mango margaritas winking at me from the bar. So here I am sitting in my boy's checks from BHS on Lake Austin. The sun is in its late afternoon phase, making the water glint and the houses on the hills reflect its embrace. We drift home listening to Tom Jones, our celebration still in full swing, and stop at KFC for Claude's supper. We get back to find the kitten sleeping.

I flick through Jenny's new *Cosmopolitan*. There's a piece on America's most eligible men, one for each state, with contact addresses. Mr Nevada is particularly juicy and lives in Las Vegas. If I weren't about to settle down into a job I could meet up with him when in Vegas. Fuck the job. I must be mad to consider settling down from this trip of a lifetime. So I write Mr Nevada a letter suggesting that we meet when I get there, whenever that will be.

Date time! Harry picks me up in his new BMW Z3 convertible. Good move, I think. He immediately lets me drive it. Another good move. I do my usual trick of hurling it down the highway at 90mph to see whether he is white-knuckled by the end of it. He's fine. As we zoom off at each light I keep wondering whether his Stetson will zip off his nut. It doesn't. We drive to a restaurant by Lake Austin. There is a fantastic view and we get the best table on the terrace, all set to watch the sun go down. There are tiny sailing boats on the water far below wending their way across the lake. I am sweating profusely because the sun is still bloody hot and hoping Harry won't notice. We are drinking margaritas, first strawberry then golden ones. By my second I am swimming. He has a PhD in Maths (this cowboy!), or Math, as he rather annoyingly puts it. Then out of nowhere:

'Your mother is standing in front of me shaking her head vehemently. She is extremely concerned about something you are going to do.'

'*What?*' I am somewhat Freaked Out by this.

'Your mother. I can see her.'

'Is she upset that I'm taking Claude across America?'

'No.'

'Is she upset that I'm driving like a lunatic?'

'No. Do you open up to strangers too fast? Do you take risks?'

'Yes. I think that if you take risks, and aren't scared of change, life rewards you.'

He is silent for a while.

'You are going into dangerous situations when you get closer to the isolated desert areas. There is a woman with long dark braids who has bad intentions towards you.'

'Well at least I'm not going to be raped. If it's a woman I'm dealing with.'

'She's not alone. There are shadowy figures behind her in the background. There is also an accident situation, a near miss, an almost miraculous event when your mother intervenes. She is calmer now that I have told you this, but she is not at all happy about your travelling around the States by yourself. Be careful. Be very careful out there. I also have an image of you under your car.'

(I assume this is checking for oil rather than the dead position.)

'What about Claudius? Is he all right?'

'Claudius is protecting you. He will stay with you until you have come to your senses.'

'Do you mean in regard to him?'

'No, I mean in regard to your sense of void.'

'What sense of void?'

I am engrossed and only shaken from my reverie by the sound of clapping. Everyone is applauding the setting of the sun, which we have missed because we were so involved in our conversation. We switch back to normal mode. He drops that one of his favourite things is surprise weekend trips – he flew himself and one girlfriend to New York for the weekend – the tart in my head squirms excitedly at this, luckily I don't betray anything outwardly. There is one drawback. He has ginger hair. He is a ginge. But on the other hand his other car is a Mazda MX5.

After dinner we drive to Mount Bonnell. As the dusk turns to night we climb the stairs to look at Austin sparkling below us under the stars. He drives me home and we say goodbye. As I wedge open the door to Jenny's apartment, I toot, 'I've found my husband!' in top throttle. 'You left your purse in my car,' ahems Harry right behind me. He laughs and leaves and Jenny emerges from the bathroom to find me in the foetal position, attempting to uncurl my toes and unclench my buttocks from miserable shame.

'Well?' asks Claude.

'It was great and he's a psychic.'

'Oh God. Don't do it.'

'What?'

'Listen slavishly to every word he's said and then wait for it all to happen instead of taking responsibility for yourself.'

'You've spent too long in the States, Claude. You sound like a therapist.'

I sleep fitfully that night (what's new, pussycat?) and have unsettling dreams of me sitting around a campfire with Indians, Ma appearing across the fiery circle from me, her face decomposing in a purple sombre mess as she silently watches me. The next morning I awake with a stiff back but am glad the night is over, and the sun and warmth make me feel better and much more positive.

The main question is how to cross Texas? Should we take the lonely route via El Paso? Or the more populated route of Dallas and Amarillo? Claudius thinks we should get to New Mexico via El Paso but I think Dallas because Southfork is there and also I have contacts in Amarillo. The cogs in my head start whirring over the usual: where do I stay? What do I do? I shudder at the thought of another Motel Grot and so call the most expensive hotel in

Dallas: the Adolphus. Throwing caution and money to the wind, I book us a super luxury room. Then I mention Claudius. Because the place is unbelievably posh, they are used to nutters insisting on travelling with their pets and so have no problem with the concept of the Claude.

This morning I pack up, and as usual have my sense of foreboding and sadness to be leaving people I really like, even though I know where I am going. Rather like revising for exams, once I set off I'm totally fine, it's the packing of the car and the last-minute checks which see these thoughts whip through my head like the mistral. We've been on the road three months now.

Chapter Eleven

Butch Cassidy
and the Sundance Kid

Dallas, Texas – Fort Worth, Texas

Guess what? I almost fall asleep on the road. My eyes are straining to stay open. I pull off half way through the three-hour journey and try to sleep in the car but this doesn't work at all. The view of Dallas from the plains outside is impressive, skyscrapers huddling together like forest firs, alone, indomitable and in the distance. Dallas is the one city in America that has no geographical reason for its existence. No river, no mountain, no valley. There was a railroad crossing at one time, but the main purpose is Business. If there's a place that nurtures the American Dream, a city that allows you to have an idea and get on and develop it and then congratulates you for your fabulous success, rather than perceive you as a threat, it's Dallas.

And Bonnie and Clyde lived their youth and were buried here. The press reported on absolutely everything they did. Bonnie often leaked them letters and poems in a Prinny Di-like forerunner to media manipulation. Such celebrities were they that when their bodies were brought back for their carnivalesque funerals, ten thousand filed past his, and twenty thousand past her, coffin – even though his spine was shattered and her face pulverised. Local journalists sent bouquets to thank them for their treacherous lives, the tales of which sold so many newspapers.

Claude and I arrive at the hotel to find that our room consists of a massive suite of three bathrooms, huge sundeck, sitting room, kitchen and two bedrooms, of which the master room has a huge four-poster bed. The place is the flashest, most comfortable and elegant place I've ever seen. The staff do anything we want, and are incredibly friendly, but not overbearingly so. As soon as Claudius is settled I take the Buick for a check-up.

'What can I do for you, ma'am?'

'Change the oil and give the car a total check-up.'

'Of course. How many miles on it and when was the last oil change?'

'Five thousand. A thousand miles ago.'

'Well then you don't need the check-up nor the oil change.'

'No but a psychic told me she could see me under my car and . . .'

My voice trails off. 'Never mind.' I return to the Adolphus.

It's my first night on the town and I go to meet Brandt, a friend of Jenny's, in one of the restaurants he owns. He and his brother Brady, originally from Michigan, are young entrepreneurs and they own all of Dallas's trendiest spots. I have not yet met an American who was actually born in the city s/he works in. The mobility here is extraordinary. The Green Room on Elm Street in Deep Ellum – a mispronounciation of 'Elm' by the black blues musicians who originally lived here – has walls of a deep burgundy with golden cherubs and purple grapes hanging above the bar. Carrie, a very pretty waitress, makes us some lethal margaritas. We then move through to the yellow dining room, where Dallas's thirtysomething media babes and artsy celebrities are eating and schmoozing. We wolf down spinach soup and goat's cheese mash. A friend of Brandt's, Randy (tee hee), joins us. He publishes the

Dallas equivalent of *Time Out* – the *Met*. After dinner we run from club to club checking out Brandt's various places in a cleaner, yuppier, friendlier version of a Mafia Boss check-up. We end up at the Sand Club, because the *Met* is having a party there.

The place is full of journalists getting hammered and climbing on the roof. Brandt introduces me to one of the editors. I start to read his T-shirt.

'No! You English Girl. You cannot read my T-shirt without paying.'

He screams this into my face moving closer and closer to me. There are guys all around watching me.

'OK. I'll give you what you're worth,' I say, and hand him a nickel.

'No way, man. That's just a nickel. You give me proper money.'

'Well, I've never had to pay to see a guy, but you seem desperate, so I will.'

He shouts absurdities and obscenities in my face, anything that enters his head.

'You're standing too close, baby.'

'Yes. English Girl. I am invading your private space.'

'You're telling me. Why don't you wash your teeth before you do it next time?'

He carries on and on, screaming nonsense at me. I cannot understand half of what he is saying because he is putting on some ridiculous accent and I don't know why this is happening to me. After a while the guys around shout, 'Hit Him! Hit Him!' and like a bimbo automaton I do, delivering a good hard slap across the face, which I rather enjoy, but the tirade continues to pour forth. I can feel my face twitching with nerves, I need to say something funny but nothing occurs and I have no idea what to do. Dammit, I wish I were Claudius, he would know what to do. So I just hit him again to whoops of approval from the others, feeling that this is not the way to go. After a moment he stops and disappears and that is that. Brandt notices I am shaky. As we walk on to the Curtain Club to hear some music, he is sweet and tells me I was fine, and stood my ground. Out of control and weird.

Slightly frustrating incident at Neiman Marcus today. It is just down the road from the Adolphus so I saunter in for a quick shop and find some long black evening gloves. Perfect for the Texan heatwave we're having. They are in the sale, even better, so I take them to the counter to buy them but the sales girl won't let me have them until Wednesday when the sale actually starts. They have this pre-sale thing whereby they tempt their customers with what they could have but don't actually let them have it. It's very upsetting. I huff off.

Dallas, after all, is the City of Hate, as it was here that darling JFK was shot. Claude laughs out loud when I suggest he accompany me on my day's visits. 'It's much too hot,' he purrs and settles deeper into the pillow. I check out the Sixth Floor Museum, a museum situated on the, um, sixth floor of the Dallas Book Store, from where Lee Harvey Oswald was meant to have shot JFK. The place is fascinating, detailing the fabulous couple's backgrounds, their life in the White House, his administration, the ominous fear everyone had about his going to Dallas in the first place, and then the events of his death and Lyndon Johnson's swearing in. I can't help but adore him. He was funny and young and glamorous and how good-looking is his son? The most moving image is that of the four-year-old JFK Jr saluting his coffin. With world-shocking deaths everyone seems to remember where they were and how they heard the news, as though that makes us part of the event somehow. Watching it all I just wish it hadn't happened and feel that nostalgic bitter-sweet pain of knowing there is no way to turn back the clock. I felt the same way when Prinny Di died and of course with Ma, that other great world figure.

On to the Conspiracy Museum. Apparently JFK was shot in the throat by a poisoned dart from an umbrella – *à la* Avengers. There's a particularly gruelling video of him being shot, a reconditioned digitally monitored thing taken from Zapruder's original film, which repeatedly shows his head being flung back as half of it was shot off from the front – essentially a snuff movie dolled up as historical evidence. Apparently the War Machine brought it all about. Kennedy was going to try and end the Vietnam war, and the CIA, FBI and Mafia wanted to get rid of him – or something.

Back at the hotel, the lobby is packed with myriad frou-frous, waves of heavy scent and chunky costume jewellery as hundreds of women leave for the Mary Kay ball – the finale to their annual conference. They're in the lobby, in the lifts and in the loo – in fact every hotel in Dallas is crammed with representatives. As the lift doors open on my floor, I stagger back blinded by a wall of flashing coloured sequins. A circle of backs, many women deep, surrounds what must clearly be a fainted painted dame. Then several 'Kitty, Kitty, Kitty's tinkle up from the centre. I ' 'Scuse me, watch that bustle, 'scuse me, mind yerself' in, to find Claudius sitting in the centre, his eyes tightly closed in a smile, almost levitating from the violence of his purrs. Several large women down on all fours are rubbing his chin and ears. I make myself instantly unpopular as I hands on hips holler, 'Cinderella is not going to the ball.' Claude opens his eyes but looks unabashed if a trifle guilty.

The ringleader, a hefty woman in blue, her head haloed in a red football of hair, stands up.

'What is he?'

'Burmese. How did you get out?'

'Used my key.'

'Don't be smart.'

'Oh hon I'm not. Is he valuable?'

'To me, very.'

'I just know my daughter would adore him.'

'Yes, well I do too.'

'Would you like to sell him?'

'*What?* Not on your nelly. Not if you paid me. I mean —'

'But hon, I will pay you.'

'No —'

'A thousand dollars.'

'No.'

'Five thousand dollars.'

'No.'

'Ten thousand.'

'Are you mad? Absolutely not.'

'Hon, I'm not mad at you. He looks so affectionate and cuddly. I'm just trying to do business.'

Her colleagues are staring at this bald-faced effrontery as much as I am. Claude on the other hand doesn't mind us bickering over him at all and is watching calmly, looking slightly smug at the amount she thinks he's worth.

'Listen, ducks. My cat's not a normal cat.'

'No, I can see that.'

'Seriously. You need to understand how his fur works. Every texture is a message.'

She looks suitably weirded out, giving me the moment I need to snap him up, trot back to the room where the maid's trolley is propping open the door and plonk him on the sofa in front of the stereophonic cinema-sized TV screen.

'Made some new rich friends, I see, Claude.'

'They sell make-up. When they've sold enough they get a pink Cadillac. She clearly had several.'

'Aren't I chauffeuring you around in style already? Still, if you want to get out you need only say the word.'

'Righty-oh,' he says pawing on the telly. Jerry Springer. 'I wish the bouncers wouldn't always step in so soon. I think it would do these folks good to get one really good wallop,' he says.

I can think of someone else who needs the odd wallop.

As he clearly wants to explore, I take Claude to see the Mesquite Rodeo – he via me black rucksack, me via me legs. The streets of Dallas are not covered with boys in cowboy hats as you might hope. In fact there are none, probably because they're all here: there are hats everywhere. A couple of women with big platinum-blonde hair and perfect make-up are in front of me in the ticket queue. They are wearing identical white shorts and white shirts with gold motifs on the front, gold jewellery and gold belts to match. One turns round and even her wrinkles have wrinkles – she is seventy if she's a day – but her turnout is still perfect. There are lots of stands selling sno-cones – large artifically coloured cups of ice – pop corn, barbq sandwiches and candy floss. There are hundreds of cowboys strutting around, and that garb is all quite sexy in its correct context. Boots, tight jeans, big buckle, and those gorgeous hats.

Claude and I settle in a front-row seat, eating candy floss. I wonder how good it is for his kidneys, and I take him out of the black bag and let him settle on my lap. He makes moves to go and explore but I say 'no' firmly. It's a rough and ready place, with the huge sandy ring surrounded by stadium seating. The fun is in the heat and the fanning of self and cat with programme, the women wandering around selling young children brightly coloured baby lassoes, the men offering cool water and sodas, the cowboys showing off their tight butts, the families settling down to watch, the talking and music from the band in the corner. Claude looks over my arm at the programme which advertises perfumes called Stallion and Buck. The announcer tells us how great the place will be when the air conditioning and huge conference facilities and hotel are installed next year. Oh for goodness' sake. This constant expansion and ever-growing greed. When will it ever stop? I think as I reach for my third Coke.

The rodeo starts with a grand parade. Two girls bearing the Lone Star flag and the US flag ride out first, followed by the cowboys and an assortment of sponsor flags, cowgirls, clowns, the rescue teams, all in all about fifty people on horseback riding round and round the ring. Yee-haws and howdys compete with the thunder of hooves. I scan for good-lookers among the riders, but their faces are pretty mashed in. Some are hunched forward, some are leaning back, their legs out straight ahead of them, one guy does the funky chicken, his arms flapping in and out. When they all hoof orf, the announcer makes us stand to pray to God and sing the anthem. Then the girls with the flags gallop out of the arena. It's rousing stuff.

First, the bull riding. The bulls are *livid*. Mainly due to the rope tied around their back just in front of the hind legs. When the guys fall off, the clowns try to get the bull's attention. The riders have to stay on for eight seconds, which is a darned long time on one of those frenzied things. The bulls throw themselves around the ring and one comes worryingly close. Claudius makes a leap movement, typically towards the bull rather than away from it, but I could see this coming and so have a tight hold on his front paws. The folks around us notice and smile indulgently while commenting on the 'brave kitty' and advising 'yew don wanna do theyat now, kitty'. These bulls are as big stars as the riders. They are treated like kings and are worth a fortune. One, Kowabunga, chucks his cowboy off and immediately starts a lap of victory around the arena. The crowd cheers. 'He gets fan mayel,' the excited white-haired grandmother behind shouts into my ear. Groups of cowboys hang around the starting fences, watching as the competing one ties his hand ever tighter into the rope he holds on with. Because they hang on with just one hand, often the cowboys have one Popeye arm while the other is a normal size. The gate opens, the bull flies out and topples his cowboy into the concrete wall at quite a pace. Several others have to jump the rails very fast as a 1,600lb beast hurtles towards them. One bull stomps and horns and generally attacks his cowboy, who limps off very much the worse for wear.

It's all too much excitement so the announcer next sends in some women to show us precision drills on their nags. They have dangly diamanté earrings hanging from their ears (the women not the horses), white shirts with spangly stars on and diamanté headbands around their hats. This is no Lipizzaner show, but is fun because some of the women are so huge, they almost give their horses hernias. One has goofy teeth and glasses, and her yee-haw is glass-shattering in volume. As they ride past, clumps of horse shit fly out of the arena and into: my clothes, my hair, my handbag. Claude watches each clump whizz past like it's a bird, his eyes flitting this way and that. The smell of horse sweat and shit is powerful, intoxicating even. The announcer introduces the girls: Boicille, Sherry, Cherry, Shereen etc and then says, 'If you laak what you see you're allowed to let erm know bout it.' Clap clap clap.

Next the bare-back riding. A twenty-year old – just like Claude! – comes out. The cowboy holds on with just that one powerful hand and flips back and forth like a rag doll on the horse's back, his back almost flat on the horse's rump. They have to keep their spurs moving, they mustn't lose a stirrup, and they can't touch with their free hand or they get disqualified. When the buzzer sounds, the guy looks for the rescue teams, two men riding horses on to which he can jump to escape the gnashing maddened beast under him, except he misjudges and flies off the back of the rescue horse. 'It's so exciting when things go wrong,' says Claude as he digs his nails into my thighs, making me wince. Seeing these men being hurled about, I can't help feeling they must just be bonkers. It's not at all unusual for a guy to have his entire biceps muscle torn clean away from the bone.

The Tijuana Stud Poker consists of four cowboys playing poker in the ring. They have to sit playing for three minutes while the fifth player ambles around them – that being Poncho, a ravenous and frothing-at-mouth bull. The last one to leave his seat is the winner and the others chicken. Poncho goes berserk, flings the card table and two of the players into mid-air. Everything goes flying, sombreros, the lot, but the Mexican music carries on regardless. It's great and Claude chortles snortily to himself.

I give Claude the option of a day trip with me, but he is addicted to the luxury of the Adolphus and refuses to leave the room. So I drive to Southfork, home of 'Dallas', alone. It was originally built and owned by the Duncan family. They were minding their own business eating lunch one day when Lorimar Productions landed on their lawn in a helicopter. JR Duncan (yes! that was his name) told them to 'Git offa ma lawen'. They came back a week later with a cheque book. Then when the series became popular, fans would drive out to the ranch at all times of day and night to see if JR (Hagman this time) was there. They'd peer in at the windows, take pictures of the Duncan family while they were *sleeping* and swim in the pool. What kind of loser do you have to be to a) believe the character on TV is real and b) swim in his pool without asking? The interior was in fact never used for filming, so we all gawp at the $30,000 interior decoration, feeling slightly deflated. It's amazing how little taste a lot of money can buy.

Really you can't beat the top hotels. While at Southfork I suddenly get a premonition that Claudius is not all right. I phone the marvellous concierge, Rob, who has a cat himself, and ask him to look in on Claude.

'Anything else I can do for you, ma'am?'

'Yes, Rob, please just give him a good tickle under the chin because he likes that.'

'Certainly, ma'am. Do you want it upward or downward motion?'

'I think upward is his preferred. You can try downward. No, I'm sure upward is how he likes it.'

'I'm on my way up to see Claudius right now.'

'Thank you so much.'

'And there was a message for you from Kathy in Austin. Apparently Mr Nevada called and left a number.'

I make my way back to the Adolphus. In this haven of luxury, where everyone is very rich and the staff assume I am too, the issue of Tipping has adopted monstrous proportions. As I stumble into the hotel I pretty much tip anyone who so much as smiles at me. I have no recollection of what is tip-worthy and what isn't. I think petting Claudius is, but instructions to a nearby restaurant – does that warrant $5? And how much do you tip? Do you tip the doorman who is incredibly nice to you? Or the guy who actually gets the car out of valet parking, who is quite surly and almost throws your keys at you? And are they being nice purely because of the tip? All so difficult and potentially embarrassing. And do you run around with ready fivers in your hand? Or do you scramble through your bag, rifle for your wallet, open it, watch all your change go flying and then sort out the notes – no this is too much, no this is too little, all while the guy waits there cap in hand, missing other potential tippers . . . ?

Money runs out at the Adolphus at a terrifying rate. So Claude and I move on to Arlington, bang between Dallas and Fort Worth, to stay with friends of Gail, of motel and slobbery dog fame. Kim and Burn live in a comfortable one-storey home in the heart of suburbia. They have two vicious Pekinese and feed nuts to their garden squirrels.

They met through a hospice because they both lost their spouses to cancer: she had been with Micky for thirty years, he with Jo-Anne for forty. Kim is pretty with short blonde hair and very long *natural* nails. Burn is older, tall, with baggy poochy eyes.

We're at Lucky's, a chain café, for lunch. I pile up with the usual, barbecued chicken, potato salad, beans, fruit, whatever else I take a fancy to, but lose my appetite and can hardly eat when Burn chooses a table right next to – aaargh! – a woman with extremely long thick greying plaits. I explain to Burn and Kim about the psychic. 'Weyell,' says Kim. 'She maght think you kinda strange too. After awl, you have gotta sweater on in the middle of a heat wave.'

'That's because of the air con,' I explain, keeping an eye on the woman.

Later Claude and I are messing around in the garden. Kim comes home from work.

'Guess what big mistake I made today?' she drawls to Burn.

'You told Dave we had company.'

'Yep. That's right.'

Dave is Kim's nephew. He is forty-two and wants to be a country/rock and roll star and practises his songs on any new victim he can find. We decide on some sign language to show each other when we've had enough because he's bound not to stop until our ears are bleeding. I suggest rubbing the side of the nose. The doorbell rings. Dave's small blue eyes twinkle from behind large specs. He immediately gets out his guitar.

'Hello Burn,' he pipes up. 'Where're the dawgs?'

'Ah put em out. So they cud howel all they liked.'

'Ril ferny, Burn. Ril ferny.'

Claude settles on my lap. He loves music. Dave strums one chord and Kim looks at me from the kitchen and rubs her nose vigorously. I start giggling and simply can't stop,

especially when he murders Led Zeppelin's 'Going to California'. I enjoy a couple of songs but start to tire when he yodels out an entire concert. Claudius jumps down after just a few minutes and trots to the bedroom, almost slamming the door behind him. Dave plays very loud, very long. He looks into my eyes and I don't know where to look. I see hunger in them – not for me, but for fame, approbation, something scary, I don't know what. He plays well and his singing's OK, but neither justifies this need. It's not even the fame he wants, he says, he just loves the music. He has records which DJs play on the radio – they even call him at home now. He has a recording contract but there is no pressure to produce anything. I wonder whose idea it was to give him some talent but fill the rest of the chasm with need? What a cheap trick.

'Yew cin tell your folks back home, you met a cowboy who plays acoustic guitar Led Zeppelin,' he says hungrily as he takes his huge guitar off his thin little legs. The guitar has a hole in it from a guy who stepped on it by mistake.

'Sure it was bah mistake, Dave?'

'Ril ferny, Burn, ril ferny.'

Slightly embarrassed, I make a speedy exit, and drive to Fort Worth. Naturally there was (and still is) plenty of squabbling between Fort Worth and Dallas because of their proximity – they are only thirty-two miles apart. In 1873 the Fort Worth Democrat took the piss out of Dallas's crime rate, urging people to visit the burgeoning city: 'No one has been killed in Dallas since the day before yesterday, that we know of.' The *Dallas Herald* countered with a slur on Fort Worth's slumped business prospects, saying that a visitor there had seen a panther asleep on Main Street 'unmolested and undisturbed . . . For a perfectly boring excursion take the train to Fort Worth.'

First I look at Sundance Square in Fort Worth – so named because Butch Cassidy and the Sundance Kid used to hang out here between raids. This was the red-light district though it has now been much cleaned up and sports Pier 1-type lifestyle shops. The outlaws' favourite bordello was Miss Fannie's in Hell's Half Acre, as it was then known. The majority of crime at that time was drunkenness – very few people had anything worth stealing. Cowboys on a trail would spend a couple of days relaxing here, blowing their month's wages on a bath, a haircut, a meal, a drink, a gamble, a dance and a whore. When their hangover dawned they set off on the 400-mile Chisholm trail to Kansas. Hell's Half Acre was also a draw for the railroad workers and buffalo hunters. The Hole in the Wall Gang had their picture taken here, and it was perhaps due to this one small moment of egotism that they were caught as prior to this no one knew what they looked like, which is why Paul Newman has cause to say of his pursuers, 'Who *are* those guys?' Those are guys who know who they're looking for – *celebrities*!

I move on to the Stockyards, the heart of Cow Town, as Fort Worth is known. This was where the Wild West began because of a treaty whereby the Indians agreed to keep west of a line that went straight through Fort Worth. After the civil war there were three million head of cattle down here that needed transporting to the starving northerners. Anyone who found cattle and branded them could keep them. Though only $2 in these parts, once they were up north they were worth as much as $40.

The buildings are low saloon-type jobs, they just need swinging doors and cowboys falling out of them. I make several attempts at buying purple cowboy boots and I find a pair – but they're only just big enough for Claudius. So no luck there, although the woman at Ponder Boots says she'll make them for me for about $600 if I want. I back out hurriedly, not only because of the quoted price but because I notice she has – aaargh! – long dark plaits . . .

I check out the Stockyards Hotel wistfully, because after

the Adolphus, I may never be able to afford another hotel again. Bonnie & Clyde stayed here in room no. 305 in 1933. Amazingly they didn't rob the bank over the road. The room has Bonnie's gun behind glass and newspaper clippings about their capture and death. I suppose these two so totally capture the American imagination because they are on one endless road trip, free of all constraints, especially moral ones, doing what they want when they want.

I wander around the place, around and around, not really taking in the Rodeo Plaza, with its Western shops, or the Mule and Horse Alley, up which the horses were herded. I like the Livestock Exchange Museum, which holds countless oddities among its old sepia photos and barbed wire, such as the Dress of Bad Luck. It was first worn by Marie whose husband David promptly left her when gripped by gold fever. Their daughter, Evelyn Henrietta, then wore it and her fiancé died a few days before their wedding day, on his way back from WWI after the fighting had finished. Their granddaughter, Alta Marguerite, wore it to her wedding and her husband Daniel died six months later of multiple sclerosis. Finally the family cottoned on and put it away but in 1949 Alta Patrick Buker wore it for an historical tour and was bedridden with an unknown disease, dumbfounding doctors for a month.

Afterwards, on the way back to the car, two cowboys catch up with me for a chat. They are charming-looking, one blond and boyish, the other tall, dark and handsome. We smile at each other, say hello and they introduce themselves.

'Ahm Robert Parker and this here is Harry Longabaugh.'

'Howdedoodie?'

'Pardon us?'

'Nothing. I'm Clare.'

'That's a perty name.'

'Thank you.'

'Howd'ya like Cow Town?' Robert is skipping along backwards in front of me as I walk towards him, his brown lizard boots heel-scuffing as they go.

'It's fine.'

'Do ya like cowboys?'

'How do you mean?'

'Ah mean nothin by it, ma'am. Ahm wondering if you like the man with roughness in his blood that cuss the land. He ain't uncouth, it's just roughage. He cain help but cuss hisself, his horse and the land.'

'I like him just fine.'

'We cowboys awl live a long time. You hearda Charles Goodnight?'

'Nope.'

'He's the first big ranchman in Texas. One of the Grand Old Cattleman of the Wild West. Made the Panhandle safe for other settlers. Lived till he was ninety-two years old. Drank a pot of coffee a day. Yessir, ahm gonna quote that to mah doctor. And Fort Worth was named after William Jenkins Worth whose soldiers of the US cavalry came this way in 1849 and didn't leave till 1853. Did you know that, ma'am/Clare?'

'No I didn't. It's very interesting.'

'Our pleasure. Ah lak your accent.'

'Good-oh.'

'Would you like to go dancing tonight?'

'Where?'

'At Billy Bob's Hawnky Tawnk.'

'I'd love to. What time?'

'We'll see y'all here at 9pm.'

'Okely Dokely.'

'Scuse me, ma'am?'

'Nothin'.'

I skip home rather excited and encounter Claude sitting

in the garden sun. I tell him of my day, and at the idea of
the date with the two cowboys he guffaws loudly.

'What?'

'Nothin'.' He turns on his heel and meanders into the
house.

I get ready but this time wear clean blue jeans and
purple T-shirt with the ironic words *Bond Girl* embla-
zoned across my diminutive chest, and carry extra cash for
drinkies. No scary Gucci stilettos. I don't want them to
react as Bird and Clit did.

I drive back to the Stockyards and there they are waiting
for me, and my, they are beautiful men. I laugh at their
jokes, carefree and happy.

'Nice car, ma'am. Where from?'

'Buick.'

'Very comfortable. You must be a wealthy woman.'

'Actually I'm on a tight budget and am planning on
selling it when I've finished driving.'

'Well it's very nice. Take a right here. This is Billy
Bob's.'

I take a right into a large car park where pick-up trucks
and various cars are already packing the place.

We wander in and they 'howdy' a few guys who all take
a good long look at me. We sit down and order some beers
at one of the many bars – this is the world's largest honky
tonk so there are plenty to choose from. There is quite a
crowd forming. A petite waitress with pockmarked skin
and long curly blonde hair comes up to our table.

'What can ah get you folks – well if it isn't . . .'

'Hey how are ya, darlin'?' Robert stands up briskly. 'I
thought you moved to Dallas a while back.'

'Yeah? Well you thought wrong.' She looks narked, he
looks nervy.

'Couple of beers for all, darlin'.' She storms off. When
she gets back she eyeballs me for a while, takes in my *Bond
Girl* T-shirt, raises her brows so that they hit her hairline in

a 'Ya really think so?' face and stalks off angrily. I don't mind at all. She's just jealous, and me? Eeeny meeny miney mo, I don't know which of you two I like mo'. Robert starts shouting across the music:

'Texas is big, huh?'

'Seems to be.'

'Ya know why the ranches are so big? Cos the land is so arid it takes a lot of it to feed just one cow. The grass ain't thick. Me and Harry know guys whose house is six miles from the gate of their ranch. And that ain't even big. Hell, there are still ranches that are 800,000 acres big. The biggest ranch here is owned by the King family. Texas is the rags-to-riches place, what with folks all discoverin' oil. But oil is no longer king here.'

'What do you think about the Indians?'

'What about em?'

'Well, the land . . .'

'Oh we took their land. They didn't believe in owning the land so we jess took it. What we did was kill the buffalo. Thes what killed em. They had nothin' to eat or keep em warm after that.'

'And what about the cowboy lifestyle?'

'It ain't easy. They work hard. They haveta trap wolves, and mend fences, brand cows and doctor em, and put out salt licks. The boys working on the land, they don't make a lot of money, but they love it. They're free. Some are drifters, some have families. They live in bunkhouses on the ranches. Things have changed though – there are four-wheel drives and jeeps and helicopters, and the auctions here are done by video. But the main way of herding cattle is still by horse. There's a lotta work tado.'

'And what do you guys do?'

'I'm a rancher and Harry is in insurance.'

'Yip, thes raght.' The first words Harry utters to me.

We crack on with the beer. Robert continues his history lesson. It's great but I'd prefer something more personal.

'Between 1845 and 1849, they gave out Texan land. Granted 640 acres in any one time . . .'

After a while I need the loo, so I shout to Robert:
  'The loo? Where is it?'
  'The *what*?'
  'The loo!'
  'The leyew?' He looks at Harry as though I am speaking Swahili.
  'I think she wants the bathroom.'
  'Oh – over theyar.'
  I walk away and on my way take a look at the Hall of Fame, where country stars have put their handprints.

In the bog, the waitress approaches me. 'Miss, ah don mean to pry, but you better be careful with those boys. They're kinda known around town, banned in here. They musta slipped in. Truth is, they're car thieves. They take unsuspecting tourists like you and rob em and they'd do worse if they could, ah don know, ah heard nasty rumours about what they do to girls. A year back my friend Sandy come inta town. Real perty accent, sounds English but ain't, comes from Maine, they make a beeline for her, give her plenty ta drink and then bully her in the car lot when she don wanna give them the keys to her car. Thas how they know me, I wasn't working here at the time. Miss, you tek mah advice and git outta here while you still can.'
  'But they're so sweet.'
  'Sweet mah sweet ass. That ain't sweet, honey, thas clever. They ladies men and they play on that to make a dishonest living outta the likes ah yew.' She emphasises this by prodding me with her finger just under my shoulder.
  'That dark un, he's mighty clever and likes history, he does all the talking, makes yer think he's all high-class and

clever. Takes yer mind off things. It's the blond one that does the dirty work outside.'

We walk out of the ladies, and standing right there, perhaps within earshot, is Robert. He can see something's wrong.

'What she say to you?'

'Nothin'.'

'Let me tell you someut.' He takes me by the arm back to our table. 'She and I were dating a while back and I broke off with her. But she's still a bit sore about it and probably don like the way ah've been looking at you. Truth is yer so perty I cain take mah eyes offaya.'

'Thanks.' I smile weakly. Now I don't know who to believe.

I get back to the table and feel woozy from the beers. They hand me another.

'I'm fine, thanks. I shouldn't be drinking, you know I am driving.'

'Now don't you worry bout that. We're all friends. We'll drive you back home. Harry here works in insurance and is covered for everything.'

'Oh I don't let anyone drive my car other than me.'

'Well now like I say that don't matter cosa Harry's insurance. You don't worry. Let's all have us some fern.'

He stands up and holds out his hand. Seems like I have to dance with the devil. I don't know what to do but he grabs my hand before I can pick up my handbag and pulls me on to the dance floor. There is a huge crowd and the music is diddley diddley in that country way and we start polkaing around. He's so good-looking I can hardly take my eyes off him but I strain back to the table to see if Harry's still there. He's not. I pull away from Robert and run to the table. My bag's gone. I whip around and spy

Harry nowhere, only a sea of hats and big hair. I make off towards a bulk of a guy in the same colour shirt as Harry, only to swing round a total stranger. As he launches into pick-up mode, I spy Harry near the door.

'Harry, I want my bag back.' I am stone-cold sober.

'Ah's jess bringing it to yer.'

'I was over there, Harry.' I point in the opposite direction. There are people around us watching. Harry sees this and gives it back to me. I look inside and the car keys are sitting next to a battered Tampax.

'Hey hey, whas the problem here?' Robert is here, there, everywhere it seems.

'It's all fine,' says Harry. 'Ah's jess bringing it to er but ah ain't sure where you was . . .'

'Come on all, let's sit down and calm down. Clare, what's wrong? You're all antsy like he's trying to make off with yer purse. Are yer crazy? He ain't no motherfuckin' queer.'

We go and sit down, but I'm no longer enjoying myself.

'Excuse me, I'll just compose myself in the bathroom.'

I wend through the crowds in the direction of the loo and when they can't see me I run.

'May I help you?'

'Yes, I'd like to report a couple of guys that I think prey on unsuspecting tourists in this area.'

'Name?'

'Clare de Vries.'

'Where ya from?'

'London, England.'

'What happened?'

'Well . . . Billy Bob's . . . waitress warned me . . . handbag incident . . . etc.'

'So you have your bag?'

'Yes I do but I think you should know about them, in case it happens to someone else less savvy than me . . .'

'Well, miss, this sounds like a lotta speculation to me, but I'll file a report if you like. And who are these guys?'

'Robert Parker and Harry Longabaugh.'

Great snorty guffaws at other end of line.

'Excuse me? Is there a problem?'

'Yes, ma'am. Sure is. They died in Bolivia about a hundred years back. Better known as Butch Cassidy and the Sundance Kid. Any other information you want me to file?'

'No. No' – wearily – 'forget it.'

Slam.

'Claudius! Claudius. Do you know who Robert Parker and Harry Longabaugh are?'

'Who *are* those guys?'

'You *do* know. Why didn't you tell me I was being taken for a ride?'

'What am I? Psychedelic? I didn't think you'd fall for it.' He turns away purring.

I still think something should be done about this so I make an appointment to see Steve Murrin, the mayor of the Stockyards. It rains while we drive there, and once out of the car, Claude holds me up by chasing and playing with the hundreds of crickets that the rain has brought out. They are jumping and flying about, as is Claudius, looking more like a kitten than a nineteen-year-old. Steve – whose skinny, skinny legs are tucked into jeans tucked into long cowboy boots – has a mouth which is entirely hidden by the longest droopiest moustache in follicular history. Thinking about what to say, I realise how damn stupid the whole thing makes me look, so instead I point Claude out to him. He watches silently and then murmurs:

'Ah'm a dawg mayen mahseyelf.'

'Oh. May I ask you something? Why do you wear your jeans tucked into your boots?'

'Jess 'cause.' Then after a moment: 'Mah deddy used to.'

'How many head do you have?'

'I don rightly recall.' He looks at me sternly. 'That's askin a man how much money he has.'

'I'm sorry, I just thought Americans didn't mind talking about money . . .'

'This ain't America. This is Texas.' Behind his hard eyes I detect a twinkle, but apologise again as the last thing I want to do is insult a cowboy. When I leave he gives me the number of his niece and nephew in Amarillo.

Claude and I set off.

Chapter Twelve

The Accidental Tourist

Quanah – Amarillo, Texas

We drive Route 287 north towards large open skies and yellow plains stretching for miles and miles. Low-slung telegraph poles border the route and the odd piebald horse or small bunch of cattle ignore us as we roll on by. We listen to the local radio – 'At least half of this country's leaders are in the grips of a Luciferian contract. Devil worshippers are in our midst! Embrace the Lord Jesus into your soul.' After three hours we stop at Quanah Parker, a tiny town seventy miles west of Wichita Falls.

The very friendly woman at the motel desk, old smily yellow tombstone teeth, gives me the key to a room that stinks of drains. The bugs on the carpet are covered with a thin layer of dust: this room has not seen a vacuum cleaner since it was built. Well, it's just one night until we get to Amarillo.

I leave Claude to unpack while I look for some dinner. Quanah is entirely shut up, even though it's only 7pm. Not a soul in sight. The old museum is down by the railroad tracks. The town is made up of wide roads with one- or two-storey buildings. I stop at the Medicine Mound Restaurant, where the napkins are red bandanas and the floor is covered in peanut shells.

Quanah Parker is named after the last great Comanche Chief whose mother, Cynthia Ann Parker, was kidnapped by Indians as a little girl, brought up as one of them, and then later kidnapped by white men when she was the mother of three children. She greatly missed her Indian life and died of a broken heart. Quanah led several war raids against the whites, but because of his lack of power against their guns, he surrendered and lived on a reservation. He learnt English, became an astute businessman, wore white men's clothes but always kept his black plaits – aaaargh! – and wore diamond studs on his shirts. He had seven wives and more than twenty children. At one time he was urged by some white busybodies to give up his six wives and adopt the monogamous form of marriage. 'Choose your favourite wife and tell the others to leave,' they urged him. 'Go on. Tell the others to leave.'

'You tell em,' Quanah replied.

After the steak, I survey the gift shop for booty and buy an 'I Love Texas' sticker and some Texas-shaped sunglasses. It has just started to rain, for the first time in the Panhandle's scorching summer, answering the signs outside churches that cry: Pray for Rain. I get back to the room to find huge jumpy beetle things that resemble spiders trying to get into the room. I calm the potential heart attack and go in to find Claude sitting gingerly in the middle of the bed, refusing to relax with a 'It really smells in here' look on his face. 'Just one night, kitkat,' I say before slipping into the damp musty sheets.

Today we were up bright and early – er, not. Today I stumbled from my bed with thunder crashing in my head, my pillow still wet from last night's tears – no, that's Elvis. Today Claude and I set off from Motel Nightmare, with beetles still skipping about on the floor, for Amarillo. As we drive along, he points out tiny purple and pink flowers on the median. It's a cool 86° outside, quite chilly really. Huge cargo trains with a triangle of bright lights at their head speed alongside us – the railroads run parallel to the road for miles and miles. I overtake one pulling fifty army jeeps all lined up one behind the other, the driver and I wave and he blows the horn – a long, evocative, adventurous moan.

The road is pretty uneventful, one small town after another, until we get to a place called – Claude! I can't believe it and swerve over to take Claude's picture beside the 'Welcome to Claude' sign, allowing the train to catch up with us. Claude looks at me and murmurs:

'All this sentiment. Really, is it necessary?'

I insist that we look around, so we go to the Claude Museum, which is next to the *Claude News* whose door has the sign: 'At lunch. Call me at home if you have news.' I carry Claude in to face four old biddies sitting behind a table, one of whom has the obligatory lipstick way up over her lips. So they do that here too – what the heck, they probably invented it here. I introduce myself to Miss Lips and describe my trip through the States.

'I had to stop here because my cat, my companion, is also called Claude – and I can't believe there is a town of the same name! So here we are. May we take a look around your museum?'

'Why surely, my deyar. Oh what a sweet kitty. What's his name?'

'Claude, Jayne Leigh. Didn'tcha hear her?' pipes up another.

'Oh, we had another English girl here just a while back. She might still be here.'

'I don't think so, Jayne Leigh. That was Miss Carla Redding and she died back in 1976. Go ahead dear and look all you want. We'll watch the kitty while you walk around.'

'Oh, that's OK. He'll probably follow me around.'

'Oh, well that is so nice. Where are you headed for?' asks Miss Lips.

'Amarillo today and the rest of the States in a few days.'

'Oh that is wonderful. And I wonder what made you stop here?'

'Her cat, Jayne Leigh. Didn'tcha hear her?'

'Your kitty?! Why he's so perty, what's his name?'

I leave them to battle it out and Claude sits watching them for a while, clearly amused by the shenanigans. It's a sweet museum, with cabinets devoted to the history of the town, the local battles with the Native Americans, the growth of Charles Goodnight's huge JA Ranch, and then several cabinets commemorating local dignitaries, sponsored by their descendants, full of old artefacts, stoves, irons, lace dresses, dolls. As I walk around I can hear the women debating whether Miss Carla Redding died in England or not. It took them the entire time I was walking around. Claude started his tour rather later than I did, in fact five minutes before I was ready to leave, but luckily he wandered around the wrong way, so in fact we met up just near the exit. Perfect. As we drive away from Claude, he notices two men outside the police station in stripy all-in-ones digging in the road and remarks that I'm not the only one to go out in me pyjamas.

Amarillo has this enormous highway, I40, running straight through it. The infamous Route 66 runs through Amarillo too – and is covered in antique shops and brightly coloured stores making the most of their historical position. There are hundreds of huge signs in people's gardens with varying messages:

Undead end
Where are the wicked young widows tonight?
Gloria is lying in a pool of blood with her head cut off

I have contacts here, name of Stanley and Wendy Marsh. He has single-handedly put Amarillo on the map, and they are the Big Cheese family around here. I am pretty sure these signs are Stanley's doing. He is known as an eccentric, interested in art for the masses. I have to call them but am feeling shy so I think I'll do it tomorrow.

We settle in a motel built in the shape of Camelot, white and pink with fairy-tale/cartoon turrets and ramparts. And only $23 a night! I hope it continues to be this cheap out west. I do the usual search for purple cowboy boots and still have no luck. I call Steve Murrin's nephew, Dale, who is a ranch manager. He invites us out the next morning – bright and early at 5.30am – to ride with the cowboys on the famous JA ranch.

'Forget it!' trumpets Claude from the other side of the room.

'But you love dawn explorations, kitkat.'

'Forget it!' he bleats.

'All right, all right, I'll go alone.'

I buy new 501s specially for tomorrow.

So today I tell slumber to get lorst at 4.30am. Not an easy task let me tell you. I put on my new blue jeans, my beige desert boots, my bandana round my neck, my cowboy hat on my head, my address book in my back pocket (I might need it for cowboys' numbers) and I am ready to go ranching. The only sunglasses I have are the Texas-shaped ones. I look a bit of a tool. Dale picks me up in his white Chevy pick-up truck and we drive out – it is still dark. The ranch is just south of Claude – Claude! This is one of the oldest ranches in Texas, started by John Adair and Charles Goodnight. It used to be more than one million acres, but now is just 160,000. It takes us a good while to get there and as we arrive the sun is just about coming up. We wait for the boys to arrive. Barry is first in his pick-up truck, towing a horse. He's good-looking with a huge moustache bending down over his cheeks and up again towards his ears.

The other guys turn up. They all have worn moulded hats, not the stupid brand-new thing I have on. I drive the

Chevy to the weighing station that they are herding the cattle to, and promptly fall asleep. I wake to loud moos and feel the sun on my cheek and poo breath on my tongue. The cowboys have the cattle all penned in and are racing them up the aisles, so to speak, pushing fifteen of them at a time on to a weighing machine. Cody is at one end, his face like Dumbo's, a very long curved nose and large ears surrounding small brown eyes. He makes farty raspberry noises at the cattle to scare them into the pens. Then blond Billy, with small crooked teeth in a large smily red-cheeked face, weighs them and shouts OK, and Barry lets them out and counts them up. They continue doing this with maybe 200 cattle, and then put them all back in the other pen in order to cut them. This takes a while, as Dale decides whether they are Barry! (to run in front of Barry to the pen – therefore to graze) or By! (to run by Barry to a truck where they are loaded up for slaughter).

'How many cows are there?' I ask Billy in a friendly interested manner.

'They're bulls,' he replies. 'They've had their horns cut so they don't hurt theirselves.'

With the cutting done we drive them back to the proper pasture. Dale lends me his horse, Sodapop.

'Mind the mesquite!' he shouts after me as I canter off with the others.

'OK!' I shout back, wondering what mesquite are.

The Western saddle is strange, but very comfortable and the covered stirrups mean there's little chance of falling off. Compared to these, English saddles seem designed to kick you off at the first opportunity. I've ridden all my life but you'd never know to watch the bouncing lump I become. One heifer escapes and I gallop after it, my hat wobbling up and down releasing lines of sweat into my eyes. 'Keep with it,' hollers Barry. I do and finally it seems to curve back and join the herd. I can't see the others paced out in a line, riding back and forth towards and away from each other to cover the area to make sure no head is left behind, but I know they're there somewhere and suspect that they have more to do with the heifer joining back than I realise. Just then Sodapop stumbles while trotting and I lose my stirrup, my balance and whump to the ground, landing on my back. Ow. Dammit. Embarrassed, I climb back on fast hoping no one saw and trot off to find the others, my back killing me.

We ride on and on over the dusty land through the cacti and shrubs, watching the Llano Estacado in the distance, imagining the Native Americans hiding in the canyon to escape the Rangers. The sky is endless. The mesquite, Barry explains trotting up, are the trees with huge thorns to the right and left of us. A century ago, there were no trees in this area at all, but they grew up as fires became more controlled.

The sun is getting higher and hotter with every minute. We drive back to the headquarters, a large comfortable farmhouse. This ranch is in the Palo Duro Canyon and stretches as far as the eye can see. There is a bunkhouse and two other houses for the permanent cowboys, a post office, a shop and a few other buildings – a self-sufficient town. We eat lunch in Carroll Jack's house. He prepares potato salad, beans and steak for us. We drink Coke or iced tea. These cowboys work the land because their Deddys done it beforem. The guys are shy and polite and don't talk much in front of me. I've been to plenty of cocktail parties and I'm not shy to start a conversation.

'I understand that you have jackalopes in these parts. I read somewhere that they imitate the human voice, or something? That cowboys singing to their herds at night can hear lonesome melodies repeated faithfully from the mountainside, but only on dark nights before a thunderstorm.' I look slightly pleased with myself for remembering all this.

Carroll Jack looks around at the others before turning back to me with a gentle pitying look in his eye.

'Thes jess a story, ma'am. A tale for the kiddies. They don exist.'

'Oh. Oh no, I see. I was just wondering. Yes yes now you mention it I thought it a bit strange at the time.'

Now I think about it, shyness with regards to starting a conversation can often be a good thing. Mental note: only speak when spoken to.

After lunch Dale and I drive around the ranch checking on the water supplies, checking the weeds and looking at the mares that breed the horses the cowboys will be breaking in next year. Finally we drive back to the hotel. I'm exhausted but Dale has at least three or four more hours' work to do. He invites me to a party later that evening.

'When you get down to it, there is not a huge difference between the cowboys and myself,' says Claude as he cleans his whiskers after polishing off two original-recipe KFC wings and half a breast. 'He lives pretty much by instinct. It's a simple unquestioning life driven by instinct and natural love of the land and animals, both of which he's in harmony with. In modern day you see people yearning for a simple harmonious life such as mine and everyone harps on about the Indians' way of life since *Dances with Wolves* (not that I see anyone willing to give up their air con) –'

'Or their KFC.'

(ignoring this) '– but the thing to remember is that both cowboys and Indians worked very heavily on instinct, like animals. Really to live an individual and independent life, instinct is the one thing you can't do without.'

'Or food.'

'Yes, food helps.'

'And warmth.'

'Oh do shut up. There is a certain romance in the independent and carefree life we lead, us cowboys. I go where I want, by projecting ideas into your head –'

'– Hello? Planet Earth? Come in –'

'However the glamour of the cowboy riding off into the sunset, surviving all weathers and needing no one is somewhat undercut when you consider how rarely they took a bath. Which is the main difference between them and myself.'

'And you're feline and they're human.'

'What?'

'Nothing.'

I change four to five times, unable to decide on what to wear for the party Dale invited me to. As I take my jeans off I put my hand in to look for the address book. Nowhere. None of the pockets. It must have fallen out when I fell off Sodapop. It's somewhere out there with the mesquite. Even if I drove the hour to the ranch I would have no idea where to look. It has Stanley and Wendy's number in it and if I'm to have a good time in Amarillo I have to get hold of them. I try Directory Enquiries. Of course they're ex-directory. I have no idea what to do. Bugger.

I turn up at Dale and Carolyn's and they are nowhere to be found. After a while I panic that I've missed them but then they sheepishly appear from upstairs. Newly-weds, huh? I think to myself as Carolyn and I shake hands. She has thick brown eyebrows above bright blue eyes, her dark straight glossy hair is tied to the side with a diamanté clip. Her teeth are bright white and she looks like a prettier version of Joanie from 'Happy Days'. We drive to the party which is not yet happening where a mad dog Otto, who is too hyper to pet, runs around sticking his nose up the girls' skirts. For a moment I have the fear. All these people know each other and can easily slip into their groove. If I'm going to have a good time I have to put in a lot of energy and make an effort. I get on with it and after a while start swinging with the rest.

Things start livening up. Jock turns up – he hasn't had sex in two years everyone tells me. Cole turns up – he's back on the sauce though he shouldn't be and promptly proves this by falling over the patio steps on to the grass. It's a bad deal, murmurs Jenna, the pretty blonde next to me. But he has fallen like a stunt man, so soft and curly that he has barely bruised himself. Garth comes in – he is tiny and ginger-haired. After a while my own intake of sauce kicks in and the conversations around me become gobbledegook. Everyone discusses going to see Robert Earl Keene play – an old room-mate of Lyle Lovett's and much-loved cult figure among Texan youth – and pretty soon people are filing out, getting in their cars. Someone mentions Stanley and Wendy and my ears prick up. I must ask them whether they have Stanley's number when I get to the honky tonk, the Midnight Rodeo. I get a lift with short ginger-haired Garth, and we join the queue a good way behind the rest of the party. Suddenly a drunk cowboy further ahead in the line starts pushing and bad-mouthing some guys in front of us.

' 'M gonna spill your guts like pigs. I'm gonna, I'm gonna . . .'

The security guard and a couple of others grab him and wrestle him to the floor. He puts up a fight but eventually his hat falls off forlornly and he is pinned to the ground, huffing and puffing, his hands bent spastically behind his back. The guard clamps handcuffs on him, brushes himself down and hollers, 'The party's over, folks. There's nothing to see here. Party's over.' We get shuffled off, and as I do, I lose ginger Garth and everyone else from the party, who have already gone inside. I can't stand out here in the dark for ever by myself so I take a cab home to Claudius.

'Claude. I've lost my address book and my new friends. I have great contacts somewhere out there, but absolutely no access to them.'

'What's so great about them?'

'They're incredible people. He's created all these sights. Look, I'll show you tomorrow.'

I take Claude to see the sights. These are pieces of artwork Stanley has created out on the land for all to see and enjoy. The first is the Cadillac Ranch. Constructed in 1974, ten Caddys from 1949 onwards are buried nose-deep into the ground so that the tail and half the body are sticking up into the air. The cars are weathered, rusted and covered in graffiti.

'You see, Claude, the cars are tilting at the same angle as the pyramids. People come from all over the world to see them, and pontificate as to their meaning.'

'If they have one.'

'One summer, holes in the ground signed "unmarked graves for sale or rent" were found near here. Unruffled by the vandalism, Stanley remarked to newspaper reporters: "It's summer and people get frisky." It's that attitude that makes me want to meet them.'

Off to the Flying Mesa. Stanley commissioned a 284' × 8'-high painted steel band to be erected in front of Goat Mountain Mesa so that in a certain light, the steel blends in with the sky and gives the impression that the top of the mountain has been chopped off and is floating, genie-like, a metre above the rest.

The last site is Ozymandias. Two huge stone legs stick up out of a field off I27. They look as though they were part of a huge statue that has crumbled to pieces. I read Claude the historical marker which explains that Shelley and his wife discovered the legs while riding across the Texan plains one day. He was immediately inspired to write the poem 'Ozymandias'.

'I agree,' says Claude. 'We have to meet these people. What a shame you lost your address book.'

'Oh don't rub it in for God's sake. I'm cross enough already.'

Back at Camelot, Claude suggests I ring the friend in England who originally gave me Stanley and Wendy's number. She isn't home so I leave a message. Half an hour later the phone rings.

'Hello?'

'Do you have a cat in there?'

'Um?'

'I'm sending up a housekeeper now. Your friend called and when I couldn't find your name in the computer she said you had a cat with you. Forgot to mention that when you booked in, didn't you? You'll have to leave.'

Oh for crying out loud.

'What about my phone call?'

'You'll havta leave NOW.'

Slam.

'Claude, bad news.'

'Let me guess . . .'

Fuckit what a bore. I slowly and wearily pack up the car and Claude wanders around behind me. We get in and pull out of the drive on to the I40 slipway. As we do, a large jeep whams straight into the side of the Buick. Claude and I wang forward, me towards the steering wheel, Claude from the seat to the floor. Oh my God everything is going wrong. My beautiful car. My beautiful cat. My beautiful laundrette. Don't cry, don't cry. A young guy is getting out and coming up. That car is weird. It's covered, every inch of it, in God Bless John Wayne stickers.

'Are you OK?' He has a 50s quiff, three-piece suit and trilby on.

'My car is mangled.'

'I'm sorry, I didn't see you pulling out. You were going very slowly.'

'Cos I don't know where to go. I've just been chucked out of this bloody place because of my cat. Who are you?'

'I'm Jimmy Dean Jimmy Dean.'

'What?'

'You'd better come back to the big house with me while we work out what to do. This is my boss's car.'

'I like the stickers.'

'Wild, huh?'

Claude and I climb in while he hooks up the Buick and we drag it to his boss's home twenty minutes down the road, whom he calls on the mobile while we drive. A large black gate with the words 'Toad Hall' swings open to allow us in. Peacocks are wandering around the lawn. There are hundreds of those weird signs:

It is nice to have a dry toilet seat
Signs of the devil
I shadow box with frightening speed – left jab left jab
zip zip right lead right hook left hook uppercut
The operator of the guillotine is inevitably some
efficient male

Up the drive in the middle of the garden is a Volkswagen Beetle, buried nose into the ground.

'Look Claude! It's just like the Cadillac Ranch.'

'Yeah, this was a birthday surprise to Stanley from his friends.'

'Stanley? Stanley lives here?'

'He's my boss.'

'And Wendy?'

'That's his wife. She's coming out now.'

She comes up all apologetic and sweet, but I'm beaming like a loon, thrilled to have found them in this fated manner. I explain who I am.

'Yes, we were expecting you!'

'But how? Address book! . . . friends of yours and mine! . . . lost! . . . Claude!'

'We knew you were coming.'

Claude and I look at each other. Was Jimmy Dean

Jimmy Dean sent out on purpose to bang into us? Maybe she doesn't realise that I'm also the victim of the accident? Oh who cares, we're here now. Wendy invites us to stay while my car is repaired. She installs us in the guest house at the back, which has a hot tub, a huge kitchen, several bedrooms to choose from, a full fridge and cat food and litter already prepared. We choose a room decorated with a picture of a pair of tadpoles cooing over their newborn swaddled tadpole baby. 'Well this is the life,' murmurs Claude as he squeezes through the door to check out the garden. 'Come and look!' he meows. I follow him to see a 1959 pink Cadillac parked outside. I turn on the hot tub and get in. Through the glass walls I can see a yellow submarine in the back field. It is an old station wagon that has been painted yellow and has a periscope sticking out the roof. Octopuses (octopi?) and fish swim across the doors. Toad Hall is on the Frying Pan Ranch, which has been owned by Wendy's family for generations. One of her ancestors invented barbed wire, which pretty much wrapped up the West for the settlers.

Later I meet Stanley. We talk about writers – they have an extended library with every book under the sun, all of which they have read. Wendy invites me to go plum-picking next day. Her hair is on the big side, and she has beautiful eyes, large, blue, and elegant long fingers like Ma's with immaculately manicured nails on the end of them, and a couple of whopping stones surrounding them.

'Do you know what? I would really love to get up early and come pick plums with you tomorrow, but I want to finish *Archy and Mehitabel*, and therefore don't really feel it's the best time.' 'Juh right, Claudius. Whatever,' I say, holding up my thumbs and fingers in the W position.

Jimmy Dean Jimmy Dean and I go for a drive in the pink Cadillac. There is plenty wrong with it – you have to steer like a child play-acting or a 1920s movie actor, turning the wheel constantly from side to side – just to keep straight. The brakes are very dodgy. In spite of this the car is a masterpiece of beauty and I feel strong pangs of love. When I go home I discuss with Claudius whether I should ask Stanley to lend it to me or not.

'It's beautiful I agree,' he purrs, sitting on the boot, his paws turned outwards slightly. 'But there's no air con. Anyway, I don't think it would make it out of Amarillo by the looks of the engine. Your desire to see the States surely is greater than your desire to look good as you see the States? Hmm, well, knowing you, that's not a given . . . still I'd be cautious if I were you . . .' He climbs into the interior and pads around before settling to sleep on the front passenger seat.

When he wakes we go down to the lake. It lies in a field away from the guest house and is so isolated that I don't bother with my swimmers. My tan has been neglected recently and I have to do something drastic about it. Claudius settles under the deck chairs and sleeps in the shade, changing positions every now and then. Looking at his whiskery face, his soft forehead which he bumps into my cheek at night, the soft patches of baby fur on his legs, his rabbit-like back paws, his huge front paws with their long, long nails, his clear green eyes, the noble line of curving head like a sphinx, I feel strong pangs of love. He has eaten solidly and slept well for days now. He is very affectionate and sleek again. I hope this lasts a long time and isn't the precursor to some hideous imminent health scare. He seems either to be in peak condition or on the brink of death. I dive off the wooden landing plank into the cool green waters and swim towards the huge inflated water trampoline. I climb on to it ungracefully, showing my bott and everything to the world, and then jump up and down a while, exhilarating in the naked wind, under the clear Texan sky. 'I Love Texas!' I whoop. 'I Love Texas! I Love Texas! God Bless You John

Wayne! Wenny! Stanny! Caw Caw! Aaaargh!' and hurl myself into the water.

Jimmy Dean Jimmy Dean keeps me company while I pick up the repaired Buick. I then stock up on petrol, cat litter and Cokes to keep me awake while driving. Being trailer trash, Jimmy Dean knows the layout of Walmart blind-folded, saving me quite a bit of time. I've often wondered while wandering among the aisles, hopelessly lost, if young Americans are issued with maps of Walmart at school and then have to answer questions such as 'Take me to the pet section from the CDs' and 'Next to which section are the cosmetics?' at a special end-of-term exam. Jimmy Dean Jimmy Dean explains the concept of trailer trash. These are the people who leave school early, have kids early and generally don't buy into the American 'improve yourself' thang.

I buy Wendy and Stanley a book to say thank you and goodbye. Wendy gives me presents of a God Bless John Wayne sticker, two miniature bottles of water, a book for a friend of hers to deliver in Santa Fe (a subtle and thoughtful way of giving me contacts there), biscuits, a jar of plum jelly, a map of Santa Fe telling me how to get to Banana Republic who are having a sale imminently, and an umbrella. This latter stumps me a bit because we are in the middle of a heat wave, a record breaking one at that, but maybe she thinks I'm homesick and this will remind me of England. We hug goodbye and I set off once I've attached the John Wayne sticker to the bumper and adorned the inside of the car with peacock feathers found on the lawn.

It is getting on. We're in the middle of August. Only a few hours' drive away is the excitement, glitz and glamour of Las Vegas. Maybe a few dinners with the mob. Maybe a little gambling. Whatever.

Chapter Thirteen

A River Runs Through It

Las Vegas – Santa Fe – El Rito, New Mexico

As we drive off Claude stinks out the car with two wopping great poos and then scratches the litter until most of it is on the floor and not in the box. We take I44 which is the old Route 66, but has been turned into an interstate and therefore is devoid of atmosphere. Soon we are into New Mexico and the landscape changes dramatically. Mountains rise in the distance and the flat yellow plains have given way to red earth. The trees are healthier and bushier than the mesquite. The odd lush green plain intersperses desert scapes. At Tucumcari I fill up on petrol and look at the map. We're very close to Las Vegas. Excitedly we drive 104 north, a one-lane road snaking ahead in a straight line for miles until it starts winding in and out of the mountains, revealing enormous plains either side. The curvature of the road means I have to slow down considerably and even so Claudius is sick. I stop and let him wander around, and air the car, but feel horribly guilty. The road is very isolated. In 100 miles I see maybe five cars, if that. The odd building is dotted here and there, but no villages, not even a hamlet, for miles and miles. One house has a huge 'GAS' sign outside, the paint worn off by the rain and wind, two lonely old-fashioned pumps standing on a clump of grass under the sign.

We approach Las Vegas and it is very run down and not

at all what I expected. No flashing lights, no nothing. We slide past the Thunderbird Motel which seems a bit of a dive and finally stop at the Palomino hotel, choosing it because of its animal name. It is run by friendly Indians whose accents have not the extra 'y' of Texas or the Cajun tone of Louisiana, but a slightly clipped upward-lilting intonation that makes each sentence a question.

Claude and I stretch our legs before I recce the town. There is a pretty square with the Plaza Hotel (a pleasant old-fashioned place) in one corner and a bank at the other. Dusty cafés and shops selling antiques and Western wear line Bride St leading out of the square. There aren't many people about and the place has a fusty run-down old West feel. I drive around 6th Street and Douglas Ave, admiring the bright green window frames on the one-storey red adobe buildings before driving on to look at the large old houses along South Pacific. Cars are older and boxier than elsewhere. Makeshift signs on plywood or painted on to white bricks advertise Chris Auto Repairs or Kelly's Kountry Kitchen. There are no casinos to be seen. No money, glitz or glamour, and certainly no Mafia and their molls hanging around. I am definitely not in Las Vegas. And yet I am. According to the map.

I stop for dinner at the best restaurant in town, in the Plaza Hotel, and get our whereabouts from the waiter.

'This is not how I expected Vegas to be.'

'What did you expect?'

'You know, casinos, glamour, girls in short golden dresses.'

'That Las Vegas is in Nevada. We're in New Mexico.'

'Oh. Yes. I see. I thought I must be mistaken.'

'This town's only claim to fame is that Doc Holliday owned a bar here and Teddy Roosevelt's Rough Riders held their reunions here.'

'Who was Doc Holliday?'

'A gunman, gambler and dentist.'

'And the – um . . .'

'Rough Riders were a volunteer cavalry Teddy Roosevelt got together: cowboys, athletes, policemen, a bunch of guys . . . Geez. All my life I'm trying to escape Europeans. They're just so crazy. They're just wacked,' he says walking away.

Back to curl up with Claudius, and consider what to do. 'Well there isn't much choice,' he says, kneading my arm with his very long claws thereby almost drawing blood. They are now so long that when he walks on the pavement he clips along like a proz. 'We're not in the wrong place. We're just not where we expected to be. I think you'll find there are wonderful hot springs near here for which this Las Vegas is famous.'

When he yawns his toothless gums are rather black and I have a mild panic attack that this Means Something, like his kidneys are about to explode. I make a panic call to my vet in London, and he calms me down telling me it's nothing to worry about. Claude meanwhile is staring into space. Everything about him brings me pleasure. When his eyes are closed in happy slits, when he's stretched out on the car floor, when he looks well-fed and soft and brown, every mood and gesture I look on with affection. I have no idea how long he has with me. I can't think what I'd do without him. I think about him dying and reduce myself to tears within seconds. Really I should be a character actress because I have all the method tools for any reaction at my disposal thanks to him.

Today I leave Claudius in bed so as to have a steak and eggs breakfast at the Spic and Span diner. As I walk out, a tramp at the door asks, 'Coffee?' 'No thanks,' I say, upon which he shakes his head rapidly from side to side about fifty times, saying 'nnooooo' in a low moo-like intonation, his lack of teeth causing his chin and lips to wobble right then left, right then left.

*   *   *

Claude and I drive to the hot springs five miles up the road. A neat white-haired couple with very posh almost English accents in a huge Oldsmobile are climbing out of the car just as we are. She wears a long clean denim skirt and he has trews and shirt on; they discuss the various appointments they have in Santa Fe later in the day, a cocktail party, the opera, etc. They survey the scene. A guy with straggly ginger hair and full beard in an old pick-up truck is studying a map by the road with a Mexican guy. A dreadlocked black guy and his sundressed and large Mexican-hatted white girlfriend are climbing out of an old bus that has been painted with flowers and whose windows are covered with grimy green half-drawn curtains at the back. They take this in and pronounce that they don't have their bathers. 'I don't think you need them here,' I say. 'Don't be shy!' knowing full well that this isn't their scene. I get into the stars-and-stripes bikini and position Claude by the healing waters so that he might get a few drips on him while I lower myself in. The water is boiling. The tubs are not very big and there is only one other person in them: a Mexican whose tiny towel reveals his red dangly scrotum. He stands gingerly on the side with just his lower legs immersed in the water. Ginger Hairy Hippie from the pick-up truck comes over.

He has been travelling around for two months, his first holiday in four years, and had just been to the Rainbow Festival in Arizona. He speaks slowly.

'Who was there?'

'Lots of brothers and sisters.'

'What did you do?'

'Lots of good sex. Lots of good food. Lots of dancing. Lots of talking. Lots of music.'

'Where do you live?'

'Colorado. I've tasted the magic though and once you've felt it' – he rubs his fingers together as though rolling a joint – 'you can create it anywhere.'

'Right. Are you getting in?'

'No I've been in. But if you want the full experience you should do as the Samurais do, stay in the hot water for as long as you can take it then go down to the cool water by the river and do the same. You do the whole process three times and then you go and have the best sex of your life.'

'Okey doke. You stay here and watch Claude and I'll immerse myself.'

I slip down the muddy grass and hurl myself in the river flowing below the Montezuma Castle. It is so freezing, it penetrates my marrow and then burns it. I start hopping from hot tub to cold spring until my head buzzes. I stroke Claudius with wet hopefully healing hands.

'Do you mind?' he keeps saying.

'I brought a cat here once,' drawls Ginger Hippie. 'He had a big swelling on his paw so I wanted to heal it here.'

'Did you take it to the vet?'

'No, I'm totally homeopathic. I thought he had stubbed his toe.'

'Sounds like a spider bite to me.'

'Yeah, that's what it was. Anyway eventually with herbs and things I cured it, but then you know what happened? I took him back to the mountains – he was like Claudius, a real good traveller – and one night I heard the coyotes come out and then two short screams and I knew. I felt the cord that attached our two hearts snap and he was gone.'

'Didn't you go and look for him?'

'No point, I knew. Anyway they eat everything. They don't leave no whiskers.'

'Oh my God I think I'm going to be sick.'

'That's the heat. You'll be about ready for some beer and lunch.'

I like his vibe. Two other hippies join Ginger Hairy Hippie and me luxuriating in the waters. They are older – about 50/60 with long, long grey, formerly blond hair. She in a flowery dress which she whips off to reveal pretty much everything and he in swimming trunks. He is formerly good-looking. She wears plenty of silver and turquoise jewellery. We start talking and foolishly I ask them what they do.

'What do we do?' he spits out. Hippies hate being asked what they do, it's who they are that's important.

'Are you an artist?' I flounder stupidly, picking the first stereotype that comes to mind because he's staring at me unnervingly.

'Well, she is. I have a book out.'

'What's it about?'

'Meditation. On golf.'

'Oh . . . interesting.'

'You know, using golf as an analogy.' He swings his arm out and takes a swipe at me.

'We're retired actually. She was a hairdresser and I was a psychologist.'

I look at her hair and it's very long. She twists and twists it to get it out of the way. Will it be a plait? I watch carefully. She carries on twisting. She could still tie it in a certain way and there'd be no difference between a plait and the tail. Twist, twist and clip. It's a coil on top of her head. I let out my breath . . .

'But she still cuts hair and I still listen to people. I want to be a stand-up comedian now – that's the next step for me.'

'I'll tell you a joke,' pipes up Ginger Hairy Hippie. 'This bird is ill and so his owner puts him where he'll get better. Takes him to the woods and leaves him near a pile of elk shit. Goes away. Bird starts squawking. Wolf comes along and eats him. Moral of the story is it ain't always your enemies who put you in the shit and ain't always your friends who get you out. But once you're in, sure better keep your mouth shut.'

A hideous silence follows this until the hairdresser titters politely.

The psychologist rises to the challenge.

'I'm Joe. Joe Ken. Go to my psychiatrist with a problem. He says you're in denial and need treatment. I say to him you've got a Mercedes Payment . . .'

Eventually I can't take this any more and dress to leave. Ginger Hairy Hippie suggests a picnic in the Plaza. We buy beer and Mexican food ('All right, you guys? You OK? You have a good day, OK?' says our Mexican waitress) and make our way to the Plaza, ignoring the large 'No alcohol permitted' signs and sit on a bench like the other tramps around. Claude eats his lunch from his bowl and then wanders and we drink beer and eat the taquitos. Ginger Hairy Hippie has a huge hunting knife that he takes out to cut the orange cheese food (seriously, that's what they call it here) and sweaty salami we have bought. We talk and get a little drunk. It starts pissing with rain and lightning races across the sky. Maybe Wendy's umbrella was a good idea after all? We transfer to my car where Claude falls asleep under the pedals. Alex tells me about UFOs landing in New Mexico and Jackie Gleason going to see them with Dick Nixon, and then building his strange mother ship home in Miami because of it. As he talks, various bits of food fall into his red beard. He keeps topping up my glass with dark Mexican beer. Listening to tales of the Very Large Array near Socorro, huge discs that are part of the Space Project, I feel pleasantly woozy. Eventually all the windows steam up as the rain continues to batter the roof: apparently the hail in these parts can be so heavy it ruins car roofs. We talk of the stars and the universe.

'What makes you a hippie and not me?'

'You have to live your life integrated, so that your heart and head are at peace. I do a job that doesn't pay taxes, I have a little less income and give up a few creature comforts so as to do that.'

'Like what?'

'Hot water and electricity. Not getting a new truck.'

For a moment I ponder the imponderable: no water, no electricity, no Gucci.

'Why don't you travel with me for a while? Where are you headed?'

I would love to. He's incredibly cool.

'In the direction of California.'

'I can't go there. I'm wanted on a five-year jail sentence.'

'Uh . . .'

'Just for growing marijuana. I've been caught twice though. How about a joint right now?'

I really want one but have a drive ahead of me and already feel plastered. Santa Fe is calling. The urge to get on and see more is always needling me. I like him and part of me wants to hang out. I am pretty sure that if I do, I will end up in bed with him. I call it a day and we swap addresses.

'Scaredy cat,' says Claude as we drive off in the direction of Santa Fe.

The I25 cuts through the mountains all the way from Las Vegas to Santa Fe. It's very pretty even with the lightning zigzagging across the sky like a child's painting. The rain beats so heavily I have to stop driving because the windscreen wipers, on at full pelt, are no match for the water. Everyone else is stopping too. I have booked myself into the Hotel Santa Fe, which helps the Picuris tribe of Indians who own 51 per cent of it. The reception room has a Mexican country kitchen at one side with sheaves of corn hanging down from the ceiling and brightly coloured ceramics. Our room has a pine four-poster and Claudius settles on it happily.

He suggests a night at the open-air opera, but decides at the last minute not to join me. I drive out of town. As I walk into the opera, two teenage girls in velvet dresses are holding up a ticket. Their friend hasn't turned up and they are trying to sell it. I give them all the money I have, which is $16. The ticket is worth $102, ten rows back, dead centre. I can't believe my luck. Tonight is *Madame Butterfly*, apt considering the number of butterflies joining in on stage. The cool night air starts creeping in so during the interval I get from the car any extra clothing I can find: a Jasper Conran white jacket, a pink Benetton shirt. I look a bit of a tramp with all my layers on, in contrast to the usually-so-casual Americans who are all dressed to the nines tonight. The girls who sold me the ticket are sitting next to me, all straight-backed with crossed lower legs. They are smart young gels from a naice family.

'My first opera!' exclaims one. 'I can't wait!' Then, when the First Act was through:

'The Intermission? Already?' pretending she isn't bored to tears.

Madam Papillon is a little heavy going, I find, a bit like drinking Scotch the first time. I'm unimpressed by the 'wait for unfaithful husband and then kill self when finally realise he used you' story line. The elements seem to empathise with Madam Butterfool's plight more than I. When she stabs herself to death the lightning spins through the sky as blade touches heart and everyone 'oohs' appreciatively.

I call one of Wendy's contacts. She is friendly and interested, says we should meet up and tells me to call back. I do and she has changed her mind 100 per cent and says she can't see me, Goodbye. Strange. I wonder what I've done. Another contact here, an English guy, doesn't return my calls and my spirits start to slump when I think of the good hippie times I could be having with Ginger Hairy Hippie. Serves me right for not going with the flow but dashing off to another city instead. Right now I could be smoking a joint and having great sex. Then getting slit to pieces with his hunting knife. Whatever.

'Don't give yourself a hard time about it,' says Claude.
'You win some you lose some. You're travelling. These
people are busy with their own lives to lead. Go out and
have a good time without them.'

'No. I'd rather sit here and feel sorry for myself, thanks.'

We go to bed early and I dream of a passionate affair
with Prince Charles, where I am totally in love with him. I
wake up thinking what the fuck is that all about?

So with very few social prospects on the horizon today,
Claudius and I walk around town. He decides that I
should carry him the entire time, because of the cars,
and by the end my arms look like Popeye's. I take him
to the Plaza to see the red adobe buildings and juicy
jewellery shops.

We visit the Loretto Chapel, which has this incredible
circular staircase. The legend is that the dimwit who built
the place forgot to put stairs between the gallery and
downstairs. The nuns didn't know what to do, so they
did the only thing they could: pray. Eventually a guy
comes along who builds this staircase which turns 360°
twice, with no central support pole. It's pure and perfect
geometry. When the job's done, he disappears, taking no
payment and leaving no name. The gels are convinced it's
St Joseph, the saint of carpentry.

Before dropping him back home, Claude and I wander
past the San Miguel Mission, the oldest church in the US. I
get irritated by such churches because they signify the
forced conversion the Indians had to put up with. Claude
is not beset by such theological problems, and merely
squints at the stained-glass windows.

We have to leave our hotel – the room is no longer
available. I move us to Las Palomas, a collection of
charming casitas. Here Claudius and I pretend to be at
home, as we have our own little kitchen, living room and
bedroom all in a one-storey adobe house. The warm

colours and curved edges of the windows and door frames reflect the light in a friendly manner. We have a little fountain outside our front door with white fairy lights to twinkle at night. There are sea-green tiles around the sink, lizards painted on the walls, Indian floor rugs and coloured corns on the cob pinned on the walls.

Once we're settled, Claude accompanies me to see a couple of ancient pueblos – these are communities of Tewa-speaking American Indians in the vicinity of Santa Fe. The first, at Tesuque, has low brown adobe buildings and a simple church heading a dirt square. It is totally deserted apart from one guy sweeping the street. He sees me get out of my car and gestures to me to go away, get out, never come back, fuck off and die. I presume these people do not want to be stared at like monkeys in a zoo, as we become more and more fascinated by a nature-loving way of life, having kicked the Indians off the land in the first place. Feeling somewhat sheepish, I drive off.

The next pueblo is San Ildefonso. Again a simple adobe church with a thin wooden cross above it is the village's most important building. A few young boys are kicking a football around under the midday sun and a young horse is running untethered through the pueblo. The Indians make some money from trading their black pottery. I look into one of the shops and pick up a tiny jar. It's $79! ('$79! "And it's not even leather!" ' comments Claude later.)

Our next stop, after a very scenic drive, is the Puye Cliff Dwellings. An easy path leads to the holes in the cliff wall, and further up the cliff are *kivas*, underground caves used for religious ceremonies, accessible by stairs hewn into the rock by years of feet pummelling them.

'All Christian churches point to God in the sky, but the Indians believed that Mother Earth was all important, so their sacred places are in or under the ground,' explains Claude. The trail is paved to keep the tourists away from areas that might suffer from erosion. The only setback is that this makes it all very sanitised and easy and gives the impression that even the National Parks are controlled environments – that nothing is truly wild and free. Claude is amazed by the turkey vultures and violet-green swallows pottering around.

Driving back we encounter another extraordinary thunderstorm where the clouds visibly pour themselves down from the sky in a grey mass of insulation wool. I like to choose as my topic of contemplation not Why We Are Here or How to Access a Higher Power but instead to mull over all the rows I've ever had with my various true and false friends, pondering each betrayal and wound, my eyes twitching in deceived and deserted anger. Some of these could have happened years ago, but no matter. They come back to haunt me as fresh as an egg. I try to get a grip and expel the bad vibes from my thoughts, I search for some way to forgive and forget but my demons continue to prick me with their rusty little tridents leaving me powerless and childlike. Or I like to think about sex.

The mood frustrates Claudius a little. He doesn't enjoy it when I'm lacerating myself. In protest he digs up all the plants in Las Palomas's garden and pees in each little hole he digs until he feels better. He's having a great time sniffing and digging and I'm shrugging and smiling apologetically to the maids who are watching in horror, knowing that when he's finished he'll walk his muddy feet all over the light rugs in the casita. I think now is a good time to check out.

Well, still no new friends. So what now? We drive out to Ten Thousand Waves, the yin yang Japanese health spa up in the hills behind the city. We're hit by herbal smells as we enter, which send Claudius's senses into overdrive. Not helpful as I'm smuggling him in in my rucksack. The bag starts moving as I hear 'That's now, sniff sniff, wait a minute, sniff sniff, I think that's, sniff, no hold on, sniff sniff and what's that? Must be new sniff sniff . . .' I whip him to the changing rooms before the guys behind the desk see me. Men who work in these places seem to fall into two categories: peaceful, whole-wheaty, organic, speaky-slowly, back-straighty, bottom-sticky-outy types or arrogant, stand-offish, attitude types, which is ironic considering these places are about healing that fragmented energy. Anyway, either type always seems good-looking so I have no complaint. Claude and I take a jacuzzi, well I mean I take one and he watches from the side. The tub is outside so that I breathe the fresh air and watch the sky and listen to the cicadas while directing those bubbles you know where. I'm sure everyone must misbehave in jacuzzis. They're so 70s rock star. Claudius is fascinated with the bubbles and keeps pawing them as if he's going to join me. I tell him it's best not. Then I put Claude in the car while I go for my massage. The masseuse puts her whole body weight into undoing three months' worth of back knots.

I barrage her with the usual questions:
    Is there anything wrong with me?
    What about that knot? What's it mean?
    Is there a cure for cellulite?
    Where's the closest KFC?

I phone the only number I have for New Mexico, a photographer living in El Rito, a friend of a friend of a friend in New York. He's a couple of hours north of Santa Fe. He says sure I can come up for a few days. On the way there I stop at KFC for some lunch for Claudius and, after eating it, he pees *blood* into his litter tray. One look at this and I am in severe panic mode. I know that El Rito is in the middle of nowhere and that there'll be no vets up there so I have to look for one now, *en route*, as we drive through Espanola. I find a normal doctor who directs me to an animal shelter that directs me two miles out of town to the animal hospital. I drive more than two miles but cannot see it. Back I go to the animal shelter which gives me the same directions. Up and down that road I drive, up and down ten times, faster each time, crying louder each time. Can I find the bloody thing? Of course not. I shout to the gods, beg and cajole, whimper and roar, and finally I see it. It's good to know that even after being on the road for three months, in an emergency situation I am very calm and don't reduce to a pile of mush within seconds.

The doctor (doctor! in England it's mister or missus) does the usual thing of suggesting hundreds of dollars' worth of X-rays, blood tests, urine samples, thises and thats. I ask her just to give me some antibiotics and we finally leave for El Rito. On the road I am so relieved that Claudius isn't dead, and that basically it's probably nothing more than a urinary infection, that I fantasise about the party I'm going to throw him for his twentieth birthday. It's next April so I only have eight months to plan for it.

Cocktails: moscow mules? champagne cocktails? margaritas?

Fairy lights: white? coloured? purple?

Dancing: Mancini's 60s jazz? Vampyros Lesbos? Air?

Location: London? Paris? New York?

By the time I have whittled down the invitation list to Claudius's 200 favourite people and decided on which cocktails to serve, I have left the turning for El Rito, road 554, miles back. Back I go to look for it and again am in such a reverie that I drive past these folks' house about three times. I keep taking the wrong turnings, and end up driving down steep inclines, gravelly, bumpy drives full of holes. They live in a cottage at the very end of their road, right next to the Carson National Forest. We are in the depths of the countryside. Finally I walk in and find Norman the photographer, 73, and Beth his girlfriend, also a photographer, 28 – both stark naked. Not a stitch of clothing between them. And Norman is the spitting image of Spike Milligan. A naked Spike Milligan.

'What the hell?' starts Claudius, but I say hello and introduce us and tell them about our little mishap on the way up. I try not to stare at anything hanging, but can't really help it. Norman is wearing cock rings – cock rings! Their cat Mah Jong has not taken kindly to Claudius and they put her outside to mellow out. The cats clearly aren't as laid-back as their owners. Claudius has had a stressful day, what with the vet and the drive and now the cat, so I settle him on a chair with some water. There are books everywhere: *Awakening Healing Energy through the Tao*, *Taoist Secrets of Love* and *Cultivating Female Sexual Energy through the Tao*. Their possessions are piled high on the floor and every surface: plants, dried flowers, books, dusty CDs and tapes, old newspapers, cards, drum heads, gardening gloves, boots, ropes, winter jumpers, Norman's photographs, tape measures, pens. On the way to the loo, I glimpse one lumpy double bed in the next room and a bathroom with sky blue and navy tiles. I wonder where Claudius and I will be sleeping and whether it's with Norman and Beth – in a free-love sort of way.

I have brought some wine so Beth and I go into the kitchen to find the corkscrew and open it. She has a fantastic figure. If I had the same I'd walk around in the nod as well. Large tits, curvy legs, round bum, long thick wavy hair, straight near the roots but curlier further down, as though, as though it's been in . . . oh my God . . . plaits. I try not to let panic waver my voice.

'Do you usually wear your hair in plaits? Is that why it's curly at the bottom and not at the top?'

'No, it's naturally like this.'

Phew! Back to relaxing.

We return to the main room and drink the wine and chat about the Cuban and Russian economies, subjects I know very little about, but seem happy to converse on regardless. After this we go to eat at the local restaurant: El Farolito, which has been written about by various flash mags. It's a tiny family-run place, one wall a blown-up picture of trees in winter, the opposite wall the same trees in summer. I have a vanilla milkshake and then enchiladas, very chilliish, and very good. The place is packed but then suddenly empties at 8.30, which is when they close.

Claude and I go to the cabin in the garden where guests stay (no free love after all) once Norman finds me a torch. Claude settles down and seems better than before. I squirt the antibiotics down his throat and he promptly squirts them back up at me. There is no water and no electricity (and certainly no Gucci). The cabin is lit by gas lamps and we are sleeping on a foam mattress on the floor. The perfect opportunity to test out living *au naturel*, living simply, integrating my beliefs with my actions, as Ginger Hairy Hippie will be, at this very moment somewhere up in Colorado. He is somewhat in my affections though I know deep down there is no future in it, what with me refusing to give up the image of myself in beigey autumn colours, chocolate velvet trousers, small gold hoops through ears below sleek chestnut haircut and expensive brown suede ankle boots. Why do all the men I fall for seem to have ginger hair – Harry was a ginge too, remember. Is it the Revenge of the Redheads? I've spent my life making jokes at their expense and now I find them devilishly attractive.

Claudius and I are not at all uncomfortable, although it is a bit of a change from the clean, new rusticity of Las Palomas. I read to Claude for a while who dozes under my arm. I'm on to my third Native American book and this one is full of juicy old wives' tales. For instance Indians believe that allowing an old person to chew your food for you is an honour. The idea makes me retch. If you are really unhappy about someone's death you cut off one of your fingers. The more you cut off the more you are in mourning. So your piano playing might suffer. One mother killed her daughter's baby by mistake by cutting the umbilical cord too close when delivering it. Their system was that men could make the decisions but women could have the last word. I blow out the light and settle down. I shove the eyemask on my face. Immediately I hear footsteps outside the cabin. They stop as I strain to hear them again. I wait, they wait. About five minutes later they move again. I try to convince myself these are animal steps in the bushes, but they sound just like a human tiptoeing along to get a good view into one of the cabin's three large windows to view nice juicy English girl ready to be slaughtered and then eaten, limb by limb chomp chomp chomp. And cat for pudding. Nyum nyum. I realise that the door to the cabin does not shut properly let alone lock. This scenario carries on for a couple of hours; Claudius is interested for the first ten minutes and then decides to let me deal with it. He sleeps peacefully but I drift off, doze, hear footsteps, wake with my heart pounding in my throat, try to breathe quietly, drift off, etc etc. After a while I think 'shove it' and get up to take a look. I try not to alert the potential marauder/rapist/murderer to my plan of action, but my knee-cracking somewhat gives it away. At the window I see nothing outside but black trees and the reflection of my own spooky white face against the black window. The rest of the night is interrupted only by noises of Claudius peeing gustily in his litter tray, which is a good sign as the vet warned me not to let him get clogged up.

I wake at 6.30am and we go for a walk. Maybe the country life is for me. The simplicity of the cabin is charming in first light if slightly scary at night. It is very cold but we walk down past Norman's house through a small wood, through a gate, through the long grass and find a clear river scuttling along at the bottom of the garden. As we watch the sun come up over the mountains and start to engolden the trees, Claudius tells me that he feels much better than yesterday. I am very relieved. He thoroughly enjoys the country smells, different grasses and cold water.

Beth makes us a breakfast of fruit salad, toast with ginger preserve and ginger tea. We eat together, Claude and I dressed, the couple starkers. I try not to look down again. Norman's eyes twinkle as he speaks. I ask him questions about which he thinks steadily before answering. I rather love Beth, she is totally Zen. She is now reading *Awakening Healing Energy through the Tao*, her back very straight, her beautiful unwrinkled face and hooded brown eyes set in a slight frown.

Friends of Norman's turn up, Geoffrey and Miranda. Geoffrey in light rumpled linen makes very obscure avant garde films. He's New York Jewish, in his late fifties and drives a huge brand-new Cadillac. Miranda is in a slinky terracotta cocktail dress and very high silver satin sling backs. She looks ridiculous in the country but who am I to talk? I've turned up all over America thinking I was something special. She is Italian-looking and rather beautiful, however only half of her face moves so her smile is crooked and angry. She is super thin with her veins showing through her arms.

'How is your new apartment, Miranda?' asks Norman.

'There is no standardisation. You can create any world you want to. I can dig any hole and feel any form of perception I feel necessary.'

'Your new film sounds interesting, Geoffrey,' says Beth.

'It's like centrifuging a compound. The experience just gets more intense,' says Miranda. She turns to Geoffrey. 'Apparently there is now no differentiation between the fringe worlds and the entertainment industry.'

'So what's your film about?' I ask.

'There are no actors and no story in my movie.'

'Great. So what do you have?'

'Just images and sounds.'

'Great. Miranda, what do you do?'

'I'm developing these multimedia learning tools. The media is a mask, the process is the transfiguration of mind. It's all about an energy shift.'

'Cool.'

'I don't understand a word they've said,' says Claude from his cushion in the corner, so we leave them to chat, and mosey on back to the river.

Later Beth joins us. Norman has installed an old porcelain bath there. He has built it up on to rocks to keep it steady. From the carefully placed rocks in the stream we fill up buckets of water to pour into the bath. Norman lights a fire underneath it to heat it up and then adds huge green comfrey leaves to the water. I strip and climb in. We settle on to the wooden board at the bottom of the bath, our knees up under our chins, trying not to burn our bums on the exposed porcelain. We spend the entire afternoon talking about love, life and money. At first the sun pours down on to us and the luscious green trees and the swollen stream/river. As the fire gets going our bums get redder and redder and we get hotter and hotter. We take it in turns to climb out and add brown freezing water from the stream in an attempt to cool down. After a couple of hours it starts to rain. Huge droplets hang from our eyes, our brows, our noses, our teeth and still we talk. The sky is a leaden grey against the bottle-green of the trees and grass. The relentless heat of the fire and the soothing cool of the rain are like hot apple pie and ice cream. Because of the rain, smoke pours out from under the fire, leaving its sweet cheesy smell in our hair and eyes. It mixes in with the wild mint, sunflowers and the other herbs and weeds growing by the bath and river.

When we finally stumble from the bath Beth shows me

some of her work – pictures with a ghostly 20s feel to them, both elegant and ethereal. She shows me Norman's work and pictures of him as a young man. Back then he looked like Ralph Fiennes. Ralph Fiennes to Spike Milligan is quite a jump. I am fascinated by their relationship and the age difference, but when I consider talking to Beth about it, I don't really know what to say. After all, they care for each other very much and are very peaceful together.

Another day at the river for Claudius. His tail swishes very gently against the wooden bench he is sitting on as he watches the hummingbirds buzzing past him like giant bumble bees. The crickets here are extra large and have come out due to the rain. They are particularly fascinating to him. He and I are now used to America's larger-than-life examples of nature. We hear coyotes screaming outside the door at night and couldn't care less, and we have had no more from the midnight prowler. Actually I have mellowed a bit since we arrived, probably because of the isolation, surrounded as we are just by the countryside. Now I don't even listen out for his steps. I think 'shove it' and turn over to sleep. If he wants to come in and steal anything, including my honour (juh right!) he's most welcome.

Chapter Fourteen

Arachnophobia

Socorro – Alamogordo – New Deming, New Mexico – Tucson, Arizona

This morning, Claudius and I have our last sunbathe in the early light by the river. We are excited about moving on although we don't know where we're going. Norman and Beth wave us off. They are naked – natch.

In my paranoia not to get caught speeding, which is my only method of driving, I have this habit of scrutinising any car that is vaguely boxy, white, brown, black or with any lights on top. I slow down, I scrutinise, I creep up. Once I'm past the danger zone, I tut and say to myself, 'Since when do cops drive a Cadillac/Pick-up Truck/Pinto . . . ?'

I've also adopted the slightly dangerous habit of watching the road and scenery though the wing mirrors. The roads sometimes develop wet pools from the heat reflections which disappear as you drive towards them. The desert out here is not a sandy Saharan mirage. There are plenty of plants making it seem lush, although on closer inspection the earth is but dust.

We cross the Rio Grande. The rocks forming the ravine are an earthenware red. The expanse and depth of the river are Olympian. There is nothing to do but gaze in silent awe. Back in the car there seems little point in hurtling, for the faster I go the further we are from the river.

We drive south, through Santa Fe, Albuquerque and

then into Socorro, a little Wild West town at the foot of the San Andres mountains. I can't be bothered to put any effort in, so we go to a hideous motel. Immediately I have to ward off feelings of loneliness but look on the bright side – Claudius is well, and that's all that matters – he was fine in the car and has shown no signs of blood in his pee since our drive to El Rito a few days ago. We share a scooby snack of KFC, except I have to take it back when I realise they've got the order wrong and given us spicy, which Claude spits out.

We head west on Highway 60, ignoring the signs saying 'Gusty Winds May Occur', to go see the VLA Ginger Hairy Hippie talked of, the Very Large Array. The road ploughs straight through plains spotted with white, sometimes purple and often sky-blue wild flowers. There are mountains in the distance. In New Mexico the mountains always seem to be in the distance, although sometimes you may find yourself on one, even though you had no idea you were climbing it. When the wild flowers are replaced by small sunflowers we see tiny antennae dishes scattered in the field in the distance. As we get closer we realise they are in a perfect Y shape. Closer still and they are huge: 82 feet in diamater, 94 feet tall and weighing 235 tons to be exact.

'Now then, Claude. The Very Large Array is part of the Space Project to look into the future. The dishes read radiowaves from outer space which are then assimilated by a huge computer so that astronomers can get information about other planets.'

'I think you'll find that although meant to look into the future, these robotic giants are in fact a sort of time machine. They receive light waves from tens of millions of years ago and so are seeing the way the world was almost at the Beginning of Time.'

'Oh.'

'Did you know that everything we use and are made of,

whether steel in cars or calcium in our bones, comes from the stars and has been through and in and out of the stars several times?'

'No.'

'Anyway, these dishes have told us plenty about the universe, for instance the gaps between the stars are full of stuff not just nothingness and there are some stars which are so heavy that a teaspoon of their matter weighs millions of tons.'

No honestly. I don't know how he knows all this, but he does. It's weirder than the time machines, don't you think?

Driving back, an astonishing sunset. The sun changes from succulent orange to vampire red before burnishing to dusty pink and finally bloodied purple. A misty blue is left on the mountains. When we are no longer driving directly into it, we watch it from the wing mirrors, Claudius standing on the door handle to look out.

We return to the motel and watch TV for the night, in remembrance of duller earlier times in the trip. We watch 'Miss Teen USA', where the current holder of this prestigious title shows off this year's prizes. 'Yeah yeah, they pay your college fees,' she says, 'but check out what they also give you: free l'Oréal hair colour for a year!'

Today we drive to Alamogordo, via Highway 380. Claudius and I have no more contacts for a while. We are on our own, so I predict some motel TV dinners. We take a break at the Valley of Fires, near Carrizozo. The valley is a huge part of the Chihuahuan desert that was covered in lava, not from a volcanic explosion but from lava seeping through vents in the valley floor thousands of years ago. Black rock is the earthbed for miles around. It's a bit hot for Claude but he likes sniffing around the beargrass and banana yucca, which he's never seen before. He also points out a couple of quails and cactus wrens hopping about, but being paranoid about snakes biting him, I stand a little too close. He tells me to 'back orf'.

Alamogordo is another small flat town with great mountains in the background. One very long boulevard with the usual motels and junk food places makes up the main road, off which a few roads run, petering out towards the mountains. This afternoon I leave Claudius sleeping and go to the cinema. They have no idea what a cinema is over here. They say movie theater. So I spend a few unproductive moments driving past the Cannon Bar, which is what the guys at the petrol station thought I was looking for. It looks particularly neon and Americana so I go in to ask for directions. It's a titty bar. At three in the afternoon these men are watching a girl with huge implanted tits gyrate and giggle as they sweat over their beers. I understand why they call it the Cannon Bar now. Eventually I get to the 'movie theater' and see *There's Something About Mary*, about a gorgeous girl that all these men are in love with and in the end she falls in love with the right one. I am totally absorbed in it so when I come out of the darkness into the broad daylight and the traffic of strange and unknown Alamogordo, where I know not a soul, and have not a thing to do, I feel somewhat ALONE. Not horribly alone, just a great empty gap where my chest should be. Or maybe a feeling of panic because there is nothing in the world I should be doing and therefore could face the eye of the storm for a moment or two. I feel chased by the void and wonder how to fill my next thirty minutes, before the evening routine of feeding Claudius, feeding myself, showering, phoning outer space and watching hours of boggling mind-blowing TV stretch out in all their dazzling angel-swinging glory.

I open the tap just a quarter turn and feel the loneliness drip into my heart and just as the flow starts to dribble into a thicker stick of glassy fluid I buy beer (bbbeeeeeerrr) from a petrol station. I always think it best to turn to drink at these moments. It is most strange the way you can buy booze and spirits in pharmacies over here. Yet they don't 'carry' normal things like eye make-up remover. Anyway, I also buy honey-roasted cashews and drive out to Ken's Car and Truck Sales (who?) to watch the sun go down on the horizon. After this calming experience, I go back to the motel and the TV is bloody broken, so Claude and I cuddle and think, he quite clearly about the black cat in *The Master and Margharita* and me very drunkenly about the '90 seconds and you're free to go' Revlon nail ads.

Today we decide to check out the White Sands National Monument in the Chihuahuan desert – 275 square miles of blinding white gypsum sand dunes, temptingly Caribbean and yet strangely lunar. As the sands are hurried along by the winds, everything gets covered, although some plants grow very fast to avoid being engulfed. The lizards, foxes and rabbits are all white as though proximity to the sands has bleached them. For once I actually look brown as even I can't look white in contrast to that white; and, er, Claudius looks brown, too. He finds it quite dazzling and tries to climb the sand dune with me but slips back down, so I put him in the car and leave the air con on, because the heat is immense and intense. I stroke him and talk to him in a particularly silly baby voice that makes him purr with childish pleasure. I kiss him on his forehead and he straightens his back in a proud way. For some reason I get an allergic reaction and my top lip swells up to the size of a decent carbuncle. I look like a lip job gone wrong. We retreat to the motel room.

Claudius and I are off. Where are we going? We're not entirely sure. But we're whizzing down Highway 70 in the direction of Las Cruces, the wind our only company because there are no other cars on the horizon. We've heard all the CDs a thousand times. My mind starts to wander, and when I return to earth a good few minutes later, there is a discernible gap between my last foray in the outside world and the retreat into my skull.

Why do people think that travelling is the time to reflect on Life's Great Issues and the direction your life is taking? The reality is it's the worst time to do this. You're far away from home, from the security of your friends and family. If you're lonely at home you can wallow in it and handle it because there is someone you can call, but if you do the same when travelling, chances are you'll be suicidal by morning, as there's no one around to look after you or listen to you ranting. As for Real Issues, it's as much brain power as I have to work out where we're going to be staying tonight and where the laundrette/omat is, let alone Death.

Claude suggests a stop in Deming to watch the annual Duck Races. On the way there we pass a dead white dog lying on the median – all four paws stick out like it's a toy; it had stiffened and was rolling from its back to its side, its back to its side, its back to its side. Claudius watches it purringly as we roll by. A few miles further on we approach an old Chevrolet SUV, dusty and grimy, packed full of luggage, with stickers from all over America on the bumper. I overtake slowly and it is full of good-looking young college boys. They notice me, my stickers – 'I Love Texas' is slightly embarrassing now that we're no longer there – and the peacock feathers and recognise a soulmate. We start to play leapfrog. The Buick is of course much more powerful than their old junket, which is crawling along at 65mph, but I slow down so that they can overtake and then after a few minutes overtake them. I'm 'fucking with them' in the vague hope that they'll fall in love with me and follow me into Deming, for a few wacky days of fun. Strangely, as I take the Deming exit, they carry on towards California.

When wandering around Deming's Fair Grounds, I

insist on buying purple-coloured contact lenses, even though they cost enough dough to feed me and the kitkat for four days. At the motel it takes me an hour to get them in. I finally manage and they look great, especially contrasted with the yellow and red of the pupil-surrounding areas, red from bloodshot poking, and yellow from general undernourishment and lack of sleep. Anyway, after some hefty swearing, I blink all the way to the City of Rocks. We do some gentle sightseeing because even though Claude's idea was a good one, he got his timing wrong and we have a few days to kill while we wait for the ducks.

The City of Rocks is a large collection of prehistoric rocks from a volcanic eruption 35 million years ago, which together look rather like, um, a city. The American version of Stonehenge, basically. It is pretty magnificent standing up there by itself in the middle of this enormous plain whose edges, miles and miles away, are adorned with mountains in every direction. Claudius and I ignore the 'no pets' sign and wander in and out of the rocks. It's all very *Picnic at Hanging Rock*, so I'm glad I have on something white and wafty, so that I too look like a turn-of-the-century damsel about to be whisked into the heart of the throbbing rock, never to be seen again. The trip is about thirty-five miles out of town, which is almost London to Oxford, but this is nothing now that I am addicted to driving. A mere bagatelle compared to the hours and hours Claudius and I have been holding this wheel. On the way back we listen to Led Zeppelin's 'Kashmir' again and again, the volume dial on the notch just before 'Blood Shoots from Ears', Claudius totally unaffected because his ears have a wall of deafness holding him in his world of whiskers and silence.

Today I'm up bright and early – four, five and six to be precise because Claudius will not stop scratching at the door for a dawn walk. Essentially there is nothing to report. I am experiencing some sort of lethargy. I should get out there and meet people, hang out in bars, Have Experiences, but I am tired. Too tired. Flubberingly, manically, matches in eyes tired.

Finally the day of the Great American Duck Races arrives. I invite Claude to the parade. A snore is all the answer I get. Groups of prepubescent leotarded girls, squeaking and cheer-leading and disco-dancing in John Travolta poses, in an embarrassing and embarrassed sort of way. Old men whizzing around in tiny yellow toy cars, people dressed up to look like ducks, Mexicans on horses, vintage cars, huge trucks, politicians taking advantage of the gathered crowds to campaign for the next election, girls twirling flags, brass bands, clowns throwing sweets to the children (hunger made me join the pre-teens in the floor scrabble), Harley Davidsons driven by easy riders, guys dressed in kilts playing the bagpipes (random), youth centres and church groups. The crowd walks down to the Fair Grounds to watch the Duck Races. I wander around sipping home-made lemonade and looking at the stalls selling handicrafts before concentrating on the quacks themselves.

Every year hundreds of ducks are brought to town for this one event, all of them trained by Robert Duck – no, seriously – a former twelve-time duck-racing champion with $50,000 to his name in wins. He tells me of his English parentage. 'Aren't there lots of people called Duck in Bath?' he asks. I have no idea. Robert gathers up ten quackadoodles and takes them to the front of the race tracks, where people rent one each. When the gates are lifted, the ducks race to the end to join their friends in the pen at the other end. A boy next to me asks his mother if he can have a go. 'For God's sake, son. We've just moved here from Florida. We've gotta build a house first. Give us a break,' she shouts back.

I feel awful and my breathing is getting more and more difficult, I'm wheezing like the wind in the wild. I even have to think to breathe. I've had several exciting hospital and death fantasies as a result. When I can bear the heat no more, I go home to join Claudius who is still taking the same nap he started this morning.

After another night of not being able to breathe, and waking up to the cacophony of Claudius scratching either the door or his litter tray or his inner ear, I pack to leave for Arizona, and consider driving off without him. Just for the hell of it. Just for the freedom. Just to see if I can handle it.

I don't.

As we pull on to the highway, the old Chevrolet with the college boys overtakes.

'Time warp,' explains Claudius as though the most natural thing in the world. Right. They don't recognise me and drive on. As we pass into Arizona, the desert comes into its own. The mountains have less green jewellery, their skin is beiger, and signs on the highway say 'poisonous snakes and insects inhabit the area'.

Driving along, there's a bit of a bottleneck up ahead. People driving at 60 instead of my usual 90/100mph. Tuh! I drive up but a brown truck to my right decides to pull out and pull out it does even though I am in the overtake lane. I lean on my horn but he/she can't/won't hear me. I slam on the brakes and get out of the way with a screeching hair-breadth to spare. I am livid and my heart has taken up residence in my throat. When I can, I overtake the fucker and stick two fingers out of my window – the effect of which is somewhat diminished as the wind waves my hand all over the place making me friendlier more than anything else. Then another huge red truck pulls up so close behind me all I can see out of the rear window is its fender. Fuck with me? I think. You wanna fuck with me? I slow down to 50mph. Getting road rage is not the most intelligent thing to do when contending with these mothers. The truck is touching me, I can feel it on my bumper and my attempts at slowing down no longer work. The truck is actually propelling me along from its own power, there is just a nasty smell of rubber from my wheels. I give it a miss. I'm not going to win this *Duel*, so I career off at top speed. To my horror the truck follows me and keeps up with me speedwise, but after a couple of Daisy Duke overtakes on the inside lane, I lose it because it is too big to slip in smaller gaps as I can. I'm slightly shaky. Claude sleeps through it all.

Although we experienced some cool in the north of New Mexico, things seem to be hotting up again down south, down here. It is hotter than New Orleans and Mississippi, except the heat is dry and therefore not as unpleasant. Even so, it is impossible to be outside for more than five minutes at a time. The temperature is 114°.

We stop in Tucson at the Hotel Congress which is something of a jackpot. For a start it has real atmosphere – a godsend after all the awful motels. The bank robber John Dillinger was caught here after he and his gang insisted on rescuing their gun-filled bags when the third floor caught fire. The fire department, who had been reading *True Detective* magazine, recognised them. There is no air conditioning, but fans and windows that open(!), no TV in the room and the main switchboard downstairs has been there since the 30s. To call out, you have to wait until you are connected with an outside line by the girl at the front desk. My room has a black iron bedstead and a couple of hundred-year-old photos on the walls framed in simple dark wooden frames. There's an old-fashioned wireless for entertainment and the bathroom is small and white with a huge old porcelain sink and bath.

The place is unutterably charming and everyone adores Claudius. No smuggling here. There are quite a few dogs around too, which Claudius is not impressed by, but at least he can wander to his heart's content. I settle him into the room and the first thing I do is cough up great swabs of blood. Yes, blood. Believing Death may be my next boyfriend I career off to the nearest hospital, which is not particularly near. As it is Sunday I go to the Emergency Room, wheezing and fighting for every breath. ER, which has the usual assortment of oddballs wearing saucepans on their heads, is quite quiet, but I still have to wait for hours in spite of staging several fainting fits and doing impressions of Mimi on her death bed. The air con is so cold that, regardless of what they'd come in for, on examination most people have to be treated for chronic hypothermia and pneumonic symptoms.

I finally get called through and put into a gown that doesn't do up the back so everyone can see my bottom when I walk down the corridor to an examination room. The person in this world that least resembles George Clooney walks in. She is brisk and efficient and of course the second she enters all signs of wheezing and coughing dry up without a trace. I describe instead of perform them and soon I have X-rays and breathing apparatus strapped to my kissing gear. I leave three hours later with umpteen prescriptions. I am so happy to be alive that I treat myself to the latest *Vanity Fair* – full of articles about Prinny Di, what a surprise – and some red hair colourant.

Back at the hotel and Claudius seems not even slightly relieved that I am still alive, albeit with a lung infection and orders to take it easy over the next few days. I dress up for dinner – pink French Connection dress and high-heeled beige Candies. I stride into the dining room, hair clean and sleek, red lips, no eye make-up. Fresh, friendly, fruity. Ready for conversation and interesting times. I sit and eat my miserable meal reading my article without even the slightest hint of interest or 'Who *is* she?' from my fellow diners. This is no middle-America canteen. It's a café replete with Tucson's most promising young things, in-tellectuals from the University of Arizona, early thirtysomethings, media types, exactly the sorts I would like to meet and chatter on endlessly to, not having spoken to a soul apart from motel receptionists since I left Norman and Beth. My waiter gives me a few strange looks, which I forgive because he is so good-looking and am grateful for because it's human contact, albeit disapproving. I slink out after eating my chicken satay. The worst of it is that the two doses of 'easy breathe' or whatever that stuff the hospital gave me was, has had major side effects, and these are the jitters that Little Richard would be proud of. At the pharmacy I looked like a junkie because I couldn't keep still for a second, and now at dinner, several times I prong cucumber slices only to watch them jitter to the floor, my face making contorted snapping movements like the Killer Turtle in an attempt to catch them mid-flight.

As I leave the dining room disconsolately, I hear Latino music coming from the hotel's nightclub. I can't resist going in, even though I'm feeling shy and silly enough as it is. I walk around and there aren't many people. They all watch as I (a) pretend to look for someone, (b) sham interest in the jukebox even though there's clearly a DJ at work, and (c) prop myself up at the bar looking uneasy until the barman notices me whereupon I throw myself on to him gratefully and engage myself in our conversation about what I should drink much too vigorously. Throwing dignity to the wind I exit and invite the friendly girl at the front desk to come for a drink. She is very sweet about it and declines but introduces me to a friend. He has a shaved head and I tower a good two feet above him. I ask him in a slightly desperate, wavery voice to have a drink with me and we saunter off. At the bar our conversation is stilted. I mention the hospital a couple of times in an unsubtle attempt to elicit concern from a fellow human. No luck so I ask him what he does.

'I have a record label.'

'What does it do?'

'Makes music.'

'Oh really? Uh yes no I mean I'd worked that out. What type of music?'

'Swing.'

'Swing! I love that. I really enjoy it.'

Silence.

'Um I think I'll have some popcorn.'

Yes it might help soak up those two maragaritas and beer. He is still on his first. Not my fault if the man's a wimp.

'Did you know that popcorn is made up of little men that are so angry that they explode?' he offers.

'What are you talking about?' I'm starting to get ugly, better get out of here before I pick a fight. 'Excuse me.' I pick up my beer and order a margarita and a Martini for my room. 'I have to go and take some medicine from my life-threatening trip to the hospital today.'

I exit balancing the glasses and my purse and pick up my key from Sweet Mary Catherine at the desk. As I start climbing the grand staircase up to the rooms, she shouts out good night to me. I wink at her (I *wink* at her) and roar back, 'Sleep well!', which considering she has several more hours to work is a dumb arse thing to say. I cringe my way on up as everyone turns to look at me, and trip, spilling half the Martini as I go. Strictly speaking I didn't need my key at all. Slithering under the door would have been fine.

Today I mooch around the 4th – a street with plenty of thrift shops. I lunch briefly on carrot and cucumber juice and green salad in an attempt to be healthy and then fart my way back to the hotel.

This evening I down several margaritas but not alone! I'm with this guy David who looks after the cyber café downstairs. I had been pootling about on-line, Claudius moseying around the café, when David started talking to him because he wants to know Claude's breed. He's the lead singer of a rock band called the Sand Rubies – I've never heard of them. He understands irony and all sorts of Monty Python stupidities and we surf the web. Soon we discover that our common ground is hypochondria. I tell him about my recent brush with death and he tells me that it is more likely that I have the killer hanta virus than a lung infection. After confirming this by finding the symptoms on the web and checklisting each one, we conclude that I have but a few hours to live. So we spend them at the Golden Nugget, a low-down honky tonk on the other side of town, where very few of Tucson's élite are currently hanging out. Instead Andy, otherwise known as Andrew, wanted for gun and drugs charges by the law, is slaughtering people with his wicked pool playing. David and I start playing against a redneck couple: she bottle-blonde, crooked teeth and unfriendly, chewing gum and air guitaring (a *girl* air guitaring!) to Lynyrd Skynyrd; he with fluffy shoulder-length blond hair and a T-shirt saying 'Floss Twice Daily' with caricatures of two girls with huge tits in bikinis. At first I thought it said Toss Twice Daily. Andy, who's not bad-looking with his long dark hair and twinkly blue eyes above a chipped front tooth and rugged stubble, sidles up and delivers the feminist trilogy:

'How many women does it take to screw in a lightbulb?'

'I don't know, Andy.'

'Two – one to do the lightbulb, one to suck my dick.'

'I see.'

'What noise does a woman make when she's comin'?'

'Er . . .'

'None – she's sucking my dick.'

'Marvellous.'

'When is a woman truly happy?'

'Let me guess . . .'

I don't actually remember the end of the evening with David because I lost count of the margaritas. Anyway, I woke up next to Claude this morning so it was all OK, I guess. I have a cracker of a hangover. I take Claudius down for breakfast in the café, walking slowly so as not to disturb too many alcohol-soaked atoms. We sit outside.

I order the usual: fruit salad and porridge for me, chocolate milk for Claudius. I ask them to open the tin of tuna I've brought down and put it on a saucer for him. He kills the chocolate milk, has a couple of mouthfuls of tuna and then saunters up and down the pavement. I eat most of the breakfast standing up leaning over the rail to keep an eye on him. Three times he walks to the end of the pavement and turns the corner, meaning I have to get up and run after him, terrified he's about to get run over. Each time I find him sitting just round the corner waiting for me, purring, and each time I ask him please not to wander out of my eyesight as it's unsettling my breakfast experience. He ignores me. The guy at the table next to me looks like Bryan Ferry, short black hair and dark blue eyes, the killer combination. He has an enormous white dog at his feet, also with ice-blue eyes. This is no dog. It's a wolf. He tells me that he lives out on the edge of the desert.

Meanwhile Claudius, bored, has wandered back into the hotel. He has waited by the door until someone opens it and then, thinking they are his personal doorman, just saunters in. Marianne, the very cool manager who has made the hotel what it is, comes out with him and asks me not to let him wander so much. I say goodbye and take him up to my room, feeling a twinge of wanting to see Man With Wolf again. I go back downstairs, you know, just to hang around, no reason, and start chatting to Marianne. Man With Wolf comes in, makes a beeline for me, and even though Marianne is in mid-sentence blurts out:

'Do you want to come to Mount Lemmon with me tomorrow?'

'Yes I'd love to.'

'I'll pick you up at eleven.'

'Fine.'

'I'm Michael by the way.'

'I'm Clare.'

'Hilaire?'

Oh not again.

'Clare.'

'Curler?'

'Yes that's right. Curler. My mother, Carmen, thought Curler more feminine than Roller,' accompanied by a 'who is this guy?' shrug to Marianne.

'I'm sorry. What was it?'

'Clare.'

'Claris. OK.'

Driving to find Claudius his KFC, I'm in rather a jolly mood. Ah what a good boy. He's my best friend. I think he is exceptional to come across the States with me like this. Not that he has much choice. Still, I admire his ability to stay cool under the changing circumstances. What strength of will and loyalty. He's always the same old kitkat.

After settling him, I head out of town. The road climbs windingly to reveal mountains right in front of my nose and then the desert stretching in the distance – a green spiky desert with hundreds of saguarro cacti – huge cartoon-like cacti standing twelve feet high with arms sticking up in curves (if they're old enough that is – they only start to grow them after seventy years) like enormous alien telegraph poles. The Sonorra Desert Museum is an outdoors museum where all the animals and plants are in their natural habitat. My favourite exhibit is the prairie dogs, overgrown guinea pigs that hug, kiss and touch each other on greeting but sometimes get carried away with aggression and eat each other's babies. Their territorial call is often given with such gusto that when they throw themselves up to give it they fall over backwards. Such passion in little things.

I relearn many fascinating things that Mrs Harrison

taught me for O level biology but which I never really took in because I was always thinking about sex – some of the many plants and animals that live here: jojoba, mesquite, organ pipe, pincushion cacti, green lynx spider, desert tarantula, coyote, woodrat and gila monster. There are even whiptail lizards, an entirely female species, which have sex by themselves to produce identical female lizards, only I don't take in all the blurb about them because I'm thinking about sex, mainly with Wolf Man.

Back at the car I slap my head in a Homer 'doh!' way. Unbelievably thick, I managed to leave the car door open. I'm lucky the Buick didn't get stolen. Not that there's anyone for miles around. I drive off. After about ten minutes I am bored with the Native American music I have been listening to, seemingly since the Dawn of Time, and look down to locate my CD folder. There it is on the floor next to a long, thicker than average black pencil poking out from under the seat. I look down again and notice it is covered in stiff lighter brown hairs. I swerve the car to the side of the road, and brake as fast as possible without sending the tarantula, which is in my car, hurtling forward from under the passenger seat towards any area where it might be able to climb up towards me. I fumble for the keys but the door won't open because I am in such a panic I haven't put the car in 'park' and this is the only way it will allow the doors to work. Engine back on, slam it in park, key off and out, open door, hurl self out. Start screaming like a hyena – a really meaty throaty scream that arises from the depths of my stomach like some creature from the bog. When I finally shut up my throat feels lacerated and hurt. I have no idea how that thing got in there unless it either crawls up vacuums, or, and this thought makes my heart stop still in fear, it can *jump*. There are no sticks in the desert as there are no trees so I open the boot and get out the radiator seat I had uselessly brought over from England for Claudius, but which of course he hasn't used because we have continually been in heatwaves. I take off the sheepskin cover and use the metal frame as a poking device. I approach the car, breathing heavily. I open all the doors and look in, but I can't see it. Of course not, because all of a sudden I've been transported into a horror film and seeing the enemy would be just too damn easy. I crane from as far away as possible to look under the seat and there it is. I stare at its beady black eyes and it stares back. It is huge, horrific, the stuff of nightmares. I poke it until it starts running. Towards me. It scrambles not up the stick and up my arm as I fear, but up the middle board and on to the driver's side and then out of the door on to the hot road below.

Screaming, I run around the car in a very, very wide circle to see where it is. It is there waiting for me, standing its ground like it owns the road, rearing its end like a scorpion. I poke it until it runs under the car and then rush to shut all the doors, hop in and screech off. Maybe it is clinging to the underrails of the car like Robert de Niro in *Cape Fear*. Just to be sure, I stop and look back. There it is in the road, standing stock-still, seeming to breathe heavily in spidery indignation, until it slowly lifts one bent leg and then another and then another until it cartwheels off the road back into the desert. I drive off shakily. Five minutes later my mind is webbing itself in paranoia. What if there's another spider in the car? What if it laid eggs in here? I stop and get out for a final check. All clear. To calm down I watch the sun go down at Gates Pass. The sky is a howling red – blood everywhere, streaking into orange and gold further up. It wounds to purple and finally night.

Back home I tell Claudius about it all, making the spider doubly big and my behaviour half as cowardly. He says he is thoroughly glad he missed it all. We fall asleep and wake up fourteen hours later.

Man With Wolf is coming to get me in half an hour. Lights! Mascara! Action!

Chapter Fifteen

Psycho

Tucson – Phoenix – Sedona, Arizona

It's 11.10 and Man With Wolf hasn't turned up so I wander around the clothes shop in the lobby. I am psyched. The shop is run by slightly camp Jeff.

'So what can't you live without?'

'The shopping process. But I don't have much time, I'm waiting for someone. They are, however, late.'

'Late? Oh no! They must pay.'

'And pay they shall. In blood and tears.'

'You must whip them.'

'I shall whip them to shreds, that's a given. That's what happens to people who keep ME waiting.'

I turn round to see Man Without Wolf listening to the entire thing, down on one knee.

'Oh, huh, er, see you later,' I mutter to Jeff.

I like to see men on their knees but not quite this soon. And he has a bowl of flowers. He cares too much. We both do and there's something over-premeditated in our countenances. Unrelaxed. Instantly I know that I am not looking at my Future Husband and feel an unobtrusive fart of disappointment.

'These are for you,' he says pointing to the flowers in the middle of a display of T-shirts.

'Oh thanks,' I say slightly embarrassed that Jeff and others are watching. 'Are they yours or the shop's?'

'No, I picked them for you on the way in.'

'How sweet, let me just put them in my room.'

'Sure.'

I start to walk up the hotel stairs, as does he.

'I'll just put these in my room, won't be a moment,' I repeat but he doesn't take the hint and follows me to my room. We go out to his pick-up truck. It's brand-new and white.

'I borrowed this from a friend because mine isn't good enough.'

'Why not?'

'Oh. You don't wanna know.'

Bloodstains? Decapitated heads? Yes I do wanna know.

We get in and it refuses to start. A look of panic sweeps his brow.

'Shall we go in mine?'

'No, do you have any jump leads?'

'Yes, I'll get them.'

We jump-start it. I park mine and hop back in. We move forward three feet and the engine goes dead. He stares at the dashboard in frustration.

'Shall we go in mine?'

'No, I'll just jump it again.' So I go get my car, repark it in front of his and the whole process starts again. When the engine's running I find somewhere else to park and we set off. We pull out of the car park and into the road and the pick-up breaks down again. Beads of sweat decorate his brow like fairylights.

'We'll take mine.'

'Yes, but I'll just have to drive this to where my friend can pick it up. So we'll have to jump it again.'

Eventually we're on the road and we drive for thirty minutes, he in his pick-up, me following in the Buick. Again I am following some stranger miles into unknown territory. We pull into the car park of a middle-America restaurant. We walk in. He addresses the girl at the front of house.

'I came in this morning to secure a table. Name of Mark. We're a little late.'

'I don't see your booking. You'll have to wait, sir.'

'But I was in here an hour ago reserving a table.'

'You'll still have to wait, sir.'

'I want a table NOW.'

'We don't have one to give you, sir.'

We go to the bar and Mark looks crestfallen and about to cry. I'm slightly giggly. Since the clothes shop I've stopped caring, but he clearly hasn't.

'Mark, this is great.'

'Everything is going wrong. I wanted it to be the perfect date.'

'It's fine. Really, it's absolutely fine.'

I'm about to order my usual plethora of margaritas but realise it's just gone 12.30 and maybe Mark isn't an alcoholic as well. In any case the girl comes over and leads us to our table. There is a vague French garden theme, the tables and chairs are green wicker and covered in flowery table cloths. Identical plastic flowers in a small glass vase wilt on each table. The air con is up high and the place is quite crowded. At a table next to us, six very old, paper-white, flabby-gulleted men and women are finishing their main courses. Several waitresses come in carrying a cake with candles on. They form a circle around the old fogeys' table and speed-sing, clapping frantically as they go:

> Zippedy Doo Daa, happy birthday!
> Zippedy Doo Daa, happy birthday!
> ZippedyZippedy, Doody DaaDaa
> Zippedy Doo Daa, Happy Birthday!

This jolly if repulsive scene is in marked contrast to Mark who is again finding the forces of evil working against him.

'I'd like the jalapeño stuffed peppers.'

'We don't have those, sir.'

'Yes you do, that's why I came here.'

'We've never had them, sir.'

Ignoring him as though starting again might make things different:

'I want the jalapeño stuffed peppers.'

'Like I said, sir, we don't have em, never have.'

'Go away.' He puts his face in his hands.

'Madam?'

'Chicken caesar salad, honey mustard on the side.'

'I'll have the same,' pipes up Mark.

'So here we are,' I say cheerily. Mark stares at me. I can see the whites all the way round his blue orbs. This is professional staring, not just a haphazard gaze into space. He looks as though he'd like to slip out of his skin and try on another.

'I last went on a date eighteen months ago.'

'Oh.'

'I liked you because you're English and I watched "The Avengers" as a kid, and Diana Rigg always seemed to be a woman whom you could trust to go away and do things on her own and not fall apart when her man wasn't there. And you wear very little make-up.' Tee hee. 'I'm a driver. I deliver things. Pizza usually. At night.'

'OK.'

'I also used to be in the army, the paratroopers. I've broken almost every bone in my body. Except my spine. The last time I broke something was three and a half years ago when my girlfriend drove us both off a cliff.'

' 'Scuse me?'

'I was giving her a driving lesson.'

'Didn't you teach her not to drive off cliffs?'

'It was a twenty-foot cliff. We split up soon after that. Another time me and seventeen others were dropping off a plane in a military exercise. There was a tornado but they made us jump anyway. We all ended up in hospital but were made to sign release forms saying we had not done the manoeuvre properly so that the general in our command wouldn't get it in the neck – that's what Clinton's administration is like. But my military career was pretty much ruined by my wife anyway.'

'Your wife?'

'Yes, I was married for eight and a half years.'

'Oh, what happened there?'

'I came home one night to find she had been raped and shot.'

Silence. No more slapstick. I can almost touch his pain, he has laid it on the table for me to examine. It must be this palpable suffering that makes him so ill at ease. I suddenly feel plugged into life, that this is what it is really about, surviving hurt that's too much to bear.

'Four months after Sheena died my neighbour shot my dog.'

'I'm sorry. I'm so sorry.'

He talks and talks until pictures of his wife marching to war and Bill Clinton lying bloody in his home and wolf hounds driving off a cliff swim in front of my eyes.

'Can I get you anything else? How about some pecan pie or Chocolate Devil cake?' We skim back to earth to hear glasses and knives tinkling about and our waiter standing in front of us with an asinine smile all over his face.

'No thanks. Shall we get out of here?' He has not touched his salad.

'Yes let's.'

We both bolt up and head towards the door.

'Shouldn't we pay?' I ask.

We sit back down and deal with the bill. He tries to pay

but they don't accept his credit card. He flashes me the whites of his eyes.

'I'll pay.'

'No, I invited you.'

'Really, it's fine I don't mind a bit.' But he is terribly upset by this and apologises profusely.

We drive to Mount Lemmon where we sit gazing out on the overlook. Man Without Wolf continues to talk. And talk. And talk. Somehow we get on to drugs.

'Ah *drugs*.' There is love in his voice.

'Do you do drugs?'

'No.'

'I thought not, you're very clean-cut-looking.'

'Ha! Well, take these,' he says opening a tin box taken from his bag and extracting two long thin brown hair plaits that taper to split ends at the bottom.

'Now hold them to the back of my head.'

'Eeeeyuwwwwhhh. Creepy.'

'That's what I used to look like.' He turns his head and stares, the two plaits falling limply on his shoulder. 'And I had a beard.' He shows me his old driver's licence to demonstrate. He looks just like a serial killer.

'I asked another girl out on a date. She was a drummer in a band. When I first saw her I really liked her style. She looked at me in this incredibly hungry way. I tell you, that's a great way to seduce men. Look at them hungrily. Anyway, when I next saw her I asked her out on a date but she didn't remember who I was. Turns out I was in my Domino's uniform that time. I was delivering that night. That was six weeks ago. You know she's playing on Saturday night. We could go and watch her play. She could see us together and get jealous.'

'If she remembers who you are. Hmm. Sounds like fun. I think not.' I realise I've been kidnapped by Ego. Even though I don't want him, I'm insulted that he wants to use me as an accessory to this other woman's supposed emotional downfall. Still, he knows nothing more about me than my name, so I start to tell him something else, talking over him in fact in order to make my point. Unfortunately I choose all the dark secrets, the baby-eating incidents rather than nursing-my-mother-when-sick stuff. Not that it matters. Half way through he comments with a sigh:

'Yeah, all this therapy stuff. I'm not very good at it.'

'Not unless you're the one doing the talking,' I round on him snarling. 'I just wanted to feel there were two of us here and not just you' is what I start telling him but internally I'm shouting: Don't be an egomaniacal bitch to this man, even though it's the state you feel most comfortable in. His wife got shot, for God's sake. Just then an enormous spider runs past and I freak as I get out of its way, almost hurling myself off Mount Lemmon in the process.

'You need something to calm down. You need the Gong treatment.'

'Mm?'

'It's a church that specialises in emptying thoughts from your head. You sit in front of a huge gong. They strike it and the vibrations pass through you. Just as you are thinking 'Wow, man' they strike it again and more vibrations pass through you. They do this until your head is empty.'

I could do with something to empty my head right now. His conversation has overloaded my skull and my head is asking permission to explode. Doom and Gloom. It's all too intense. I keep looking for an opening to suggest driving back, but he doesn't draw breath. He certainly needs to get a few things off his chest. I feel inadequate to help him.

'Seduce you.'

' 'Scuse you?'

'I thought it was time I got out there again. This whole thing was about me trying to seduce you. I thought you were safe because I knew you were leaving town and that I could practise on you. And now we've spent the day together but I've used you as a therapist. I've poured all my stories out regardless of whether you wanted to hear them or not. I've treated you badly. That's why you're annoyed.' He starts crying.

'Mark, it's OK. Really, please don't be upset. There's no harm done.'

'The plan backfired because I realise I'm not capable of these casual relations people have with people and now I feel attached to you. I've not told one person all my stories before.'

'It's because you've opened up to me that you feel attached to me. I've opened up to people in the past and felt close, but it's probably just gratitude that you've been able to open up in the first place. So few people tell the truth about themselves to themselves that it's doubly nice to do it to someone else now and then. It gives you the impression that you're connected and not alone in this world. Please, Mark.' He starts sobbing. 'It's all right. People use each other all the time and this is not the worst example of it.'

'I'm sorry. I'm sorry. I'm sorry.'

'Please don't apologise for everything. It's not your fault. Nor is it that your wife died. Anyway, I'm sorry I've been a bad-tempered bitch.'

He starts howling.

I feel confused. Low, depressed, so humble next to his honesty and yet equally repelled by it. Why do some people experience so much more than others and then are flawed by the pain? I know he's desperately trying to connect with people, but the air is too raw. I drive down Mount Lemmon at 60mph even though the signs and

corners allow for just fifteen. I'm desperate to be alone,
however, and therefore overtake vehicles around other-
way bends and generally drive like a lunatic. From the
corner of my eye I can see him kicking the floor in fake
braking thrusts. When we get back I drop him outside his
own van.

'I'll call you in the morning,' he says.

'OK!' I shout driving off.

Back with Claude. 'How was your date?'

'Don't ask. Of course he turned out to be a loon from
the planet Zog.'

'I could have told you that just from his staring eyes.'

'Well, why didn't you then?'

He rests his paws on my arm, licking them and con-
tinuing on to my skin. A comforting if raspingly painful
cat-bath.

I am woken by the phone in the middle of the night.

'There's no orange juice down here.'

'Hello? Who is this?'

'It's Mark.'

'What time is it?'

'9.30 in the morning. I'm in the lobby.'

'You're at the hotel? Oh. I thought you were calling
first.'

'I have something for you.'

'I'll be down in ten minutes. Claude, hand me my
slippers.'

I get dressed and go downstairs to see Mark sitting on a
sofa next to a huge bunch of flowers.

'Oh how lovely! Thank you so much!' I gush.

'Actually they're the hotel's.'

'Oh . . . sorry.'

'I bought this for you. I thought you might want to
confront your fears . . .'

He holds forth a glass jar. It contains a tarantula. There is silence in my head but – from the horrified looks on other people's faces – not around me: I am clearly making some appalling noise that Genghis Khan would be proud to call his own.

'No, that's ugly. Take it away, that's horrid,' are my outside words.

My inside words are: yeah right. I'd like to confront my deepest fears

(1) before breakfast
(2) in the lobby of this hotel
(3) with you at your instigation – how fucking WEIRD.

Back at the room I let out a few more belly screams to get it all out of my system.

'Your lungs are better. Maybe we should move on tomorrow,' says Claude.

'Where to?'

'Somewhere that reminds you of me.'

Phoenix.

The journey to Phoenix is relatively calm apart from a Spook Car. These are cars with blackened windows which stick to your tail, drop back and then come to find you again a few minutes later. The trick is to either (i) drive very slowly so that they get bored and pick on someone else, or (ii) drive very fast in an attempt to lose them. The latter is the worse choice as this is in fact what they want you to do so that they can enjoy a little racing, but inevitably it is the one I always opt for. This time I decide to just pull over and let them carry on. But they don't. They pull over and stop right behind me. The driver doesn't get out. The windows are too black – I can't see who's playing silly buggers with me. This freaks me even more.

'Claude what shall I do?'

'Let me deal with this. Don't turn around.'

I peek at him through the mirror. He climbs up on to the back ledge and sits calmly, staring directly into the black of the driver's view. He doesn't move an inch, he just stares. After a while the car pulls out and drives off at top speed.

'Fantastic kitkat! Could you actually see in?'

'Drive on.'

Phoenix is another large city and I'm bored of them. We stop for lunch with our only contacts here: Diana and her husband, Jeff, friends of Gail's. Jeff is a short teddy-bear of a man. He is almost a body builder and has smooth circular ears sticking out from his head. Diana is short, blonde and very good-looking, straight white teeth and symmetrical handsome features. They have moved from New Jersey for the weather and are starting their lives again. They've taken a few pay cuts to fulfil their dream but they're managing and are proud of their lack of fear of change.

Their home is a modern apartment in a complex complete with swimming pool and all mod cons – the sort of building that makes a town soulless – nice, clean, modern, bland, but this is part of the American dream, comfort, stability, accessibility, and they've worked for it and are right to be proud. In their living room they have pictures of each of them with Arnold Schwarzenegger. 'Getting autographs from famous people is one of my hobbies,' says Diana. 'I once jumped into Telly Savalas's limo to get his.' She has a collection of plates decorated with cows and a bird called KC. Their former bird, Sunshine, died three months after their move to Arizona – and not having found anywhere suitable to bury him, Diana keeps him in the freezer. 'Wrapped in aloominum,' she explains.

'Yeah, we love animals,' says Jeff. 'My cousin Kelly has a dog that holds on to a rubber ring and she can swing him round in the air like a wheel. She's been on David Letterman.'

Could it get any hotter? It's 120° outside. Heading for Sedona, Headquarters for Heebyjeebies the world over, enormous red striped mountains rise up, lone mesas unfettered by valleys, rock formations worthy of the gods, masterpieces of geology. We book into luxury (it's time) at the Bell Rock Inn, which has two pools and two spas. Claudius is excited at the hundreds of new smells, all of which have to be identified and captured at least three times. We walk around the gardens and then look around the town. Claude likes to talk more than look at maps so of course we get lost a couple of times but finally make it to a shop called Earth Mother Father. They sell 'Vortex in a Can', which is gathered unharmfully by non-smoking vegetarians. Tinkly music, whiffs of incense, pictures of unicorns, mythical lands and rainbow pyramids – and a garden which Claudius explores. The loo out there has a sign on the door saying 'vacant sister' one side and 'occupied brother' the other – an exercise in trust evidently because I try the loo and the lock works perfectly. A couple walk into the shop behind us, both with long loose hair, rainbow trousers, and Jesus Creepers on their feet.

'How *are* you?' says the woman behind the desk.

The man hugs her and they stroke each other's shoulders. He nods slowly, smiles and closes his eyes before saying, 'I am good. I thank you. The spirits are good.' Claude and I look at each other. We are both struck by an intense desire to punch him in the face.

I decide to have a reading; I suggest that Claude have earconing and then parasite cleansing, although he could Heal the Wounds in his Heart, or watch a Swim with Dolphins video. That's when he's not attending the Angelic Healing Clinic – no appointment needed, Love Donation!

'Your aura demands it,' I explain.

'I'll have a chat with the sun and listen in to yours,' he says, settling down on a log near a tree. 'And then I might give this a hug,' he says closing his eyes, yawning. 'Now bugger orf.'

I start with a palm reading. I intend not making it easy for her by giving too much away but the bespectacled, hair-bunned woman asks lots of questions.

'What does your father think about this?'

'Not much.'

'And your mother?'

'She's dead.'

'Yes, I knew you were going to say that. What star sign are you?'

'Virgo.'

'Yes, I can see that in your hand because you are an earth sign.'

Pauses and thought and then:

'You are a healer and going to express yourself artistically.'

'Well, I've never drawn a picture in my life and my photos are ghastly.'

'Have you ever travelled astrally?'

'Er, not as such, no.'

'Well, you will travel a lot. And you're going to have a child soon.'

'Oh God, I hope not. Maybe you mean my cat Claudius? He's out there communing with the sun.' She looks out of the open window. Sure enough his head is up, he has smelt something interesting and is yearning for more.

'Aye, Claudius. You gave him this name for a reason.'

'Yes. He needed a name.'

'He is a king. He always has been. Since Egyptian times.'

'Yes! Yes! I've always known it.' I prattle on about him until she interrupts with:

'He can paint. Buy him the book *Cats That Paint*. One

cat got his favourite female cat to pose for him and when she died he refused to paint again. Another stared at himself for two hours before doing his own self-portrait.'

'Right.' (Juh!)

'Cats are here to help us into the New Age.'

I check on Claude and pat him. He is attracting everyone out of the shop to stop and stroke him which is annoying the shop keeper who wants business and Claude who wants peace.

'What's new, pussycat?'

'I can't help it if I'm beautiful,' he sighs.

'I thought that was great.'

'Really? Even though you told her everything, your English accent makes it obvious that you're travelling and she believes in *Cats That Paint*?'

'Yes kitkat. Apparently you're a king, too.'

He stretches up importantly and looks immensely pleased.

'Leave me, I must sleep.'

I woke up four times between three and four this morning thanks to Claudius whiskering my nose, and finally succumbed to a sleeping pill. So today has been a hazy dozy nightmare, shitty shitty with nothing solid behind it.

In fact I am experiencing psychic meltdown. You might also refer to it as getting out of bed on the wrong side. You might also say the childish part of my character is very much in the driving seat. Suffice to say I am feeling out of control, unloved and angry. All day I am fighting one anger rush after another. My demons are playing Monopoly in my belly and losing their tempers with each other, throwing little green plastic houses and red hotels around, slamming the board over each other's heads, scattering fake money in the air.

I can't take much more of this so I book myself into the

Enchantment Resort for a massage. Claudius of course spends all day catching up on his sleep on my bed. The resort is situated in the Enchantment Canyon, which is a 'vortex', an energy centre. Originally a sacred place for the Indians, there was some objection to its being built. In spite of high-profile visitors such as JFK Jr and Pamela Anderson (Pam!), the place has had financial problems in the past with management changes every few years – as though the spirits do not approve of the rich whites taking over these ancient sites for profit.

My masseuse, Uschi, seems to be clairvoyant. She knows from feeling my chest that I sleep badly and am often up between three and four in the morning. She even describes my character to me to a tee. She pounds the knots out of my back.

I then visit the Crystal Magic shop and, in spite of the heebyjeebies who are out in force, I feel healed by some genuine talent and therefore fit enough to be clement towards them. I buy:

Purple sunglasses – for colour therapy: they make the world seem so much prettier.

Bumper stickers saying: 'Immortal. And you?' and 'Something Wondrous Is Happening' because of its purple spangly background.

4 tiny blue star candle holders.

5 gold candles.

2 books on astrology/numerology/cards, which apparently Pam is into as well.

A spangly silver star hangy thing for the car, the New Age version of furry dice.

Feeling much, much better I run to tell Claude all about it. He is watching reruns of 'I Dream of Jeannie' in which Larry Hagman looks young and gorgeous.

*   *   *

Today we hike to Boynton Canyon. Due to rain last night, the weather is cool in among the trees. Claudius is in the rucksack but spends most of the time barking orders at me. 'Mind that branch! Go to those blue things! I want to smell them. Let me down!'

We climb higher and higher into the canyon. The smell of the juniper and piñon smoothes the cool air. The deep green and silvery teal colours of the trees contrast with the red mountains behind, so close and so big, some seem to have faces carved into them. We see huge yellow butterflies, blue jays and numerous insects and lizards. The path has yellow and red and purple wild flowers clustered here and there, as well as prickly pears and cacti. Some trees leave small lilac berries that harden when they fall to the ground. As I walk I feel complete, without burden, free, happy. Claude gets used to the rocking motion and after a while smiles, closes his eyes and then dozes in the sack.

'Get down. Stop it. Please. I can't see.'

We're in the car and Claudius is playing with the New Age silver thing. He hits it so hard that it swings across my line of vision like a pendulum every few seconds. It's very annoying as I'm driving. He ignores me and, as it slows to a dither, he raises his paw and whacks it again like Martina Navratilova. Maybe he's senile. Maybe he's regressing.

We watch the sun go down from Airport Road, pulling off on one of the lay-bys and climbing to the top of a rock for a panoramic view. We are surrounded by several heebyjeebies, one of whom is playing an irritating flutey pseudo-Indian tune on a recorder, but the peace is tangible.

Claudius and I watch beer drinking TV. The 'Guinness Book of Records' is on. A guy has just beaten the world record for carrying bees on his body. 87lbs' worth of bees swarm all over his face and body and down his pants, hundreds and hundreds of them so that he looks like a monster from 'Scooby Doo'. All in the heat of the day. How damn weird do you have to be to do that?

Lights out. Intellectually it was best that my mother died: we didn't want her to suffer, she had a good, if short, life, etc etc, but emotionally there is some unaccountable anger and it bubbles around inside causing toil and trouble. If Claudius dies, I will be *livid*.

Chapter Sixteen

Spellbound

Grand Canyon – Arizona

Next destination: the Grand Canyon. Highway 89A twists up through the canyons and the red rocks disappear as quickly as they materialised. Several thousand feet up, the cool of the Kaibab National Forest breathes over my silled arm. Highway 180 to the Grand Canyon is deserted.

Once settled into our hotel, we attempt our first hike, a relatively easy affair through a small stretch of forest to the edge of the canyon rim. Claudius sniffs the silver sage grass, cacti and yucca on the edge of the Grand Canyon park. He points out the yellowing barks of the aging ponderosa and Red Indian paintbrush flowers. He even sees a couple of white-tail deer, though luckily there are no incidents with any of the black bears, coyotes, skunks or porcupines hiding further in the depths of the forest. We're bumbling along discussing Prinny Di, what to do tonight, the latest nail-wrapping techniques, when we come to the edge and are gob-smacked into silence.

The canyon stretches ahead and down for miles, bathed in a ghostly blue light. I take pictures, knowing they will never capture its majesty or sacred atmosphere. Faced with such natural magnificence it is difficult to doubt a God. The canyon is not just a large hole, it is made up of various gorges. The inner gorge alone is 1,000 feet deep, but it is dwarfed by the surrounding canyon which is a mile high. In the middle of the canyon are various smaller canyons and ravines around baby mountains which resemble small temples. The oldest rocks, at the bottom of the canyon near the river, are two billion years old and made up the earth's crust at one time. These are known as the superrocks. On top of these are alternate strips of red layers and sheer beige rocks, with the odd tree clinging to a ledge.

'Here we are gawping,' says Claude. 'But some Indians thought the Kaibab was too sacred even to look at, and when they showed the first Spanish explorers the canyon, they would only stand in the trees a way away from the edge. They called it kaibab, meaning upside-down mountain, because that is the shape that would have been left had an upside-down mountain been plumped in the earth here.'

'Is that how it was formed?' I ask, dumbfounded by the beauty.

'Well, it's one story. Another Indian myth is of a bull trying to find a weevil in a hole. It bored the ground with its horns until the canyon was formed, and the earth it displaced became the San Francisco peaks. Of course the more scientific version involves the southern edge of the Colorado plateau rising with the Colorado river cutting through.'

'That peaceful muddy meander down there could cause all this?'

'It's a roaring torrent of white water. Its speed and volume and the huge amounts of gravel, sand and mud it carries cut through the rock as scissors through paper.'

He looks at the view now and then but smells closer to home and is more interested in chasing after the many chipmunks and squirrels running around. So he *is* regressing. Like a superstar he draws the usual amount of attention as he walks along – and refuses point-blank to get in the knapsack, but wanders along a couple of metres behind me. I do most of the hike with my head twisted round checking on him. It's a miracle I neither bump into trees nor fall off the edge.

When we're tired, we stop at the El Tovar terrace for a margarita (Claudius chooses water) as the daylight fades. This is the oldest flashest hotel in the park. Apparently one woman once complained that 'they had built the canyon too near'. Claudius wanders off to say hello to each table, and ask what they're all drinking. There's almost a 'He's mine', 'No! He's mine!' scenario with one woman who falls so deeply in love with him (declaring him the prettiest kitty she has ever seen) that I literally have to wrestle him from her arms in order to take him back home. Like any attention junkie, he's amused rather than freaked by this.

As usual I have slept terribly and feel like death warmed up. Also, Claude has developed the habit of stretching first thing: it's more like a shudder and every time he does it I think, That's it. He's had a heart attack. My panic once got the better of me and I pinched him until he mewed just to be sure he was still alive. Why is my health giving out? It is incredibly frustrating. I yearn for my own bed. Even though this is an impossibility from the quarantine-and-Claudius point of view, a master plan has started to form in my head. There is hope yet of returning to England with him without quarantine. It's risky but would be worth it. I must think.

I don't feel quite up to a hike today so I quell my better environmental instincts and take a plane across the canyon. Joe, our pilot, comes out to greet us. Not unlike Richard Gere in *An Officer and a Gentleman* – he is unutterably good-looking, in his uniform with captain's hat and aviator specs and short-sleeved shirt. Being both oversexed and underfed, as it were, I have to pick my jaw up off the ground and follow him to a plane small enough to be powered by a hairdryer. As we take off, I let Claude out of the rucksack and settle him on my lap. He digs his nails into my thighs, bringing tears to my eyes. He is a little nervy, I am merely in love. I scour Joe's fingers for rings: seriously, he's the best-looking man I've ever seen.

There is another couple in the plane as well – a Japanese pair, who have taken a back seat – Joe has seated me up front, next to him. The plane rattles our bones as it takes off, and is buffeted by every gust of wind in the sky. A pigeon hitting it would fly off unawares as the plane ricocheted to its plummeting death below. Joe starts playing atmospheric music, Enya and such-like, and gives us a spiel about the canyon and the forest and the wildlife. We are up for a little while and are all thinking the same thing: yes, yes, but the canyon? Then we spot the edge of the forest and know it is coming. It approaches, we approach. All silence into slow-motion, and then, a slow orgasm, we fly over the world's greatest creation. Joe says in a deep husky voice, 'Welcome to the Grand Canyon,' and I almost pee my pants. My eyes water over with sentiment (and lust), as when dramatic film scores overdo the corny. I can't help myself. I look at Joe.

'Kiss me.'

'What?'

''Scuse me?' (I chicken out).

'Yes?'

'Do you feel the way we do when you do this?'

'Gets me every time, ma'am.'

Pause.

'Joe, what is the strange blue light that bathes the canyon?'

'Pollution. It gets sucked in from LA and San Diego. Sometimes a hike down there is no better than a walk in a city.'

'What a shame.'

Pause.

'Ma'am?'

'Yes, Joe?'

'What is that cat doing on your lap?'

'Oh my gosh, I brought my cat by mistake! I didn't realise, I am sorry.'

'He's not meant to be up here.'

'No? Oh well, never mind, he's here now. Let's not ruin this lovely time together!'

'It's very dangerous. We'll have to go back down.'

'But look, he's loving it.' Claudius is making strange cat-sees-bird noises at the other little planes flying around in the distance.

'If he were to go berserk, we could all die.'

At this suggestion Claudius looks at me the way he does when I introduce a potential boyfriend to him and his catometer is swinging at zero.

'Claudius go berserk? The canyon flattening out is more likely.'

Unfortunately we go back down immediately. Joe is angry, though hiding it. The Japanese are not hiding it. They want their money back. In case the company tries to charge me for anything, when we get down I forego the certificate I would receive saying I've had the ultimate experience blah blah blah, and the chance of getting Joe's number, and bomb it back to the car, Claudius bouncing around in the bag in a most ungainly fashion.

Well, we've seen it from above. Time to get stuck in and actually follow one of the trails carved by mineral prospectors at the turn of the century. So today we take our hearts in our hands and start the Bright Angel Trail – intending to do it fully, which supposedly takes three hours down and at least four hours back – and that's just to a plateau, not all the way down to the river – that takes a couple of days. I'm weighed down with water and food in a bag on my back and Claude in the rucksack on my front. I develop BO almost instantly, what with the strain of it all.

The trail winds down gently in long hairpin bends, past the Kolb Studio (built by a couple of photographer explorers at the turn of the century) which clings to the side of the canyon. Soon we seem to be dwarfed by the cliffsides. Claude points out the mule manure dotted here and there on the trail, evidence of people having an easier time of it than we. Exhausted people on their way up are too tired to say hello. There are signs everywhere warning about heat exhaustion. Plenty of people die from hiking during the heat of the day. You have to set off before ten or after four – especially as the canyon gets hotter as you get lower, and temperatures down there can reach 120°. I'm worried because even though I'm built like a hiker, muscly legs and arms, I'm actually a bit of a poof when it comes to walking long distances. This is twelve miles and I've never managed to walk more than two hours. On the way down a ranger tells us the cheery news that I've left it much too late in the day and will never make it back. 'Good-oh,' I hoot and carry on regardless – I don't want him to see Claude who is definitely *verboten* down here.

The more we descend, the more exciting it is to look up at the beige and grey sheer rock faces and watch them change to pink, brown and violet hues. I have to keep Claude's bag open so that he doesn't get too hot, and his head swings round and up as he looks at the sides of the canyon. As I walk, I make sure to look each and every man in the eye, on the pull, even when under severe physical stress. There are several good-lookers out there as well. We are walking down in the company of two French guys and three Americans, a father and two late-teen boys who are too shy to speak. We don't walk together but keep overtaking each other as we stop for rests now and then. Each time we banter briefly on a different topic: the heat, the water, the views, keep going! I reach the second resthouse and decide to go on to the Indian Gardens, further down. I'm playing it all by ear, pacing myself, being flexible so as to avoid *death*. The further down I get the more careless I am about hiding Claude. I walk past people but I can see a few 'ahh'ing and wanting to stroke. At the Indian Gardens, 3,000 feet below the rim (so called because the Havasupai once farmed here), we catch up with the mules which are all tethered to a post while the lazy (lucky) riders eat their lunch in the shade.

I am pooped, but think it a shame to get this far and not go to the Plateau Point, which is another mile and a half. Claude encourages me, which is easy to do considering he is bright as a button and hasn't walked a step except to take the odd pee. Mentally I am psyched and refusing to give in to blisters, pain, fatigue. The blood is pounding through me, as though in a manic game of hide and seek, searching every darkened nook in every limb for hidden energy, urging it to come out. My forces are rallied. A vast smile spreads on my face that refuses to dispel. I'm tripping, I must be in the Zone. We walk out to the plateau, the walk is flat and rocky, we are no longer descending. The heat is heavier down here and the sky seems to hum with energy, being blocked in as it is by the canyon walls yearning on either side. The energy moves endlessly to some indistinguishable centre of the canyon. My heart pounds my ears with a ceremonial beat.

Claudius doesn't seem awed by the immensity of the canyon. It's just another part of this universe he accepts without question or fuss. He is simply humming a little tune and enjoying the ride. It must be wonderful to live with no doubt in your soul. He is so sure of himself. He knows his purpose: to accompany me on this transAmerican lark. Why else would he have lived so long? I feel as if I have been working up to this and yet sometimes I have no idea why I'm doing it.

From the plateau the Colorado river is still a thousand feet down, but the inner gorges are as magnificent as the larger ones and we can see the river white-horsing along the rocks. Claude and I lie out on the plateau, which consists of sliver upon sliver of rock, and eat our picnic of cheese, cold tortillas, apples and chocolate. I cut up bite-size pieces of cheese and chocolate chips for him. He eats some but is more interested in the squirrels that are trying to steal our food.

My legs are sore and tired, my toes bruised and painful. I only rest for half an hour, my restless little soul yearning for the thrill of making it back to the top. I take off my shoes. To my horror, as I do so, one of my big toenails falls off. Clean off like a toothpick. Or something. I put my shoes back on, pack up and try to walk but it is bloody painful.

'Oh Claude. There's no way we're going to make it to the top like this. I'm in too much pain.'

'Well, you have to get back to the Indian Gardens. If we're lucky the mules may still be there.'

'But it's a mile and a half away. I can't do it.'

'Let's hear none of that. One foot in front of the other, come on.'

I start back painfully. It rains, which helps at least to cool me down, but once we make it to the Indian Gardens, the sun is beating down on our heads like a wave of nausea. I stay in the cool of the cottonwood trees for a few minutes while I regroup my ailing forces. Claude feels very heavy all of a sudden. Luckily the mules are still there. I explain my problem to the mule master and beg for a ride up.

'No. No can do. There are no spare mules and all these folks have paid for theirs.'

'Please.' I'm about to cry.

'No. Sorry.'

I begin walking up, but as I do I hear a ranger approach the mule master.

'Have you seen a boy around hiking with a cat called Claudia? I just got word on my radio that some folks on the way up saw a cat using the canyon as a bath-room.'

'For God's sake!' I swing round angry. 'I'm a girl. A GIRL. I'm not a boy. Claudius is the boy, and he's ClaudIUS not Claudia.' I take small steps, but keep moving.

'Stop, please!' he runs after me. 'Animals are not allowed down here.'

'What are they then?' pointing at the mules and attempting to stomp off – difficult with only nine toenails.

'You have to evacuate the canyon immediately.'

'Give me four hours and I should be at the top.'

'Excuse me, miss. We want you up faster than that. You're taking one of these mules with me.' The mule master looks pissed-off but there's nothing he can do in the face of such angry authority. Claude and I smile at each other. Bingo. We enjoy a delicious pain-free ride to the top. It still takes a while to get up, and the ranger can't stay angry and quiet all the time. I can feel him mellowing – it's impossible to stay angry when surrounded by such beauty. And the canyon.

Ha! Anyway I tell him about Claude and my trip and by the end we're the best of friends. He even lets me off the fine that would surely be coming my way, if I promise not to do it again.

I am now thoroughly addicted to hiking and all things canyonesque. I take Claude home, full of hikey muscly dykey confidence, thinking how toned and pretty I look. Something of a heart-stopping shock then when I see in the mirror that I've forgotten to put my mascara on and look the spitting image of Struwwelpeter. No wonder he thought I was a boy.

On the news tonight, there is a story about one of *Cosmopolitan's* Most Eligible Men going to the slammer for raping and beating his girlfriend. We wait with bated breath – luckily it's not Mr Nevada. I phone him to

organise a meeting, as we are approaching . . . You Know
Where.

This morning we leave the canyon and drive towards
Route 66. We stop at Seligman for lunch at a café with
brightly coloured chairs and tables out in the covered yard
and Mexican flags hanging from the ceiling. Some French
guys all Harleyed up in new skull and crossbones bandanas and crispy clean black leathers are reliving the Route
66 thing. Claudius pokes around in the yard among the
rusty old classic cars and an iron bedstead with paper
flowers stuck into it. The loos have TVs and phones in
them and classic pop pipes in. The door leading to the
cubby hole where you order food has handles on both
sides, confusing the French boys who spend a good few
minutes trying to get in. The two old guys behind the
counter are barmy.
  'Yes, ma'am.'
  'A cheeseburger, please.'
  'A cheeseburger with cheese?'
  'Yes please.'
  'Two cheeseburgers.'
  'No, just one.'
  'But with cheese?'
  'Yes.'
  'Then that's two. Anything else?'
  'Just one, please. Yes, a Coke.'
  'Small, medium or large?'
  'Small.'
They hand over a tiny thimbleful. They write the order
down in disappearing ink.
  'You're A.'
  I forget my letter and go back in. 'Have you said mine?'
  'Yours is tomorrow's order.' They suddenly squirt
mustard all down my front – a long line of yellow toy
tape that gets its scream anyway. I ask for a straw and they

offer me hundreds. I pay and they give my change to the guy next to me. The whole thing is mayhem. Claudius meanwhile has climbed under the fence into next door's garden and I have to negotiate with him to lure him back out. It's double KFC for the rest of the week. I take him in to meet the nutters and they offer to cook him for me. Horrified, we leave. We continue on Route 66, listening to 'Matthew and Son' by Cat Stevens over and over again. We pass through quaint little towns called Tuxton and Valentine and Claude poos, which brings the party atmosphere down a notch or two.

We are trying to get to Nevada, you know what happens there, but as everyone from the petrol-station attendants to motel receptionists to sexy pilots have told us different journey times, three, five or six hours, we drive for about three and a half and stop for the night at Kingman. Kingman is in the middle of the Arizona desert, a long strip of motels and fast-food chains, but all in the spirit of Route 66, so flashing, colourful lights and crazy memorabilia give us a hint of that mecca of lights in Nevada that we are searching for.

Claude is tired after the journey and wants to sleep but I want to see London Bridge at Lake Havasu City an hour away. Yes, apparently London Bridge really was falling down – er, sinking an inch every eight years – and London decided to sell it to the highest bidder, which was of course some barmy American. Robert P. McCulloch Sr bought it for $2,460,000 in 1968 and then transported it stone by stone (22 million pounds of them) to Arizona where he literally created a city, Lake Havasu. It was the only bridge to be built on dry land, as they then created a waterway under it. Nowadays Lake Havasu is a weird 18–30s resort watersport playground place in the middle of the desert. There is an entire fake British Village, complete with pub, pillar postboxes and red phone boxes. The main hotel has several tit-jobbed fake-blonde girls in it and guys with dyed blond hair and tattoos playing volley ball. I have a beer, watch them and lust after them, even though they are quite vulgar: one lies down under a fountain so that it shoots up between his legs making it look as though he is, you know . . . I drive back as a huge yellow full moon climbs into the sky behind the strange rock formations between Lake Havasu and Kingman. And tomorrow?

Vegas Baby.

Chapter Seventeen

Viva Las Vegas

Las Vegas, Nevada

We drive the drive we have to drive to Vegas. Highway 93 takes us through real desert, moonscape desert, with not a tree in sight, but miles and miles of rocky mountainous vista, strange and forbidding. It is very, very hot again and we take a break at the Hoover Dam. Claudius perches on the overlook and stares at the hundreds of carp gathered below us. Once in Vegas, Claude chooses the Luxor Hotel as the Egyptians loved cats. It is a huge pyramid right at the end of the strip which is lit up at night by lasers flashing up its edges. I smuggle him in: quite easy as all these hotels are enormous. We're on the seventeenth floor and he feels right at home among the *faux* Egyptian fixtures and fittings – it's deeply swish. There are hieroglyphics wherever there is floor or wall space. Our room is plush but is nothing compared to the interior of the exterior – interior strictly speaking but so huge it might as well be an exterior. Huge Rameses figures hold up the portals, through which bell boys and valets are trying to deal with hordes of people trying to get in and out of the place. There are enormous fountains inside, several restaurants, a casino, a post office, several shops and a health centre. You could live here for years without ever leaving. There's even a couple dressed as Antony and Cleo wandering around, with gold make-up and black eyeliner, having their picture taken with tourists. The gift shop sells Cleo outfits. I can't resist getting one, complete with black wig, gold skirt, boob tube and eye liner.

Begas Vaby is the world's greatest adult theme park because each hotel is more magnificent than the next in a desperate attempt to lure people in to part with their money at the tables. The Mirage has an erupting volcano. Huge swathes of water and fire spume the air with orange and red lights every fifteen minutes. There are white tigers and lions and dolphins in the private garden of Siegfried and Roy – the hotel's resident magicians, camper than a row of tents. The Bellagio's water fountains race miles into the air. Treasure Island has a full-scale pyrotechnic water battle with pirates versus the British, culminating in explosions and the actors hurling themselves into the fake sea below. Yes, surrounding Treasure Island is a fake sea, not just a pond but vast tracts of water. Caesar's Palace has a huge Roman atrium inside with a sky that changes from night to day and statues that move. A set of horses with chariot and fountains lead up to the huge sky-stretched Greek Palace. New York New York is a plasticky miniature version of New York complete with Statue of Liberty and the Manhattan Express, a rollercoaster that winds in and out of the skyscrapers. And the lights. The lights are incredible, flashing, dancing colours.

As for the gambling, even the 7-11s outside town have five baby slot machines. And nothing is too strange. A Little Off The Top is a hairdresser where the stylists are dressed in lingerie. The Little White Wedding Chapel has a drive-up wedding window. The things to do: race cars, drop 225 feet, bodyfly in wind tunnels, sky dive, chocoholic around the MGM Grand where 30,000 square feet have been dedicated to chocolate. You need never stop and think.

It's ironic that the controlled environment is what the Americans seem to be best at – even though they have the most beautiful natural environment with every geographical aspect imaginable at their disposal. Maybe the pioneers experienced such a hard time that fear of the great wild is now ingrained into the American psyche, so they gain immense satisfaction from dominating even the most forbidding terrain. Vegas is, after all, in the middle of the desert.

I try the hotel's restaurant, which is an As Much As You Can Eat buffet. After downing three plates of food in a most unladylike fashion I hit the tables. It's not quite the Sharon Stone experience I was hoping for. The majority of people are cellulitey wrinkly old fogeys wearing shorts, sneakers and spangly T-shirts, smoking or drinking Coke, pouring cupfuls of quarters into slot machines.

So I buy tickets to a show. Well this is Vegas. Am I right, baby? When I invite Claudius, he makes a paw gesture that translates roughly somewhere between 'oh phooey' and 'clean my litter tray'. Trent Carlini is the Dream King. His leaflet has two pictures: Elvis one side and Trent the other. They are indistinguishable. Underneath is the caption: 'This is Elvis. This is Trent. Any questions?' Trent opens his show by saying that when Elvis died, he felt like a son losing his father. He comes out and the audience does not go wild. They need to assess exactly how like Elvis he really is, and a few of us are hoping that by some miracle Elvis really will walk out from behind that curtain. Not only does Trent sound exactly like Elvis but he looks very like him, which is a great bonus. There are moments when I can fool myself that he is the King. He sings fantastic Vegas songs like 'See See Rider' and at the end the curtains fall to reveal the gaming tables as he belts out 'Viva Las Vegas'!

Afterwards I have my picture taken with him. He is very good-looking: well, he looks like the King, right? We chat and I persuade him to have a drink. The King! Drinking with me! After his adoring fans have dispersed I join him in

the bar next door. I order what he orders: water, unfortunately. He doesn't drink.

'You're the greatest impostor I ever did see!' repeating
the words of an excited old black lady in the audience.

'Actually, I don't like to be called an impersonator. I
prefer Presley Artist or Elvis Stylist.'

'Okely Dokely. Whatever, you're great,' I toot. He
smiles that crooked curled-lip smirk that makes millions
weak at the knees. I guess he's heard this before, if the
reactions of the audience are anything to go by. There
were women telling him that he had brought Elvis alive for
them.

'Elvis is a way of life,' he yodels. 'He's the song two
people made out to in a back seat, he's a musical mecca of
490 songs.'

I want to know all about him (Trent), his age, his
marital status, how he got to do this, and start bombard-
ing him with questions. He starts with 'No personal
questions' and I think, *Hello?* Who *are* you? but he lets
slip that he is married with three little girls at home in the
burbs. I stifle a look of life-shattering disappointment.

Before he started doing Elvis, he was a pop star in Italy
and his own career was going places. 'I was chased out of it
by people telling me how much I looked like Elvis and
wanting me to be him. At first I resented it because I have a
lot to offer musically, but later I gave in because it's not what
you like it's what they want that sells. Right? But I'm no
Elvis wannabe. This is pure entertainment. I'm not trying to
be Elvis. It's all about where you focus. I'm not an Elvis
(pron. Elveyes), one of those non-entertainers who wears
his clothes out in the street and at home. I'm a tribute artist.'

I fly two feet above the ground back to the Luxor and
tell the King about the King.

Today Claude didn't eat his breakfast and when I ask him
to accompany me to the Liberace museum, he seems quiet

and pensive so I tiptoe out alone. I'm worried but, not wanting anything to be wrong, I try to put it to the back of my mind.

Adoring devoted fans, overmade-up and over-perfumed old ducks, run the place. They point me towards the piano room. Liberace had a rhinestone piano! Every inch of it (apart from the keys, obviously) covered in rhinestones. The next room has his costumes, one of which weighed more than 200lbs from its beads – the King Neptune costume. His Purple Costume took six months to complete and the six seamstresses working on it had to wear dark glasses to protect their eyes from the glare of the rhinestones. Back in 1975 he was spending $750,000 on Black Glama costumes made of 200 female minx – eyuw. There is a cabinet showing the rings he wore, rings the size of eggs. When asked how he played with them, he chipmunk-smiled back: 'Very well, thank you!' The final room contains other objects from his home, his cars and his picture albums and correspondence (his signature included his name with a piano and candelabra on it). Of course he had a rhinestone car as well as a piano, and a mirrored car and Rolls-Royces. Pictures from his home manifest the soul of kitsch etched into his every gesture. Fur rugs on the beds (for his twenty-six dogs), a car in the living room; he even had a copy made of the Queen's crystal and gold glasses after a visit to England – and then had the mould destroyed.

He became what he became through three major changes in his act. One, he added a candelabra; two, he played something upbeat and fun in a serious classical concert and, three, he started wearing extraordinary costumes after he hit the headlines in the 50s when he wore a gold lamé jacket for one recital. I'm admiring his costumes when a tiny girl next to me, no more than five feet high, leans and whispers: 'That's what my wedding dress is like.' Her accent is thick Bronx.

'It is?'

She's pointing at a cape with a collar stretching to the ceiling, covered in rhinestones and feathers with fur cuffs. 'Yiya. But white.'

'Aren't you very young to get married?'

'Are you kidding me? I'm twenty-one. What about you?'

'Um, twenty-eight.'

'Married?'

'I should coco.'

'You Australian?'

'With my beautiful accent? Are you mad? I'm British.'

'Yiya. Like the guys on Treasure Island's battleship – did ya see it?'

'Yes.'

'That guy who salutes as the ship's sinking and then is still there saluting when they haul the ship back up from the sea. Remember? Are all you guys like that?'

'Absolutely. Yes.'

To cut a long chitchat short, before I know it, I'm off to a Vegas wedding. Tonight at the Graceland chapel.

I arrive early so as to get a good seat but needn't have bothered. Cindy and Chaz have not got many invitees – they have clearly eloped. There are a couple of girls, Donna and Carly, with strong make-up and short tinny dresses revealing thick thighs propped up in black leather platform shoes. Their hair is ringleted and lacquered within an inch of its life. Chaz (22) is a flash young mafioso, with a 50s hairdo and wide collars and cuffs. He is accompanied by his best friend, Scott, a spotty, cocky bird who makes eyes at either Donna or me, and maybe both. I think it's me, Donna thinks it's her, in the end he's probably not that fussy. The music starts and Elvis leads Cindy up the aisle. Elvis! Elvis in his later years, you understand, and therefore quite podgy. Elvis in his wig-slipping years, you understand, and therefore slightly balding on one side. Elvis in his short years, you understand, and therefore not looking very much like Elvis at all. Sure enough, Cindy's dress is draped with a white satin acrylic cloak with some sparkles and frou-frou maribou feathers hugging the slightly wilting stiff collar. She looks adorable, being the reet petitist thing you ever did see, although I wouldn't like to see her near a match. That cloak'd shoot her in instant flames to the roof. A non-denominational vicar marries them before you can say Yehoodi Menyewhin and then Elvis sings to them for about twenty minutes before photos and then limoing out of there. I love it. I clap and cry 'yee haw' when I think it appropriate, which is in fact not as often as I do it, but Cindy and Chaz are too happy to notice, though the two Brooklyn girls do and stare. Cindy chose this chapel because Jon Bon Jovi and Lorenzo Lamas had married there. (Not to each other, you understand.) We go to the Harley Davidson café to celebrate. A huge motorcycle with red flashing lights sticks out of the building. The Brooklyn girls ease up and are fun and friendly, if a little wary of me and jealous that Cindy has found a new friend on her wedding day. After an hour we are all sloshed and making toasts to each other. I stand up. 'I only met you today, Cindy and Chaz, but on behalf of England, we love you guys.' The Brooklyn girls stand up. 'We've known you all yer life Cind, and a dirty piece a shit you are too – haaaa,' they holler. 'Only kidding, we love you guys and Chaz, you treat her good or don't never show your face round here again – haaaaa.' After a while the waitress comes over, sticks her pencil behind her ear, crosses her arms and yells at us to 'simmer down'. Teenage weddings. How nostaligic I become, remembering my own.

At the very end of the evening, how shall I put this, drink has very much got the better of me. I'm in no mood to return to the hotel, so Scott and I go gambling. On our way to the tables at Caesar's Palace he tells me Vegas myths, such as the time Kerry Packer came to town, won $50 million and gave out $1 million worth of tips to the casino staff, just like that. He asked one waitress how much her mortgage was and on her reply immediately wrote out a cheque for that amount. After this, I am psyched by the idea of winning a fortune. Caesar's Palace is rather swisher than the Luxor – and lots of people are in dinner jackets and evening dress. We settle down to some blackjack. I run out of money almost immediately, so I ask Scott to lend me $50. He runs off for some chips for me and returns with a great pile: he must have asked for $1 ones, rather silly of him. I'm usually very good at this, when playing my friends in Notting Hill, but somehow things are different here. I lose heinously and repeatedly. After a while I get the bit stuck between my teeth, I'm convinced I'm being diddled. Scott can see what's happening and is whispering for me to back out now, but I refuse and go on and on until I have but one chip left and have to bow out. It's shaming. I reach into my bag and write him a cheque for $50.

'Is that a tip?'

'No, it's what I owe you.'

'I don't think so. More like $5,000.'

Pause.

''Scuse me?'

'I lent you $5,000.'

'I asked for fifty.'

'That table has a $100 minimum – see the sign? I thought you meant 50 chips – 50 times 100 bucks.'

'I didn't.'

'Too bad.'

'I, Scott, um, how, oh God, I don't have it.'

'Well, I can think of a thousand ways to get it in this town.'

'I beg your pardon? This is ridiculous. How could you possibly have thought I meant 5,000 dollars? And how come you have that sort of money?'

'Mind your own jello, baby. What do you think this is, some sort of playground? You seemed to know what you were doing.'

'But I didn't! I was pretending because I didn't want the table to think I was a beginner.'

'Yeah? Well, you live and learn. Maybe next time you won't lap up the sauce like a kitten the way you did tonight. Geez.'

'Claudius.'

'Claudius? Who the fuck is he?'

'He's my patron. He'll have the money. I'll have to get it off him. He's back at my hotel waiting for me.'

'A patron? I know what ya sayin'. Ya see. I knew we could work this out. I'll come with you.'

'OK.'

We make our way towards the Luxor, after breaking through the little crowd that formed around us to hear our altercation. So glad they all think Claudius is a pimp too. What the fuck am I going to do when he realises Claudius is a cat and no more loaded than I'm Cleopatra?

At the lifts up to the rooms, I turn to him.

'Scott. Claudius would be very angry if he saw I'd spent the evening with someone else. Could you wait for me here?'

'I'll wait for you outside your room. Not down here.'

'But I might be some time. I'll have to do a lot of, um, talking, to get 5,000 off him.'

'I understand. I'll wait right here. If you ain't down in half an hour, I'm coming to get you, and believe me, I'll find you.'

'Scott, please calm down. I'll be down. Anyway, I'm in room 1713.'

I bomb it up to my room, kicking myself for having given him the right room number.

'Claude what am I going to do?' I wring my hands in worry.

'You have very little choice. Do you have $5,000?'

'Of course not. You know that.'

'Well then, there's only one thing to do.'

'And that is?'

'Run.'

'Run? But it's so dishonest.'

'OK, don't run. I'm sure he'll just let you go with an IOU.'

'Are you being sarky?'

Oh my God. After thinking with Claude, peeing and changing, I have only fifteen minutes left. I have to make a decision. I call the car valet, the bell boy and pack like lightning. I change again. I have to get out of here without being recognised. Just as I'm finishing, a knock at the door. Oh bloody hell. I open it and see nothing. Then I look down. There is Mr Nevada – I recognise him from his picture in *Cosmo*. A full head shorter than me and wearing a T-shirt that says 'I love animals. They taste great!'

'I got your message and thought I'd stop by.'

'Oh. Hi.'

'Good time?'

'Not as such, no. There's a nutter downstairs waiting to kill me.' I explain everything super-fast.

'One question. Why are you dressed as Cleopatra?'

'Because I'm terrified he's going to recognise me. Please help me get out of here. Come on, Claude.' Who gets up and jumps off the bed and starts in our direction, but his legs buckle under him. I run to him.

'Kitkat, what's wrong?'

He is terribly thin and looks weak and unsteady. My heart stops. I no longer give a shit about Scott and am stone-cold sober. I start to cry, causing great swathes of black liner to ooze down my face, like a treacle river. Knock at the door again. I'm about to have a heart attack.

The bell boy arrives and takes the bags. I carry Claudius downstairs in the lift, and try to be normal and unpanicky with Mr Nevada, who although diminutive is terribly good-looking. Everyone is staring at me. I don't know how good an idea this Cleopatra thing was – I seem to be attracting a lot more attention than I wanted. On the way out I pass Scott on his way in. Aaargh! He looks but is distracted by Claudius and so doesn't click.

'Well, if you ever come to town again and you're not on the run, I'd love to meet up properly,' says Mr Nevada, handing me Claudius as I edge the gold skirt into the driving seat.

'Me too. Thanks for your help. Sorry for being so weird. I'm not really like this,' I say as I screech the car out of there like wildfire.

We have to get to LA and a vet immediately. LA is six hours away and it's midnight. I'm exhausted, but Claudius is ill and that's all that matters. I'll have to think about what I've done later. Why didn't I listen to my instincts? Deep down, I knew something was wrong.

Chapter Eighteen

LA Story

Los Angeles, California

I drive fast through the night, propelled as I am by fear and a bubbling inner panic. We stop once at a gas station to call a friend, Kitty, in LA. She is not thrilled to be woken at 6am but invites us over nevertheless. To take his mind off his illness I introduce Claude to Hollywood mores.

'This is Hollywood. Where Clara Bow apparently took on the entire USC football team, where silent star Karl Dane, in penury, was forced to sell hot dogs outside the studio that had made him a star before the 'talkies', and where Peg Entwistle threw herself to her death from the 'H' of the Hollywood sign when her career took a turn for the worse.

'Most informative,' he says. 'But what about Arnie?'

Once in LA I get very lost. Other drivers honk and hurl abuse at me. Apparently my mother was a whore and I'm white trash. Fascinating. Hollywood is surprisingly grotty but I can't help but find it glamorous nevertheless. The roads are bumpy, uneven and ridden with holes. There are huge billboards lining Sunset Boulevard: 'Pamela's Back' screams one as Pam slides on her belly above the cars. The Marlboro man looms above the Chateau Marmont hotel, while on the opposite side of the road is an anti-smoking poster: a man smelling his girlfriend's hand, a fag in his other hand. 'Your scent is intoxicating!' he murmurs. 'Yours is carcinogenic,' she replies, one eyebrow raised.

The first thing Kitty says is: 'Why are you dressed as Cleopatra?'

'Don't even ask. You'd never believe it,' I say, climbing out of the gold skirt. 'I need a vet.'

There is one down the road. We rush there and after a long wait are ushered into a consulting room.

'Why can't he walk, doctor?'

'He's old.'

'But he could walk two days ago. In fact, a week ago he was chasing chipmunks in the Grand Canyon.'

'He's nineteen.'

'I know that. But as I say he was fine a few days ago. Do you think it has something to do with his kidneys?'

'We can take blood tests.'

Soon I hear Claudius howling and mewing with pain and rush to the door. Three men are manhandling him on to his back and sticking needles into him.

'What do you think you're doing?' I storm over.

'We're trying to get blood and urine samples. He's not co-operating.'

'Claudius is a very mellow cat and for him to make that noise you must be doing something horrid. Leave him alone.'

I take him out and set him down next to me. Stressed, he immediately pees all over the floor. They use this as the sample and relieve me of $100. I get the distinct impression that they're out to get as much money as possible before scratching the itch.

Angry I take him home. Claudius stumbles to the litter tray and then the sofa. I stay with him and wait for his blood results over the weekend. I give him liquids under his skin in the meantime. I also phone another vet for a second opinion. Kidney problems do not usually manifest themselves in the legs she tells me. 'Aspirin might help if it is arthritis, but be sure to give very small doses.'

How can I explain this sensation? I feel so low. I was looking forward to LA but if Claudius is ill life holds no joy for me. I have no confidence in the vets who all give different answers. And then charge so much. I have no home. I am exhausted. I am fed up. It breaks my heart to watch Claudius stumble around, he can't even climb on to the sofa, which he clearly wants to do. I put him outside the front door on the roof so he can at least sit in the sun. He closes his eyes in exhaustion and I put a glass of water next to him. He drinks half of it, clearly trying to flush himself out. I'm sure his kidneys are the problem.

We can't go on like this for ever. My master plan must be worked out. There is a way of getting home without subjecting Claudius to quarantine. I make a few calls, assess the risk factor, which is high, mull it over, hum and haw.

On Sunday night Kitty insists we go out to dinner for a couple of hours to take my mind off Claude. We eat at La Poubelle – which means 'the dustbin' in French but no one seems to know or care about this – and are joined by two girlfriends of Kitty's, Janice and Annie. Janice has rats-tailed mousey hair and a hint of dirt under her chewed chipped dark nails. When she smiles, dimples appear just under her eyes. Annie is very short, with tight corkscrew curls and twinkly blue eyes. She is a researcher for a TV show about sex. She regales us with stories of various titty shows she's been forced to sit through and weirdos who've made a recording career out of singing about butt sex. Kitty has a crush on one of the good-looking young stars in Hollywood, whom she recently interviewed. He called her the day he got in from Outtatown but hasn't called since. She is 'bastard bastard'ing under her breath and wondering what to do. 'Should I call him?' she asks.

'No,' I reply. 'At the end of the day playing games and

keeping your dignity is far more important than true love.'
From the woman who is only interested in co-dependent
love. With a cat.

'Let's face it,' I stick the knife in, 'if he liked you he'd
call,' and twist it a little. 'And if you have to make excuses
for him and help him out, why would you want to be with
him in the first place?'

So as we're on the subject of men we talk about how
many we have done it with. Annie, Kitty and I have the
usual conservative numbers for our age, but Janice as-
tounds us with her total. Seventy-seven. She is twenty-
four. We coo with fake admiration murmuring 'slut' under
our breath. The restaurant lives up to its name. The service
is appallingly slow. Janice insists on tipping 20 per cent.

'That's what the stars do,' she nods confidentially.

Monday morning I phone the vet for the blood results.
A high BUN (Blood Urea Nitrogen) for cats is 36. Claudius's is 180. His body is swimming in toxins. The doctor
says I could give Claude liquids under the skin twice a day,
but it would be better to put him into the hospital for a few
days so that he can receive liquids intravenously. Five
minutes later I drop him off. The doctor says I can visit
him whenever I want. I visit twice a day from then on, and
feed Claudius (who refuses to touch the vet's food) mushy
kitten food which he licks off a spoon. No more KFC ever.
Pure protein is death to the kidneys.

While Claudius is in hospital, I have the chance to sleep
at night because there is no litter tray scratching to wake
me, and yet I sleep badly because I miss him so much. I
miss the loud purring in my ear and the whisker-tickling at
seven in the morning.

Back at home, alone. Worry worry worry.
    Is he going to die? Pace pace pace.
    Try to top up the tan on Kate's sundeck.
    With what force will I hit the skids when Claude dies?

Which drugs and what drink shall I consume in order to dull the pain?

As quickly as I have decided on this course of action, I reject it. I decide to hold my head up Joan Crawford high. I stalk about the roof, my fists waving at the sun, at the forces and generally in the direction of any ethereal ectoplasmic goo that may be listening. 'Throw at me what you will, life,' I intone melodramatically. 'You'll never get me down permanently. I'll climb back up and be bigger and better than before. And then I'll give you a good kicking.' I collapse back on the deck chair, shattered, spent, sunburnt.

Fed up of ruminating, I leaf through the *Yellow Pages* today and just happen to come across: physicians, plastic and reconstructive surgery. Pages and pages follow, so I go for the most obvious name and make an appointment. Well, I have to cheer myself up somehow while Claude is away. I drive to Beverly Hills for my consultation with a, um, plastic surgeon. Well, I am in LA, right? As I pass into Beverly Hills, the dreadful Hollywood roads suddenly become smooth black tar drives, silky skeins of dark ribbon, soft as a babe's cheeks. Skyscraping palm trees on wide boulevards sway gently in the Giorgio-scented breeze. Palladian edifices next to Italian villas, next to English castles next to Tara mansions next to long sleek Marilyn-type bungalows vie for the Prix de Grandeur. Sleekly coiffed box hedges stand tall, but not so tall that the general public can't see how wealthy these folks are. Gates gently clank shut enclosing blue-striped uniformed maids sweeping the sweeping steps. A couple of brand-new cars in the drives: classic sports cars, Beemers, Porsches. And Hollywood is meant to be glamorous. Not a bit of it, compared to this. The shops make Bond Street look like Brick Lane. White, gold, marble, glass, row after row of designers and boutiques. Wilshire, Rodeo, and the Regent Beverly Wilshire where Julia hung out as the *Pretty Woman*.

Toni, with perfectly overmade-up face and very white teeth, greets me at the surgery. The waiting room is plushly chintzy with plumped-up cushions everywhere. I get shepherded by an over-smiling Korean girl into another waiting room. This one's mahogany.

A large photo album on the desk of befores and afters passes my time. Girls with pretty, interesting noses had had them transformed to a Barbie slight uplift thing. The doctor comes in.

'I'm looking at your tits,' I chime cheerily. Henceforth from his silent response I refer to them as 'breasts'. Quite a contrast to Ma's last stand with her surgeon in Harley Street. There they come in dressed in a suit and you talk. Here, in case you haven't fully clocked that he's a surgeon, he walks in dressed in full operational garb including a blue dishcloth wrapped around his head and plastic bag shoes on his feet. The nurse is dressed identically. He talks me through it all. Whenever I ask excited questions, he pretty much tells me to shut up, but in Californese: 'I just wish you to know the consequences', and, 'That is a good question which I will address in a moment. Now, if you would let me finish my sentence . . .' The first thing I have to do is go to a department store, find a bra the size I want and stuff it with socks to see what it would look like. The idea makes me giggle with embarrassed anticipation.

'No two things are the same size. No two things I have are the same size.' (Really doctor. I don't wish to know.) 'No two things you have are the same size. I can only make them bigger, not prettier. So you bring the bra back to me and then we have a meeting of the minds. Because your breasts are very small I would put the bag under the muscle.' He then pulls out a plastic bag small enough to be a paperweight and thick enough to be a hot-water bottle.

'That goes in my skin?'

'Yes.'

'Is there any, I mean –'

'Let me finish . . .'

'No, but, putting that sort of plastic in the body, is that um, healthy?'

Lack of sensitivity in the nipples is the very least of possible post-op complications – though of course none of his clients have ever experienced this. Other problems are as follows: the breasts could harden – we're not talking day-old chewed chewing gum consistency here, but *concrete* – infections, haematomas, blood under the skin, scarring, and decreased muscle strength in the forearm which apparently only a world-class tennis champion would notice. Oh and sloshy tits in planes. Air stewardesses have told him that sometimes under pressure air boobles get into the solution and pop and slosh about. His large specs loom at me. I find it all slightly creepy. He has to leave the room for a few moments so I turn to the nurse.

'Have you had anything done?'

'No but I've worked here for four years and he's good. I've seen his breasts.'

Then we start my examination. To my horror my nipples stand to attention when he looks at my tits, his cigarette-stained breath warming them slightly. I shout mentally to them: Get down, you fools. Down! Now! without much luck. He squeezes one of my poor little chests into a deformed ice cream cone shape to prove how much could be added to the skin to pump me up to a nice B cup.

Next I have a chat with Shelly to discuss dates.

'So if I go up to a B cup do you think I'll be able to get B-movie actors? Do I have to be C cup to date premier-league ones?'

She opens and closes her mouth like a fish for about a minute.

'We mean dates for surgery, dear.'

'Yes, only kidding. Have you had any surgery?' I ask her as she sits down. Silly question. This woman no longer has anything she was born with. Her nose is perfect. Her cheeks are blemish-free.

'What do you think?' she chirps. She is blonde in a beige trouser-suit, with a blonde pony tail and a beige stewardess hat perched on the back of her head. White capped teeth. 'I'm fifty-five,' she says. Even with perfect face and all the rest of it, she still looks fifty-five. There is something about being on this planet for fifty-five years that translates to the demeanour, and correcting the wrinkles doesn't change that. We then go through prices. Oh boy. £6,000. I say thanks I'll think about it. And I am thinking about it until it occurs to me that even if Cindy Crawford were to walk through the door, the doctor would probably find something wrong with her and suggest a nip and a tuck here and there. Maybe I should accept androgyny. Claude loves me as I am.

At the vet this morning, I stroke and cuddle him (Claude not the vet) but he is sulking big time. He's a sorry sight: he's been sleeping in his litter tray and his legs are covered in pee. But he's alive, and there is fight in his eyes so I feel a bit more positive. His arm is bandaged up with the needle in it. The paw beneath the bandage is five times the size of the other. It is a huge monstrous alien thing. I call the vet over who has a 'Leave me alone, woman' look on his face. He gets the assistant to undo the bandage. There are lots of other cats in the other cages, one of which is a one-eyed black kitten owned by an actress who has left him here permanently. He spends his life in the cage. He plays with Claudius's drip hanging down past his cage, so I call the vet over again. He gets the assistant to see to it. I am astounded by the lack of proper care. One of the assistants points out the lion cat to me. This is a large orange cat who has no fur other than a mane, leg warmers and a tuft on his tail.

'I've never seen one of those before. Is it a special breed?'

The assistants laugh. 'He is just a normal ginger cat but we shaved him so he looks like a lion.'

'Is that cruel?'

'No.'

I am not convinced.

Tonight I go out for a brief drink with a high-flying exec from Paramount Pictures, a friend of Jeremy's. 'He's devastating to look at,' says Jeremy, whom I call to cry to about Claudius's plight. I call John but his hectic schedule will only allow for next week. I beg. He agrees. I turn up at the Bar Marmont uncoolly early. I'm in a corset (cheaper than surgery), a pink micro dress, burgundy Voyage cardi, Joseph Azagury sling backs, which charmingly sling back every two or three minutes, leaving me to hook them back on in a *Georgy Girl* fashion.

John is great-looking in a clean-cut preppy way. We drink cocktails, he a Martini, me a – I'll let you guess, sounds like Margaret and Rita, and I start to get the ins and outs of the film business. Working in acquisitions, he has to find films to buy and distribute as well as read scripts to make. Once he and his boss (he's not quite as high-flying as Jeremy made out) have found something they like they have to make ten other departments agree with them. It's a surprise any films ever get made at all. They go to the film festivals and the swish parties, and John drives a red Porsche. His manners are impeccable – opening doors and lighting my fags.

We move on to the Sky Bar at the Mondrian. This is currently the swishest place in town. To get in you have to call, leave your name and affiliated company and if they like your voice they call you back. Luckily we sashay in, or John does and I hop in bent double, one hand trying to sling my foot back in its shoe, pulling the strap over my hardened yellow cheddar of a heel.

We enter via the back door, the servants' quarters really, and then come upon the most lovely open area, with candlelit tables and a large calm dark blue pool, wide white steps with cream cushions thrown on them and huge footstools that gorgeous guys and gels are reclining on. Not just any old riff raff, but *beautiful* people. Girls whose plastic surgery is so good you can't tell, their sleek hair and little black dresses flawless, air-brushed and air-kissed. *Très chic*. John and I down a few more cocktails and then leave for home. I have to get home because, erm, actually I have all night but John has a full day tomorrow. There's some sort of pool incident on the way out, but I can't remember it fully. Something about a girl standing on my toe, us having short if sharp words, me getting hold of her shoe, maybe the pool getting involved, a slight tussle with the doorman, her boyfriend prodding John, John frog-marching me to the car. It's a little hazy now, I can't remember it totally. ANYWAY. John hasn't called today.

Time to pick Claudius up from the vet. I am incredibly excited. When I walk in, the other cats have 'What a pampered poof' looks on their jealous faces. Claudius purrs and is very happy to see me. His paw has gone down a little but is not entirely its normal size. I pay a whopping bill of $200. Claudius feels soft and spongy, so he is not dehydrated any more. I take him home. I settle him inside the front door and he stiffly stealths towards the sofa – and bumps into it. His walking hasn't improved at all. He then turns around and walks in the other direction. When he gets to the wall he doesn't stop. I try putting him near his litter tray. He bangs into it before sniffing it and getting into it. I put him elsewhere and the same thing happens. I pick him up and look at him. His eyes are huge black saucers, not a sliver of green to be seen. A faceless futureless reality bangs my forehead and beats me hard enough to create its own chasm of despair.

Claudius is blind.

Claudius is blind.

Claudius is blind.

I phone the vet and explain that Claudius still cannot walk properly but is now blind as well.

'He may be diabetic. We should do some blood tests.'

'Haven't we just done some?'

'Yes, his creatinine levels are now down. You should give him liquids once a week.'

'But what about his walking and sight?'

'He's very old.'

'Do we have to go through this again?'

'It may be his potassium levels.'

'Why?'

'Or his electrolytes.'

'But wouldn't the blood tests have told you that? Are you playing a guessing game here?'

I slam the phone down and phone my vet in London, who is very sweet. His sight loss may be due to blood pressure, it may be the retina detaching from its wall. In any case he gives me the number of his best friend, who happens to live in LA. I immediately make an appointment to see Dr Shipp. I want one last go before taking drastic action.

What should I do? Should I put him down? He doesn't look to me as though he's had enough. Will I know when the time has come? I want to keep making him better.

While waiting for the appointment, I go to the Emmys with Kitty. And yet I don't go to them exactly. She is a journalist and stands in the press pens by the side of the red carpets, with thousands of others, trying to get the stars' attention as they go in to the hall, and I stand with her. We are both in full black tie under the pounding sun at three in the afternoon. I feel vaguely foolish. There is another pen across the way crammed with 'normal' people off the street who are here to cheer. The cameras focus on them and two girls in the front, waving both hands in frantic peace signs, scream 'woooo' in a high-pitched tone that makes all the dogs in the area run for cover. Soon the stars totter by us. It's extraordinary how perfect the woman are, with every hair in place, every bag of silicone nicely cantilevered, every lip line rouged in. Hair dyed, nails manicured, wearing someone else's diamonds.

We see Kelsey Grammar, Jamie Lee Curtis – incredible body – Jane Seymour, the guys from 'Frasier' and 'ER' and 'Seinfeld' and 'Larry Sanders'. Loveliest of them all, without fake anything, is Helena Bonham-Carter. I help Kitty with a few choice teasers: 'Oi Whitney! Over here, love!': but ultimately they all ignore us. Surely the highlight of the day has to be Donny and Marie, who are still toothy, albeit a little more wrinkled than when I watched them every Saturday night in my nightie in the 70s. The whole thing takes hours under the relentless sun. At the end the press are all horrid and competitive with each other. 'I got so much footage. You didn't? Oh I'm sorry. You could use mine, only none of my questions would be relevant for you. Oh I am sorry.'

Claude and I hit Dr Shipp's office. It is tucked away in a corner of Bev's Hills and looks like a ship with wooden beams across the walls. The place is full of friendly people talking to each other and referring to 'Tony', the technicians are laid-back, and the receptionists are pretty. Tony is tall, large and rugged. He looks at me and I look at him. He speaks plainly, tells me the truth in medical detail and doesn't charge a fortune. He doesn't give me any 'diabetes, electrolytes, potassium' bullshit. He says that the toxins from the kidney failure have affected things, that Claude has lost muscle tissue due to the high level of protein escaping in his pee, that he needs a dose of steroids to help him build up the muscle in his legs, that I should lay off KFC but feed him what he likes for the last weeks in his life (yup that's how he put it), that I should give him liquids under the skin every day if not twice a day. He then chucks in some liquids and needles for free. He finishes off by saying we should concentrate on the kidneys before the eyesight as there might not be anything to be done there. I am so relieved to find a proper vet finally that I feel like crying, but resort to flirting instead.

I take Claudius back home and make him as comfortable as possible while we wait for the steroids to work. He is very reliant on me because of his sight, so I make sure he is near his litter tray, food and water at all times. If he goes for a walk I go with him to prevent painful nose bumps. I don't know where we're at. I don't know whether these are the last stages, and like Ma he'll start going downhill very fast, or whether he is just acting his age now. The fact is he is blind. I have to think hard about the quality of his life, especially for someone with as much independence and curiosity as he. Not being able to explore could be very frustrating. I know he is not in any pain, and he does not seem at all discontented. It may just be a shift of lifestyle for both of us, but I have to make very sure that his life is enjoyable. This calls for an extremely clear head.

Tonight I leave Claudius sleeping on the sofa, with his things right next to him. I've given him his liquids under the skin and he has had a bite to eat. I have to get out and have some liquid relief myself.

It is Janice's twenty-fifth birthday. We all dress up. Janice can't decide what to wear. She holds up a tight black dress and a tight black skirt with see-through flimsy grey top. The skirt takes one look at her arse and screams at the seams, 'I'll never make it. Please, please don't make me.' It starts climbing up the walls of her bedroom. 'I think I'll pick . . . eyuw . . . this one.' She takes the hapless black skirt into the bathroom. Finally we set off for Lucky Seven, a jazz club, for dinner. We have a table right at the front and are joined by two of Janice's girlfriends. Sandy has thick black plaits like a squaw, black eyes and pale skin, Michelle is half Asian, with sleek shoulder-length golden brown hair. Very exotic. Not a stitch of make-up and very sexy.

Jeff Goldblum is playing the keyboards with his band tonight and just before he starts he comes over and sits down right opposite me. Me! And then starts to kiss Michelle. Passionately. I try not to look impressed or stare. When they have disengaged tongues he shakes my hand – and then everyone else's around the table. When he returns to the keyboards, I question Michelle closely. Her ex-boyfriends include Christian Slater and Griffin Dunne. She met Griffin on a plane, Christian at the Oscars and Jeff at the Oscars as well. She was the girl Christian went to prison over. He punched her in the face. Sandy leans over and starts talking about a role she has just landed in an independent film (movie).

'So, like, the first scene you see me get out of this car and I'm wiping my mouth because I've just given the lead a blow job. And I'm a junkie and he says I don't have any dope for you, so I'm like no? OK can I have a go on your skateboard instead of money? And he says yes so I take the skateboard and whizz around on it so I'm really good at it and they're all watching –'

'– So you have to learn to skateboard?'

'– yuh but I'm great at roller-blading and snow-board-ing so it'll be OK, anyway so then when I come back and give him the skateboard back, and I've been really good and elegant on it, and then as I turn to go he stops and looks at me and then he hugs me and it's like a really emotional moment and you see they've connected. Really it's a character I can take anywhere, anyway I want. It's really cool.'

'Yeah, really cool.'

'So where you next headed?'

'Up the coast to San Francisco.'

'Oh you must meet my friend Chase, he's on his way up there too. He's totally cool. Very smart. Hot. Just so gorgeous, it's like unbelievable. Take his number.'

Jeff walks over and sits down next to Michelle and they start kissing again. I'm all nonchalant and coolly flick my cigarette on the floor. I turn to Kitty on my other side to chat when we smell something rancid and I turn to see my favourite little tote bag in flames. What I had mistaken for the floor in terms of my cigarette's demise had in fact been my handbag. A little scuffling and throwing of champagne on to the rising smoke soon puts an end to it, and I don't think I look too much of a fool in Jeff's eyes. Actually his eyes are turned and looking into Michelle's until I accidentally throw champagne on his feet in my attempt to quell the flames. He's charming about it. 'No, go ahead, really. I love having wet feet. They keep me cool while I'm playing.'

One of the reasons we had chosen this place was the excess of deeply sexy men to be found after 10.30pm most nights. Of course the night I choose they have decided to hang out at Whiskey Go-Go or somewhere. I scan the room and there is no one fuckable for a ten-mile radius. No matter. There's one boy I take a shine to: Charlie, a friend of Janice's unimpressive boyfriend. ('I dare you to take him aside and say do you realise that you're number 78?' I whisper to Kitty 'If you do, I'll give you a whole dollar.') Charlie is a Tom Cruise lookalike. I start to chat him up:

'If you flick ash in my bag I'll punch you.'

' 'Scuse me?'

'Don't worry, I've just been drinking. I always like a little fight when squiffy.'

'But I'm a really nice guy.'

'Oh good, then you'll be a pushover.' No reaction. Kitty budges me with her hips as she plonks herself on the couch.

'Move up. Or can I sit on your lap?'

'You can sit on my face if you pay me enough.'

Charles walks away.

'What did I say?'

Kitty shrugs. 'Nothing attractive anyway,' she whispers.

Claudius woke me up this morning with the delicious sound of his jaws chomping away on his food. Which means the steroids are working. He is perky and very affectionate. When I got up I positioned him in a sunspot on the roof and he purred until he fell asleep. Oh my God I can't believe it. Truly he is the world's greatest kitkat.

Four of us, Kitty, Annie, Dom (Annie's boyfriend) and I, go to Molly Malone's where we down several beers and listen to a girl that looks and sounds like Sheryl Crow, and then to a couple who are so adenoidal they might as well be singing through their noses. We move on to the Smog Cutter, a small bar run by a Korean family in downtown Hollywood. A mixed crowd of old Koreans drink alongside young beautiful model types – because of the karaoke. Oh yes. We then sit down to enjoy the bizarre combination of very good singers – a roly big-haired woman singing her fantastic version of 'Bobby McGee' – juxtaposed with embarrassed couples – yuppies singing 'Summer Nights' looking unsure and pretending they can't read the words – followed by a gay couple singing 'Freeze Frame', and finally Dom, singing 'Green Green Grass of Home' too quietly, forcing us to holler 'louder' from our drunken corner. More and more people take the microphone but for about half an hour I'm uncharacteristically quiet, looking for the closest exit – because my turn approaches. I rack my brains wondering how to sing and ruin my throat with chained cigarettes. Why do I feel obliged to put myself through this sort of thing every time the challenge presents itself? I wish I were dead. Then the old guy putting on the records calls my name. I go up ashen and almost in tears, but soon snap out of it knowing this is no way to win the audience over. Luckily I have chosen my current favourite, 'Viva Las Vegas', which gets me going the second the music starts. The first few words are a little strange as I hit the wrong register and start in the K key. I hiccup and swallow with fear. The good news is that I can't hear the song without starting to dance, and soon enough my Elvis impression is in full swing. The karate kicks go down well, as I'm wearing my new tight bronze trousers and high wedge shoes. The bad news is I position my foot badly, fall over, and scatter beer and pretzels from the nearest table to the high winds. Actually this goes down a treat and I see several groups double up with howling laughter. I then forget an entire verse, even though the words are actually in front of me, and my dancing has had to simmer down a little because of the split up my arse the fall occasioned. Nevertheless the clapping is hearty at the end and several people are wiping away tears but, hey, that's show business. I presume they're laughing with me and not at me, though it is impossible to tell at this stage. I would say from an objectively unbiased critical viewpoint that the performance is not the best the Smog Cutter has ever seen and yet I am floating on a Cloud Nine high. I can climb Mount Everest, Compete in Ice Skating Championships, Get a Boyfriend (er no), Cook a Soufflé, You Name It Baybee. As we stagger out at two in the morning, I hijack a good-looking Austrian, get his number and an invitation to his party the following night.

'I've scored!' I roar in Kitty's face who replies, 'Shhh, he's right behind you. Get in the taxi.'

Claudius walked around this morning as though nothing had ever been wrong. His legs have built up some muscle and he can even climb up and down from the sofa once he's sure it's the sofa he's about to climb on to. As he can't see I don't know how he knows this but know it he does. I am thrilled and in the most buoyant fantastic mood. To celebrate I hit Chinatown, seemingly on the edge of the earth but actually at the end of Sunset Boulevard. I buy a dress a full size too small because I refuse to acknowledge that it doesn't fit. The rest of the afternoon, I cuddle Claude on the sunroof.

Kitty and I are very hungover from yesterday but agree to go to the Austrian's party for just one hour. Somewhere in Hollywood, three apartments have been cleared so as to resemble studios. Marko (the Austrian)'s work (three paintings of random colours swished about) doesn't appeal to me, but he is very sweet and not bad-looking, so I want to encourage him.

'I like these,' I say pointing to a setup of white boxes with lights directed on them.

'They're for sitting on,' he says.

'Good-oh,' I trumpet, feeling faintly foolish. Marko is skinny with almond-shaped eyes, a head slightly on the Tefal side and breath so drenched in old and new alcohol it could jump-start you from a coma. I carry on staring at his art-splattered screens, hoping that my quiet and slow mood makes me seem rather cool and aloof.

'You seem quiet and slow tonight.' He puts a hand on my arm. 'Are you all right?'

'Oh yes, thanks.' That's when our conversation runs out.

The main party is swinging outside at the back, so we hit it. There are several interesting-looking guys, lots of artists and Europeans. One of the garages is open, pretending to be a Little Austria gift shop, with pictures of cows on flags etc. I look up and there is Ermintrude staring at me from the roof.

'Kitty.'

'Yes.'

'There seems to be a cow on the roof.'

'Did you mix your headache pills up with Claude's antibiotics again?'

'No. There is simply a cow on the roof.'

And indeed there is. It is one of the artist's installations. Fred, the bull, as he turns out to be, has in fact been in several films and milk commercials and is quite used to this sort of thing and no he doesn't feel lonely standing up there on the roof grass (an entire lawn has been installed for his comfort) staring down at us silly humans staring up at him. We leave early, but can't find Marko. Back at home I find Claudius plumped in front of the telly, sixth-sensing a programme about Power Preachers. 'Did you know,' he starts, 'that there exists a group of huge body-building preachers who entice their congregation into the House of God by performing such stunts as breaking ten rows of bricks with their heads before preaching about strength on the inside as well as the out?'

This morning I call Marko to say thank you and leave our number for him. His answer machine does a *Swingers* on me and cuts me off while I'm talking. I call back a couple of times. Eventually I give up but not before embarrassment has made me clench and unclench my buttocks several times.

Claudius continues to recover. He's eating more and has put on some weight. He even seems to sense things with his whiskers, so although he can't see, he can get around. I can't believe it. He tells me he feels well enough to move on when I'm ready.

I'm ready. I think. I feel exhausted. I'm still motoring and yet have the distinct impression that I have already lost the race.

Chapter Nineteen

An Affair to Remember

Santa Barbara – San Luis Obispo – Monterey – Palo Alto – San Francisco, California

After arranging to meet Sandy's friend Chase in San Luis Obispo at the Madonna Inn, Claude and I set off up Highway 1, our first destination Santa Barbara, our ultimate destination San Francisco. Tomorrow we are finally going to meet Monty Roberts, the real Horse Whisperer.

'Why?' asks Claude.

'Well . . . because . . . we're near his farm, and because . . . he talks to horses.'

'The further west we've moved the loonier people get. From Texas onwards everyone has been wacko.'

'What about New York, Claude?'

'Well, yes, it all tends to hang out there too.'

'And Oxford, Mississippi wasn't rigid with rules.'

'No. Nor for that matter was New Orleans totally on the straight and narrow. In fact America is full of nutters doing their own thing. But a man who talks to horses. Honestly!'

Back to grotty motels. I switch on the telly. Claude can't see the screen but he positions his body in that direction anyway and lies, a thick warm mocha tube, against my legs. We try to watch a film but the ads, which interrupt every five minutes, make me want to murder someone. Sleep, ah sleep.

*   *   *

Today is the day. We set off bright and early, and Claudius settles on my lap for the short drive to Monty Roberts's farm. The white adobe walls are covered in blood-red roses, and black clean letters announce 'Flag Is Up Farms'. Driving in we are hit by a delicious, warm, manurey horse smell. Claudius sticks his nose high in the air as he recalls the sweet pungence of the cowboys. About 150 horses are stabled here. Some are trained in the special round pen watched by the managers from a raised plank. Others are raced on the track at the further end of the farms. The rest stay in row upon row of immaculate stables. I am horribly excited but clearly not the first person here. There's a pretty woman manning the visitor's booth, selling books, videos and T-shirts of the great man.

'Hello. I've come to see Monty Roberts.'

'You can't. He's in Germany. Oh what a sweet kitty.'

'He's where?'

My heart is sinking so fast I put the *Titanic* to shame. She explains that he is only at his farm about three days a month and those three days are preciously guarded by his workers. I can't believe how stupid I've been, thinking I could just swan in and chat for hours on end like old buddies. I wander around listlessly for about half an hour waiting for the disappointment to subside, but it refuses to. Claudius is sniffing and chewing the neatly manicured grass, his day not even slightly affected by this major fuck-up. I watch his reaction and think I'll do just the same. So what if Monty isn't here? We amble off to see the stallions. Eventually I move on, having spoken to everyone in the stables but Monty himself.

Further on at San Luis Obispo I check into the Madonna Inn to find there are no messages for me. Chase is obviously standing me up. This pink-fenced white palace is the work of an entrepreneur, Alex Madonna, and his wife, Phyllis. The building is a white turreted number, with 100 rooms each decorated in a different way, 'so as not to make the same mistake twice': the Caveman Room has walls, ceiling and floor of solid rock. The Austrian Suite has Prussian-blue carpets and flowery wallpaper offset by ornate gold-framed mirrors, crystal chandeliers and white rococo furniture. The Jungle Rock room has a waterfall shower and zebra fur bedspreads.

Our room, Carin, at the top of white wooden spiral stairs, is also draped in pink.

'What's it like?' asks Claude.

'Where shall I begin? The leather armchairs are baby-pink, there's a huge gold cherub hanging above the bed with a set of candles in its hand, the bed itself is enormous, there are four gold-framed mirrors and two balconies covered in astroturf. The bathroom has pink embroidered roses on the wall and mirrors surrounded by entwined roses. Even the basins are covered in baby-pink Elizabethan rose patterns, topped by two huge Louis XIV fake gilt mirrors.'

'So Liberace wouldn't feel uncomfortable here then?'

'Not exactly, no.'

He checks out the bed while I settle myself in one of the pink leather booths in the dining room for a steak and chips dinner. It's as though Hansel and Gretel are at home or the twelve dancing princesses are about to come leaping out. The floor is carpeted in huge pink roses, and a thirty-foot gold and fairy-lit rose tree is the central attraction. It is in fact made of electrical conduit, scrap copper and spare diesel-fuel tubing. The Madonnas chose pink as their main colour because 'it's real flattering for women'. Even the sugar is pink. I may be simpering in the glorious glow of friendly fuchsia but on the inside things are rottingly dervish. I missed Monty Roberts, I'm exhausted and depleted and Claudius is blind. I'm a fucking failure.

A leaflet on the inn is my dinner companion. There is a long detailed blurb about Alex Madonna and then Phyllis is introduced as 'attractive, articulate and quietly self-assured'. I'm glad she's pretty and quiet. Best that way. There is an open valentine from she to he, celebrating his classic rags-to-riches story. The couple are central figures in the community. He erected a cross on the nearby hill which is a beacon of hope and joy to those who see it. It is anxiously watched by old ladies seeking a Christmas greeting when it is lit up in the holidays and a crippled young man swore that one day he would walk up the hill to that cross. And he did. Ahhh. These tales of peace, prosperity and good will can't soften my bitter heart. When hatred is the juice in the engine, the pupils turn to blood.

On the way back to my room I get extra cat food out of the car, drop it all over the road and end up retrieving tins from under the car.

'Hi.'

From where I am I can only see shoes and jeaned legs. I struggle out to find a tall bald guy, the spitting image of Richard Gere, with a devastating smile before me. Jackpot.

'Hi. I'm Clare.'

'Clare?'

'Yes.'

'I'm Chase, Sandy's friend.'

'Oh! Fantastic, I thought you weren't coming.'

'Sorry, I missed the bus.'

'Did you get a room?'

'Yes.' He smiles. 'Shall we go to the bar?'

'Absolutely. Let me just feed my cat.'

Chase and I converse easily in Traveller Talk, exchanging vital facts fast: what we're doing where we're going how long for where we're from. He lives in Detroit, has a whippet that he adores, a degree in English and has been travelling in the Far East. His trip has clearly been very different from mine. He paced himself as though for a marathon and has not returned a shivering shadow of his former self. He used to live in San Francisco and is going to meet friends there. He asks about my family and wants to know all about my mother. I tell him and he talks about his father who also died a few years back. We are the last in the bar when I offer him a lift up the coast with me. I return to Claudius, who is sniffing his way towards his litter tray on the bed. Sounds strange I know but flexibility is the name of the game here.

Feeling buoyed up and cheerful at the thought of this stranger's presence I check out the ladies' gift shop which has an astounding fake fur coat with my name written all over it. Sadly the lining has my bank manager's name also inscribed so I do not buy it. It's the first time I've ever exercised any self-control in the retail-therapy department and I am impressed, if depressed.

This morning Chase, Claudius and I take Highway 1 up the coast. It's a winding pretty road, climbing through hills and dales with tall waving grasses, occasionally revealing the vast expanse of Pacific Ocean to our left. The Californian sun metes out a kindly golden light that hides the wrinkles formerly etched into my forehead (like Braveheart's battle scars) by the less flattering Mississippian and Texan suns. We might almost be in the Mediterranean except an intangible grandeur of sea and sky reminds us that we are far, far from home. Claudius sniffs the sea air and we stop at one of the many roadside beaches.

'Cats don't like an unenclosed environment unless it's their own,' says Chase emphatically.

'Most cats maybe. But Claudius is different.'

'Leave him in the car, he won't like it.'

'After nineteen years of his company I'm pretty sure of what he likes and dislikes. Watch this.'

I carry him to the deserted beach, wishing he had his sight. I have always wanted him to be on the beach and here we are but he can't see the sea. His nose is working overtime however, smelling the sun and sea and sand. I dig him a basket-sized hole and pour in sun-warmed grains on the damper patches. I put Claude in there to protect him from the wind. He settles down smiling, occasionally raising his nose when a new scent tries to skim past. Chase looks at him in wonder while I run to flirt with the sea, wading in and then nipping out as the waves come to get me. Finally I dive under them, while they snatch powerfully at my legs in an attempt to drag me their way. I wade and push forward to reach a place where I can no longer touch the bottom. The side current is strong and I crawl against it. I look back to land. It occurs to me that Chase could easily pick up my keys and leave Kitkat and me stranded here for good. But he is lying on his back looking at the blue sky. Two brown foxy points sticking up above the sand are all I can see of Claudius. I push on until I am far out.

'Come back! Get back!' shouts Chase, a stick man from the sand. I turn about and swim to him. I make no progress at all. I push harder, think stronger, and still make no progress. Fear snaps at my heels and I carry on, banishing fatigue to the margins of my core, though I hear it creeping back when I'm not looking. I look back and see a wave approaching that might excite the Beach Boys, but that scares the shit out of me. It occurs to me that if it breaks on me I might drown as I can't touch the bottom. It races until its greenly glassy rockabilly quiff is curling orgasmically behind me. It sweeps me to its crest and breaks as I float along with it. I strain my head up to the sky but as I do, my legs go down and are caught in the combine wheels of undertow. I flip down and a mighty force keeps me there. I try to break free but I'm a flick of dust in this tornado. I'm bound in chains of water and sand and foam. My breath reserve has run out and I must breathe. Sand and shells are raping through my fanny and hair and nostrils. I roll on to the beach and lie a while gasping. Chase runs forward.

'Jesus Christ. Are you all right?'

'Yes. I'm fine.' I get up, totter slightly, readjust the red stripy triangles to cover my nipples and pull the blue stars from between my cheeks. I criss-cross up the beach to fall down next to Claude.

'Well my duck,' he purrs. 'What a to-do.'

'Yes, kitten.' I pick him up and hug him close and sob into his fur.

'I'd rather you didn't blow your nose on me,' he purrs, not unkindly. I sprawl like a starfish under the sun, staring at the sky and wondering why.

I'm calm. I'm cooked. We drive on to Monterey and book into the Casa Munras Garden Hotel, a sweet place, clean, simple, comfortable. Claudius stays in to sleep but Chase and I walk across the road to Margie's Diner and polish off huge plates of gravy and biscuits and burgers. We discuss the next couple of days. We could stay in town to go whale-watching but he wants to get on to San Francisco, and I agree. Something is pulling me there with a Jedi-like force. It is chilly as we walk back to the hotel so in one movement he takes off his jacket and swings it across my shoulders like a bull fighter. His looks are mesmerising. We return to the hotel.

We drive on to San Francisco and after much back-doubling and umming and ahhing we book into a cheap place. Chase does not have much cash on him so I pay for it on my credit card. Our room is disgusting, with thin torn dirty curtains, the sheets are hairy and stained. There is a communal bathroom whose loos contain copious amounts of shit and *blood*. I think *peut-être non* to myself. After more indecision, Chase tries some friends of his in the city but can't get hold of anyone and has lost most of their numbers. It's getting late and I want to settle Claude so I agree to stay with his cousin an hour south of San

Francisco. Even though I have made it to my end destination, we are already back on the road again heading out of the city in the direction we came in. Irritation. I'm not entirely sure why I'm relying on the kindness of strangers.

'How do you feel?' Chase keeps asking and I do that thing that women do. I blame my angst on deep inner emotions of sadness at the end of the trip. The reality, however, is that I'm pissed off he didn't try to save me when I was drowning, and I'm pissed off that I wanted saving in the first place. I also feel guilty about Claudius being in the car all day and know that I could have sorted us out much sooner.

'Upset that I almost drowned.'

'I'm sorry. I can't swim.' He smiles sadly and holds my hand. I smile back, happy to feel close again. I wonder how he kisses.

His cousin lives in suburbia and I am grateful to have a place to rest my head. I am so tired I am now running on neurotic, eye-pricking energy. His cousin is extremely sweet and hospitable, offering me drinks and cigarettes. He even talks about the weather – I think Americans actually do this more than the Brits. 'Well at least we're not on the bay here. As Mark Twain said: "There's only one thing colder than a San Francisco winter and that's a San Francisco summer." '

This morning Claudius and I poke around the garden while Chase cooks us breakfast. Claude gets around all right, almost entirely by sense, and seems to be having a pleasant time. While eating, our conversation is somewhat one-sided as Chase loves to talk, slowly, emphatically, crossing every t, dotting every i, lecturing almost. He talks for an hour about Japan during the war. I am yearning to look around San Francisco but Chase can't quite get his act together, so after a few hours in the house doing nothing, we finally set off in search of a pair of shoes for him in Palo Alto, a town south of San Fran. We enter Bloomingdales. He doesn't realise that I have hit every other Bloomies between New York and here, but I try to act interested anyway. He picks up a carrier from the cosmetics section. 'I want to look at the kitchenware,' he says, heading in that direction. As he passes the knives, he deftly slips two packets of Kitchen Devils into the bag and without stopping heads on up to the counter.

'What are you doing?' I whisper.

'Buying shoes,' he whispers back. 'Hello, Joan,' he reads the button on the sales girl's blouse. 'I'm Chase.' He holds out his hand to her and she shakes it, taken aback by the friendly personal approach which she is meant to adopt. 'How are you today?'

'I'm fine, thank you. Is there something I can help you with?'

'Yes. My mom gave me these for my birthday.' He whips out the knives. 'And I don't really like them. My girlfriend here' (hello? is that *moi*?) 'thinks I should swap them for a pair of shoes, but I think I want that Le Creuset set you have over there. What do you think?'

'Oh, when was your birthday?' she sings along.

'In July but I was away travelling.'

'Well how nice, where were you?'

'I was in Jamaica and Costa Rica.'

'Oh how wonderful. Well now, we need your driver's licence to do this.'

'I don't have my licence. Clare? Could I have yours?'

'Sure,' I say, reaching into my bag. 'Do you know what? I don't have it on me,' I lie, realising that I'm about to involve myself in the theft. I walk out to the car.

Half an hour later he walks out in a pair of new shoes.

'I spent $160 on my shoes,' he says. 'There's $90 left if you want to buy something.'

'Thanks.' I swallow drily. 'I'm OK.'

Back at his cousin's, I check on Claudius who is silent and looks away. Clearly not in the mood for a chat.

Today I want to go sightseeing but Chase wanders around the house listlessly, making calls and smoking cigarettes until well into the afternoon. I'm the one with the car and yet I can't get up the energy to leave. When we finally do, instead of directing me into town he leads me to a nursing home in Redwood City. 'I want to visit my grandmom,' he says without warning. She is ninety-five and the sweetest old woman who has clearly spent her entire life smiling. 'Hello dear,' she beams at me through whitened unseeing eyes, her teeth falling down almost into her handbag. Chase cuddles her and talks to her for a whole minute before using her phone to call various friends. I hang around her room smelling old woman smells, trying not to be depressed at her weakened dying state and chatting with her, but she is tired, so I wander out to the balcony for a cigarette. Chase is talking in a very intimate flirty fashion to someone at the other end of the line. I wonder where the day has gone.

Today Chase has chores to do – he wants to get his motorcycle licence – and needs a lift into town. I still want to get out there and see the city but he swears the test will not take more than half an hour and then he'll show me all the best untouristy parts. We go to the Department of Motor Vehicles and stand on line. He strikes up conversations with everyone around. His looks excite people at first but a forced eagerness in his manner scares them and eventually they turn their heads away. Time ticks on. Whenever I suggest meeting him later so that I can explore, he looks exasperated and says, 'I'll just be five more minutes. Can't you think of anyone but yourself?' Four hours later we are out of there. I have this inescapable feeling that my day has been pissed away again, through my own weakness and desire for company.

He thinks we should test out his skills and hire a scooter. At the scooter shop he tells me he has no credit card so can we use mine? The deposit is $600. I know I don't have the money in my account as my budget is running low. I mention this and he accuses me of being tight.

'It's not that. It's just that I don't have the money and I think it is going to jam my credit card.'

'Of course it won't. Don't be ridiculous. For God's sake, you're staying free at my cousin's and all you can do is bitch about money. Don't worry, it'll be fine.'

'Chase, I am not bitching, I am telling you a fact. I don't have the money to do this.'

In the end I hand over the credit card because I haven't the energy to fight.

We whizz around the city for an hour. It's a pretty place with exceptional houses in the rich areas – appropriately named Nob Hill and Pacific Heights. We drive to Fisherman's Wharf and Ghirardelli Square. We walk out on to the pier, watch the boats leaving for Alcatraz, and look back at the overgrown, sleepy, Mediterranean city near the sea, its hills in the distance. It's the least American-looking city I have yet seen: there aren't masses of steel-mirrored columns of sky-scrapers. As the sun sets, we watch the sea-lions baying, barking and flubbering about on Pier 39, sliding into the water and heaving themselves out. After the earthquake of 1989 about fifty sea-lions visited the Pier. Then when the San Franciscans made it a protected area, their numbers quickly grew to over 600. On the way back, a huge yellow moon hangs low, lower than the hills it seems, over the city.

Chase drops me outside a nearby restaurant saying he'll return in five minutes. Because of its location on the bay, fogs blow in at the drop of a hat. One has just come in to find me in a summer get-up. It is freezing cold but I am excited about a romantic dinner.

An hour later and I am somewhat less bouncy. When Chase arrives, he does not apologise for his tardiness and flirts with the waitress until I feel like knocking their heads together. He pays for dinner but then complains about it. Afterwards we have sex in the car. I'm terrified someone will see us and am convinced that this is the sort of thing the average American would like us to be thrown in jail for. Still, he knows what he's doing, which is fantastic, though I'd have preferred a more intimate setting for our first romantic encounter.

Chase wants to show me around some more so he decides we should see his old campus at Berkeley. He shows me the long boulevard leveraged with stairs that he used to roller-blade down, very straight and fast. We wander into the lecture halls. He tells me the names of the professors and where he sat. He then locks the doors, shuts the shutters and turns off the lights. A little lecture series perhaps? Or just a simple murder? Nope, it's sex again. This excites me but scares me at the same time. I would hate to be caught in this most intriguing and slightly uncomfortable position by any of those aforementioned professors. In these situations it's not a case of a quick and exciting fuck, oh no. Chase takes his time, as in the car last night. No rushing for him. I have to bite my tongue not to scream from fear of being caught. When we're both done and dusted we go for a latte (lahtay) at one of the campus coffee shops. I am beginning to think what a nice boyfriend I have, before I stop short in my tracks and realise what position he has been elevated to in my head. Just because he's in control. Dear me how silly girls can be.

We drive back into the city to eat very hot Chinese food at a tiny white bare kitchen-like place in Chinatown. We then wander around looking at the sex shops. As girls in platforms only Gary Glitter would consider wearing totter along beside us, trying to look happy, we start arguing about Catholicism. He batters his points home regardless of their truth or accuracy. I expend large amounts of energy on arguing points I know he will never concede. The shop we go into has every form of dildo, some in horrific sizes, dick key rings, fucky mugs, lezzy vids, mags, blow-up dolls (blow-up dolls with realistic vaginas! the box yells delightedly) and right at the back are the video booths, with signs asking you to please leave the place clean for the next person. We go in and start feeding quarters into the machine to watch some really nasty filth, and then wouldn't you know it but we're at it ourselves again. The naughty rebellious feeling has passed and I am now slightly fed up of sex in public places. Well at least the door locks here and we are vaguely alone, even if there are large gaps under and above the walls.

I lie awake thinking all night. I can't sleep because Chase throws his arms in my direction every half-hour and Claudius needs help to find his litter tray and food and water now and then. By morning I am half mad.

I feel this increasing anger towards Chase. Things don't feel right. We have spent every moment together in the last few days, but I never feel connected, even – or rather especially – when we're having sex. It would be great if life were a film and at the end of my road trip I met the love of my life but this ain't no movie, baby. I'm too old to let daydreams of love trip me up again. I want looking after because I'm tired, yes, but that's not what life is about, is it? I don't understand how I let this happen to me. Maybe the fatigue, maybe the loneliness. Whatever. It has to stop.

When he wakes I tell him, kindly, that it would be best if I go back to what I am used to, taking care of and being by myself, and plan to leave for San Fran at 11.30am so that I can have a full day of it. Fine, he says, but could he have a lift into the city? Sure. Why not? Why be churlish about this? I take a shower and check up on Claudius who is sleeping off the night's activities. Downstairs Chase is on the phone chatting with a friend. He hangs up at 11.20am so I start calling around to find somewhere to stay. I have no idea where to go so he suggests the Mansions Hotel. I organise a room there. I need some time to myself to think.

'Could you do me a favour? Could you help me pack our things and clean the room so that we leave on time?'

'I need to talk with my cousin.'

'Right now? You've had four days.'

'You do it.'

I storm upstairs, pack his and my things, throw them in the car and clean the room. I thank his cousin and start backing out of the drive. Reluctantly he joins me; I'm driving and if he wants a lift to town he has to come NOW. Three miles down the road he asks me to pull over. He starts to rummage in the boot looking for his book. I slam on the horn. Three miles further down the road he asks me to pull over. He wants to hitchhike back to his cousin's, because he has forgotten his personal organiser. I need directions into the city. I have no idea where I am. He starts to draw a map and then huffs back into the car. As we move along it turns out he has his organiser on him after all. What am I doing? How have I found myself in this gritty relationship? I hardly know the guy. Clearly my mind has been kidnapped by aliens. We get into the city and I park the car in the Haight-Ashbury area. I mean to meander with Claudius but Chase is behind me, criticising me in a quiet voice, and I am feeling more and more fragmented. I stop and say:

'OK. I'm off to have a little time on my own in the city.' I carry Claudius in my arms as it's too cold to leave him in the car.

'Hey hold on. Let's have some lunch.'

'Actually I'd quite like a little time on my own.'

'Let's discuss this. I want a soda.'

As he stops to buy one, I run, just run, turn a corner and slip into the first place I can. It is a hippie haven, a hotel with an art gallery at the front, the Red Victorian Inn. The nice Madame Macarthy figure at the front desk can see I am flustered. She introduces herself as Sami Sunchild, the owner. Her soft white hair in a chignon, long flowing clothes, calm light-blue eyes and long fake mother-of-pearl beads tied in a knot at her waist remind me of my grandmother.

'Why don't you take some time to recover yourself?' She smiles sweetly. 'You can look at some of my art in the Meditative Gallery and you can read my newsletter.'

I try the former, large peace signs in various bright colourful combinations, and then the latter, a poem en-titled 'After', with lines such as 'After my best friend left, After my dog was stolen, After a diagnosis of breast cancer, After taking control of my body and disappearing the cancer without use of prescribed surgery or chemother-apy . . .' and then a list of the disasters she went through to get the hotel up and running: 'After a two-year wait for a court date to recover my title, After the receiver lost money each month, After three weeks of courtroom attack', with tiny letters at the end: 'much abbreviated'. I find her list exhausting, even though it is meant to signify that she kept going and didn't give up her 'dream of creating an eco-friendly peace network for travellers'. Under the poem is a picture of her clasping a globe.

Claudius has curled up on a chair to sleep, so I look around the hotel. As it commemorates 1967's Summer of Love everything is suitably wacky. The rooms are all decorated after one heebyjeeby theme or another: the Teddy Bear room, the Flower Child room, etc. The Peace Center downstairs is where everyone gathers for breakfast – one of the tables has a loo as a seat. One of the bath-rooms has goldfish in the tank. I ask Sami what happens when it flushes.

'I'm not telling,' she replies in her quiet whispery voice. 'It's more fun to live in the question.'

Right.

'What star sign are you?'

'I don't want to be pre-pegged, I want to be experienced . . .'

'Is Sunchild your real name?'

'Yes it is. First I bore my father's name and then my husband's and then I created one of my very own.'

Sami spies Claude and then eyes him distrustfully.

'Now, did you have to bring your cat in here?'

'Well, it's very cold in the car and I have nowhere else to put him.'

'Well that is not my problem. Now I want to be sympathetic and loving, but this really isn't my problem.'

It's at this tense moment that Chase walks up.

'Hello. How . . . where . . . ?'

'I've been looking at the art here.'

'For how long?'

'About thirty minutes.'

'Well. I feel violated.' I'm getting into Californese.

'Why?'

'Because I told you I wanted time alone.'

'So you've had it. Come on, let's go to the Mansions.'

'Chase, you don't understand. I need more time alone. An eternity.'

'You'll have it. I'll just help you settle in the room and then I'll leave.'

Before we go to the Mansions I try to get some money out on my credit card. It doesn't work – it is jammed. I TOLD YOU SO the screen prints out before spitting my card back out. At the Mansions Hotel in the Pacific Heights region the charming manager, Skip, helps me with my bags while Chase smuggles Claudius in under his coat. Skip leads us through the lobby where letters from various psychics and demonologists who have stayed here searching for psychic phenomena are framed on the wall. They all testify to the presence of Claudia, the hotel's main ghost among many, who resides in the Presidential Suite. A letter from the famed spiritualist Sylvia Brown confirms that Claudia died in a grisly incident involving blades. Opposite is a wall of fame, signatures from the famous people who have stayed here: Barbra Streisand, Robin Williams, JFK Jr, Robert Downey Jr. Through the hotel we go, round corners, up stairs down stairs, past dried flowers, rich wall colours and murals with life-size drawings of various people who have contributed to San Fran's rich history. Skip leads me to – *the Presidential Suite*. It has an oak-lined library with sofa and fireplace, and views over the city. The room is dark but very cosy. The bedroom is also oak-lined with a large bed covered in tapestried cushions. Before leaving Skip gives me tickets to the hotel's magic show.

When Skip is gone Chase and I have a cigarette and then I suggest he leave me alone while I pull myself together.

'First why don't you drive me to Bloomingdales?' he says. 'I feel like shopping.'

'Why don't you just take a cab? I'll give you the money to take one.'

'It would be easier and quicker for you to drive me.'

'But I'm exhausted and want to be alone. Please take a cab.'

'No.'

Not wishing to row further and thinking the sooner done the sooner I'm in bed and free of him, we get back in the car. San Fran has roads that are steeper than Everest. Driving over them is to relive the end of *The Italian Job*. The car tips over the edge and sky fills the windscreen. It hovers in a vacuum for a few moments until the wheels touch earth again. You career down the slope to the next plateau.

After a couple of blocks of this, I slam on the brakes.

'I'm just too tired to do this and fed up of being bullied

and bossed by you. Get out. I want some time to myself. It's not such a great thing to ask. Can't you just leave me alone?'

I drive back to the hotel and settle down for some sleep in that huge comfortable bed, which Claudius is already curled up on. There is a knock at the door. Chase is back.

'I want to talk,' he says.

'I want to sleep. Please leave.'

He stares at me, his eyes glimmering and brushing against my body in a spooked-up fashion. I don't know what to do. I consider calling the police.

'I have to see you just for a moment. Please.'

'Chase, this is nonsense. Why won't you leave me alone?'

He talks. I watch the clock, counting the minutes of sleep that are passing me by. Finally he leaves. It is too late to get any sleep as the hotel's magic show is about to start. I shower briefly, dress and go downstairs to the salon where the hotel's residents are dressed for evening and sipping cocktails. The room has a large piano that is playing by itself. A life-size doll sits outside the salon, quietly awaiting the aperitif hour. It is here but she's off with the fairies. There are chargrilled vegetables and little cheese toasts and drinks.

The old boy's tricks are amusing and I go up to prepare for the first good night's sleep in ages. I get my paraphernalia together: tissues for runny nose, clock to check on number of awakenings, not that I'd need it tonight, inhaler for asthma, cream for wrinkles, food, water and litter tray for Claudius, eye mask so I can get to sleep in the first place.

Good night. Sleep tight.

Not so. At midnight, Claudius and Claudia get together and live it up big time. The temperature drops drastically and Claudius seems to lose his blindness. He dashes about the apartment as though trying to catch a long piece of rope. His youthful spirits have been fully restored, he doesn't bump into a thing and makes wicked hairpin bends with no trouble at all. Each time he runs into the library section of the suite, the door slams hard and opens again to let him out. The noise of it all carries on for what seems like an hour. After that I am somewhat freaked and don't sleep again. Well, Claude seemed to have a good time at least.

This morning I am pretty frazzled, and dying to tell Skip about the incident. Unfortunately he doesn't know about Claudius so I have to keep schtum. I want to get out before You Know Who turns up, so I check into the Motel Capri two miles down the road, because in spite of its American neon scrawly writing sign, the name reminds me of Europe and warmer climes. There is a large sign saying 'no pets' and the walls are paper-thin. It's a far cry from the Mansions.

We get out of the room quickly. Claude and I amble along to look at the Golden Gate Bridge. It is awesome, not least because it allows for six lanes of traffic. There is a large bunch of Japs standing around the enormous display cable with its myriad wires, touching them and 'aww'ing. We walk over to get a fine view of Alcatraz. As we walk, a fog flows in, swiftly, quietly, until the bridge is half its normal size, its towers completely engulfed in the white beard of the sky. Looking out to Alcatraz, I can barely distinguish what is fog, what is sea and what is sky. The whole place has taken on the wintry atmosphere of a ghost town. It's early October.

Back at the motel there is a message from Chase saying he is coming round later. I am totally freaked that he found me. I come up with a master plan and ask the receptionist to tell the guy who comes to look for me that I have checked out.

'He doesn't realise my cat is at the vet,' I explain, somewhat lyingly.

'So just say you found out I had a cat and threw me out.
I'd be very grateful. No matter how clever he is, don't let
him into my room.'

I then take a cab to Vesuvio's to get out of the way until
Chase has come and gone. As the cab moves off, I realise
that he must have seen the Buick. And that my leaving it
there is another telltale sign that I haven't left, whatever
the receptionist says. Its stickers (Las Vegas and Hollywood stickers along with the rest), peacock feathers and
New Age nonsense make it unmistakable.

Vesuvio's is a small bar in the North Beach area with lots
of young arty types drinking beer. It's where Jack Kerouac
used to get plastered on red wine before staggering out to
the alley outside to throw up. It's cosy with wooden
benches and little tables and stained-glass windows. Very
boho. It sits next door to the City Lights bookshop, whose
maze of tiny rooms are crammed floor to ceiling with
brain food. The area looks down on to the financial
district where scrapers and white lights reach up for the
sky. It's a groovy city shot. The guy next to me chats me
up. He's a comedian. Apparently.

'As Mark Twain said, "There's only one thing colder than
a San Francisco winter and that's a San Francisco summer",' is his opening gambit. He talks ten to the dozen. He
asks me question after question, so many that I can't
answer. I consider telling him the Chase saga but then
realise that it makes me look weak and foolish. Instead I
crack some terrible jokes, even though he's the comedian
here. We talk about Holland, and about how I am half
Dutch; I say how much I like Dutch men, they are so sexy,
well I have never slept with one, except for my father of
course. You need a particularly twisted and black sense of
humour to find this funny, and preferably a few years in
therapy too. He looks at me with fear and pain in his eyes.

*　　*　　*

When it's late enough I return to the motel. I hop into the receptionist to see how goes it? We share a ciggy.

'He came in.' She takes a long drag, her red nails contrasting with the thin white slim. 'He said, "I've lost my key. It's room 207." He's a good liar. And I should know. I was married to a con artist for twenty-seven years. I said, "We threw that girl out because she had a cat." Because he lies himself he doesn't believe anyone else. So he tries to find out when and where you had gone to. He came back twice and he's still in the area, so be careful. If I were you I wouldn't put any lights on up there.'

This piece of news immediately makes me twitchy so I decide to finish the fag upstairs.

As I climb the concrete steps I look around and there in the shadows on the other side of the road is Chase, waiting under a porch, watching me, smoking slowly. He must have seen me talking and conspiring with the receptionist. I put the lights on and phone down to reception. 'He's been watching us.'

'Do you want me to call the cops, honey?' she asks.

'Not yet.'

But the strange thing is, I wait and wait and nothing happens. He never shows. I must have been mistaken about his hiding in the shadows – or paranoiacally scared. I fall asleep with the lights on and sleep heartily until Claudius wakes me at eight the next morning with a tongue bath on the arm.

Bright and early, today is the first day of the rest of my life. I open the door to check out the weather and breathe the fresh (cat-litter-free) air. Chase is standing on the doormat. I stifle a little scream.

'How are you?' He is all charm and smiles.

'I'm fine.'

'Good. I thought you'd been chucked out?'

'Oh . . . Yes. Well luckily another receptionist took pity on me and let me back in when the nasty one who chucked me out had gone.' On the outside apologetic, but inside apoplectic. He could find me if I hid on the moon.

'Can I invite you to breakfast?' He smiles sweetly, apologetically.

'Um.'

'Come on, just for half an hour.'

We hit Mel's Diner round the corner where I order a huge pancakey thing, hot chocolate, orange juice, the works. It's a 50s joint, with mini juke-boxes on the table, a huge central aluminium bar and all the servers wearing red and white stripy boat paper hats.

'I have to go to Detroit. I have to go home,' says Chase. 'Would you give me a lift to the airport?'

'When?'

'In a couple of hours.'

'If you promise to leave me alone.'

'OK.'

On the way back we pass a Beauty Parlour and, feeling in need of pampering, I go in. Chase chats up the old biddies as I get my eyebrows waxed by a glamorous Iranian.

'Now. Does anyone need tweezing?' he asks to roars of delighted flirty laughter from the old birds. 'Because I'm ready if you are,' he finishes off. When the brows are finished he instructs the Iranian Madam to do my moustache.

'My what?' I ask indignantly.

'Your moustache.'

'I don't have a moustache.'

'Oh dahlink. I do my whole face,' says Iranian Madam.

'Well maybe you're the bearded lady, I don't care, I like my hairy face and anyway they are all blonde and I do not have a moustache.' Before I know it there is hot boiling wax on my lip and they are both pulling away at the cloth. It is highly painful and then my upper lip is gone.

'There,' says Chase delightedly. 'To be honest, I have been aware of that ever since we met. Shall we do the rest of her?' he asks Iranian Madam. I jump up and am ready to go.

'How much do I owe you?'

My lip feels bald and strangely plastic.

As we go out I am still murmuring, 'I do not have a moustache.'

'You know, you had long tendrils before.'

'Long tendrils?' I scream this time. 'Long fucking tendrils? Listen you psychotic idiot. If there's one thing we can be sure of in this crazy world, it's that I'm vain as hell. And if I had had long tendrils I wouldn't have needed some thieving psycho stalking weirdo to tell me. I would have dealt with it years ago.'

'I just want you to be New York clean. You should really get rid of all this.'

He makes a sweeping gesture from my fanny down.

'Do you mean shave them or just cut them off all together?' I stand with my hands on my hips in the street. 'Just because you shave under your arms like some obsessive weirdo and your hair has completely vacated your head, is no reason for everyone else to be totally bald. I'm not condoning Italian hairiness – by the way, how do you know the Italian planes at the airport? They have hair under the wings – but I am not dirty.' In spite of my anger, I am rather pleased at my new soignée eyebrows.

He offers to show me a superb view of San Fran on the other side of the Golden Gate Bridge before we go to the airport. As we cross the water, he mentions casually, 'Actually I'm not bald. I shave my head. I have done since I was first on the highschool swim team.'

On the what? I stare at him. That's it. What am I doing here?

I turn the car round on the bridge. This is an extremely dangerous thing to do. For a start the bridge is a six-lane thoroughfare. Secondly, the two sides are separated by small yellow cones, and if you are driving at any speed, which you're not meant to be, but I of course was, involves weaving through one and then taking your turn at quite a speed to avoid being hit by the oncoming cars. The jolt shocks Chase into obscenities.

'What? What are you thinking?' he asks.

'Nothing,' I reply.

Something, is the truth. And this is it. This is not the most auspicious ending to my trip. I'm fed up of this liar, this thief. I'm choosing not to hurt any more. Some pain is written in the stars but this certainly isn't. It's my choice. I know when a man makes me happy and you honeychile do not. You are out of my life and I am taking control now.

'Where are we going?' he asks. 'What the . . . ?'

'I want you out of the car.'

'For Christ's sake.' He starts protesting. 'What are you doing? What have I said?'

My mind is made up. I jump out, hop to his side and open the door. He climbs out slowly.

'Chase. You're a nut. You're an obsessive. You need passengers on your ride. But I'm getting off. Or rather you are. Whatever.'

And with those inarticulate words, I hop back in the Brilliant Buick and shoot off, slamming on the interlock system as he tries to get back in the car. My heart is beating but hot damn I feel good. I see him in my mirror staring, unbelieving, gesticulating, wondering where the ninny found the energy and/or guts to assert herself. 'Now get yourself to the airport you FUCKER!' I shout at the mirror.

I drive back to Claudius.

'At the end of the day he wasn't even a dog person,' blinks Claudius quietly. 'He was just a dog.'

Chapter Twenty

The Sphinx

San Rafael, California –
New York, New York

This morning I wake bright and late, at 11am, and just knowing that Chase is on his way to Detroit where he'll be swallowed up by a crowd of other nuts makes me grin ecstatically. So I have driven across the States with my trusty kitten at my side, and you might wonder what the moral of the story is? Don't comment on a woman's facial hair. It might just be the hair that broke the cat's back.

Janie comes up trumps with a guy called Sense (*Sense?*) who owns a boat moored at San Rafael, just over the Golden Gate Bridge, and invites us to stay there as long as we like. He greets us with:

'Well it's nice out here because we're protected from the bay. As Mark Twain said, "There's only one thing colder than a San Francisco winter and that's a San Francisco summer." ' I think if someone else tells me this I'm going to scream. Claudius and I take in a few weeks' October sun until we feel rested enough to decide what to do.

The boat has no running water, no electricity and no phone, but we are doing fine. During the day the sun is hot and shines on this little sea vessel and Claudius. Each day as we wake up he looks at me as if to say: 'I should be basking!' so I put him outside and he sits sniffing the sun, and eventually settles down, after squinting down at the sea for a goodly while. Each time I have to tell him that the green stuff is water and not grass and it will be a mighty nasty shock for him if he ever reaches it, but he doesn't seem interested in touching, just looking. Can he see it?

It doesn't seem to matter. He is happy. Affectionate and purry at night, he slants those greens at me during the day. I call Dr Shipp whenever I am near a phone, which is not that often. He tells me it is just a waiting game, I should continue giving Claudius his liquids to clear his kidneys. One day they will no longer work.

Sometimes I lie awake in our cabin, swaying with the rippling tide, side to side, side to side, as Claude snores curled up in my arms. I wonder, will I know when he's had enough? Or will my fear of his going prevent me from hearing his voice?

Coming back to the boat one day, the car in front of me doesn't slow down when a deer crosses the road from the median where it was grazing. Its hind leg is clipped and it limps away, the limb circling loosely, unnaturally, behind it. I slam on the brakes and follow it into the woods to try and help it. It watches me from a distance and then hops away, trying to hide its pain like a shameful thing.

My masterplan has taken shape. Fly back to New York. Fly back to Paris. Drive Claudius to Calais and put him in the car in the Shuttle. We will then drive to London, to our flat and he can die there, in my bed, as though the whole trip were a dream. Before I even broach the subject with him, I know his comments and my reply.

'If they catch you, they will put me in quarantine and you in prison.'

'They won't catch us kitkat.'

'Are you really willing to risk losing me just for an exciting, adrenalin-pusher?'

'It's not for an exciting number. It's to get us home.'

'But we are home. We're together.'
And he'd be right. So I don't bother.

New York, on the other hand, is much more acceptable as a plan of action. We've always dreamed of living there and dreams have a purpose. Am I right? Did Monica blow Bill?

'Talking of which, kitkat,' we're on the plane to JFK, 'I dreamt of you last night.'

'Is that so?' he says, not looking even slightly interested.

'Yes. We were sitting on the rocks looking out to sea. When the tide started lapping at our feet, I carried you carefully over the rocks making sure not to slip on the snotty seaweed until we were out of danger and back on the shore, away from the encroaching sea. Then I was on a very sunny boat, where a tall, good-looking, white-haired old man was waiting –'

'Hold on. Where am I in all this?'

'Well, you sort of disappeared once I had removed us from the rocks.'

'Oh. Charming.'

'Anyway, I was at home waiting for him –'

'Is there an end to this soon? You seem to forget that dreams are only interesting to the dreamer, who is ultimately fascinated with *herself*.'

'Shut it and listen. And Ma was asleep in bed. Then I woke up.'

'Fascinating. Now. Where are my fries?'

Claudius has developed a penchant for French Fries, but he has not clocked the fact that they don't serve McDonald's on planes.

In NY we hole up in a warm womb of a flat. Claudius sits snuggled up on my jumper on the leather armchair near the window catching up on some sleep. Every day I make sure he gets his chips, cut up into tiny worms. It's a balanced diet because I chop up small pieces of Gruyère too.

*   *   *

The streets of NYC.

The best way not to stand out in a New York crowd:

wear as many clashing-coloured clothes as possible
gesticulate wildly
shout absurdities
walk fast

On the subway no one the same. Baggy-eyed black woman bent over double, ginger-haired twenty-year girl with clear skin and sky eyes in a brown leather jacket and clean blue jeans, an Indian cheek-boned mother in sneakers and track pants with her young Superman-T-shirted boy on her lap, a black-haired blue-eyed model in sleek black and her equally stunning model boyfriend, a nutter in flip flops and shorts (it's November) shouting 'I got you, babe!' and 'Revolution!'

Restaurants, bars, cafés, delis, grocery stores. Food everywhere. And the shops. The most delightful intriguing original shops stuffed full of things to buy: blue glass star lamps, pink seed pearl photo frames, brushed velvet cushions, lilac leather skirts, high-heeled purple cowboy boots (finally!), silver fox fur hats, pink fluffy boas, silk rose brooches, except I'm not in the mood. They're just a temporary distraction from the permanence I can no longer avoid.

The blue December sky. White Christmas lights up everywhere. Sometimes they cover entire edifices (like the posters) but as often can be found in trees or shop windows, twinkling and glittering us all on to a glamorous and gorgeous Yuletide. This Christmas will be the third anniversary of Ma's death.

After a while giving Claude his liquids becomes too uncomfortable for him. He shudders and twitches and tries to get away from the needle, which he has never done before. I carry on for a couple of days but I know what he is saying. So I stop administering them. The whole point about the process is to make his life better, not worse. So we wait.

Christmas. I give him a heating pad. He gives me a pink boa.

But no card.

'Too old to write, my dear.' All his presents used to have tiny cards accompanying them, with eccentric handwriting (very similar to Ma's, actually). To darling Clare, happy Christmas, with love from Claudius, hugs, kisses, paws.

New Year's Eve. Yawn.

The anniversary comes and goes. Still we wait.

Then he stops eating his normal amounts. I give him all his favourites every day, chips, cheese, chocolate milk, tuna, chicken, beef, anything he so much as lifts his nose to, praying that I can postpone it all again. That he will fight as before like the champion he is.

'You'll know when it's time,' they say. I wait for it to seem right, but each day doubts overwhelm me. Should I do the liquids? Should I give him steroids to try and build him up again? Should I put him in hospital? Mere noise to fill the emptiness, as he has told me what he wants.

I can't imagine not having him around, because he isn't just under my skin, he's in my heart. I know he has no kidneys left. I'm beginning to feel the way I did when Ma died. There is no choice, I know he has to die and I want to fight it, but I can't. My mind is in treacle.

Meanwhile he gets thinner. Yet he doesn't seem to be suffering. From thousands of years of genetic training, he hides his pain as though I might attack him should I see a sign of weakness. What does he do with it? I don't know because he has stopped talking. But I am still listening. I don't know what to do. I wait for him to tell me, but he doesn't. He still purrs when I go near him (albeit in a whisper), and he still walks (although he wobbles), and he still eats (but doll amounts). I put the food down and he chomp chomp chomps enthusiastically, as if to please me, but after three mouthfuls, just as I am starting to relax and think he might get something down, he turns away, shaking his paws as if the food has dirtied him.

Then I start to pray he will die in my arms.

I try to listen to my instincts, *but I don't have any*. I am never more in the moment or more at sea. My thoughts scatter every which way.

That morning Claudius was on my arm as usual, and I realised I could hardly feel him. He was so light from the lack of eating that his weight hardly made an impression on my arm at all. I called the vet.

The annoying thing about that day is that it was exactly the same as any other. The sun had the temerity to blue the sky and the cabs were driving through New York with their usual honky bravado. I took a cab to the upper east side with Claude on my lap and then had to wait for half an hour in the vet's waiting room. The vet examined him and she was very sweet and told me that Claudius was not in the final stages but that he would be soon. Did I really want to see my best friend go through the hideous pain that kidney disease brings with it? No of course not. I signed the release forms and she let us have ten minutes together. During this time I just sat kissing Claude on his soft chocolatey head. He closed his eyes exhausted, he said not a word. She came back with the assistant. They got out the syringe and as they did Claudius pulled his leg away and stood up and looked at me. I panicked and the vet sent us home. I waited.

I could wait until he is in a coma of pain to put him to sleep. Do I really want all those last images of him, which I had of her, to haunt me in the same way? Do I need to put him through that just to remind myself that I'm alive? Shouldn't I do a favour to the cat that has accompanied me around the world, and fought with me through everything and been right at my side? My selfishness is the cage that carries my fear. I used to love my prison, my psychological tic, but I'm fed up of being unsure, because it keeps my dying cat in pain. I have been unsteady ever since Ma died and I can no longer bear the endless questioning. Death's a fact.

So two days later, when my childish heart had found some significance in the day, January 21st consisting of the date of my birthday – 17th – when Claudius was first mine, plus Ma's death – 4th – when he came to be mine again) I gave him a lunch of sushi eel and took him back to the vet. This time there was no wavering.

While I wait for his ashes – the crematorium said it would take ten days and I can't face the apartment alone – I go to New Zealand to visit my sister, who gave Claudius to me in the first place all those years ago. She and her husband and I go to the beach every day. Memories of Monterey could prevent me from entering the sea, but I can't be bothered to panic. My sister is so like Ma, but at the same time very much herself. I show her the photos of Claude and me around the States and she says, 'You look like Ma too.' Then one night after all the talking Ma comes back. I see her sitting in the corner of the room. She is laughing and holding a glass of whisky. In spite of her strange attire, the white nightie she died in, she is completely fine, not skinny, not ill, just a little transparent.

I fly back to New York to collect Claude's ashes and am surprised by how little the white powdery substance moves me. I sit in the tiny apartment surrounded by my packed bags ready for London and feel the silence just a moment too long. He's not here.

After the dull dread of fear, which in fact only takes a moment to drop me in its crevasse, I run out to the street and breathe. Instead of concentrating on the glitter in the shops down at this level, I look up at the intricate stone-work adorning the tops of the New York edifices, way up there against the blue sky. I have stopped running.

A Note on the Author

Clare de Vries worked as a journalist before she
set off across the highways of America.
She lives in London.

A Note on the Type

The text of this book is set in Linotype Sabon, named after the type founder, Jacques Sabon. It was designed by Jan Tschichold and jointly developed by Linotype, Monotype and Stempel, in response to a need for a typeface to be available in identical form for mechanical hot metal composition and hand composition using foundry type.

Tschichold based his design for Sabon roman on a fount engraved by Garamond, and Sabon italic on a fount by Granjon. It was first used in 1966 and has proved an enduring modern classic.